ADDITIONAL PRAISE FOR
THE UPSIDE OF AGING

"Paul Irving has gathered some of the smartest, most thoughtful minds for a wide ranging discussion of the challenging, the good, and the hopeful parts of the aging phenomenon."

**Donna Shalala, president, University of Miami;
former U. S. Secretary of Health and Human Services**

"This extraordinary book is profoundly optimistic, enlightening, and empowering. Our aging population presents unprecedented opportunities for enhancing health, transformation, and success across virtually all disciplines. If you read only one book this year on aging, this is it."

**Dean Ornish, M.D., founder and president,
Preventive Medicine Research Institute; clinical professor
of Medicine, UC, San Francisco; author, *The Spectrum***

"It's time that all of us, young and old, talk about aging in the 21st century and how we can tap into the wisdom and experience we gain to create stronger communities. This compelling book redefines aging: Getting older isn't about declining abilities; it's about increasing opportunities. It's recognition that aging doesn't limit the possibilities in front of us; it grows them."

**Kathy Calvin, president and CEO,
United Nations Foundation**

"Paul Irving brings together extraordinary thinkers who explain why we must transform our approach to aging from one that assumes dependency and disability to one of engagement, productivity and potential. They make a compelling case that we cannot afford to do otherwise."

**Dr. John Beard, director, Department of Ageing
and Life Course, World Health Organization**

"This is the moment for creating the opportunities of our now-longer lives. This book offers the optimistic and innovative lens and path forward we need, for society, for leaders and for our communities. Brought to us by energized, expert and thoughtful voices, it is a critical conversation changer for our future."

Linda P. Fried, MD, MPH, dean, Mailman School of Public Health, Columbia University

The Upside of Aging

The Upside
of Aging

*How Long Life Is
Changing the World of
Health, Work, Innovation,
Policy, and Purpose*

Edited by
Paul H. Irving
with Rita Beamish

WILEY

Contents

Foreword

The economic benefits far outweigh the challenges that come with an aging society. The extension of life, and the extension of healthy life, are positive developments to be celebrated, not feared. Their impact will be an economic boon, not a drag.

What does it mean to be old? We each have our own definition, but we probably agree that the chronological ages that used to define "elderly" are increasingly irrelevant. I've had many friends and colleagues who did their most important work in their eighties and nineties. Unfortunately, I've also lost far too many family members and dear friends to disease before they had a chance to experience full lives.

When my father was diagnosed and treated for melanoma in the mid-1970s, the doctors thought they had caught the cancer before it spread. A few years later, however, the disease recurred, and by the time it was discovered, the prognosis was terminal. I took Dad to cancer centers around the country and consulted with leading physicians and researchers before it became frustratingly clear that medical science didn't have a solution. So I moved my family from the East Coast back to California to give my kids and their grandfather a chance to know each other. Dad passed away 10 months later.

In 1993, I was diagnosed with advanced prostate cancer and given 12 to 18 months to live. It was devastating to think that the family continuity I sought after my father's diagnosis now seemed impossible. There probably would be no chance to see my kids get married and start families of their own.

But the science had improved by then, and I drew upon the network of cancer researchers the Milken Family Foundation had assembled throughout the 1980s. In addition to standard therapies, I consulted nutritionists, eliminated meat from my diet, consulted Eastern medicine, and practiced yoga. There were a lot more tools to draw upon than when my father was diagnosed.

If my father's cancer had occurred in 1993, he may have survived. Had I received my diagnosis in 1974, I may not have. The great news for my generation is that medical science advanced remarkably in the interim, and it's moving faster today than ever.

We're transforming what it means to be "old," in terms not only of how we perceive aging, but also how we experience it. The personal and social benefits of living longer are priceless, and the economic benefits far outweigh the challenges that come with an aging society. The extension of life, and the extension of healthy life, are positive developments to be celebrated, not feared, and their impact will be an economic boon, not a drag.

The Greatest Achievement in Human History

Over the past two centuries—by far the most prosperous 200 years in human history—at least half of all economic growth can be attributed to advances in public health and medicine that led to longer, healthier lives. To understand just how much life improved in the twentieth century alone, consider the life of Jiroemon Kimura, whose name you may recognize from news stories.

Born in a western Japanese fishing village in 1897, Mr. Kimura is among a very small group of people who lived through the entire twentieth century. He witnessed some of the greatest advances and most transformational inventions in human history: horseless carriages, Marconi's radio blast across the Atlantic, the Wright brothers' first flights, the theory of relativity, Fleming's discovery of penicillin, the exploration of DNA, Salk's vaccine, Sputnik, heart transplants, man's first steps on the moon, personal computers, MRIs, cell phones, the Internet, and . . . the list could go on for pages.

Kimura himself accomplished something remarkable: He was recognized by Guinness World Records as the oldest man in recorded history and was the oldest living person on the planet until he passed away at age 116. He attributed his longevity to good nutrition—light and healthy meals—and he stayed active long after his 1962 retirement from the post office, working on his son's farm.

But of all the advances during his life, Kimura participated in what is perhaps the greatest achievement in the history of civilization: the doubling, in less than one century, of average life spans around the globe.

When Kimura was born, worldwide life expectancy at birth was 31 years. It's now 70. The United States went from 47 to 79 years. When people pine for the "good old days," they take for granted just how much things have improved—most notably that we live longer, healthier, and more productive lives.

"What a ~~Drag~~ Thrill It Is Getting Old"

A few years ago, on a sunny Los Angeles morning, I drove up the winding, tree-shaded driveway of my longtime friend Kirk Kerkorian. We were scheduled to play doubles tennis, but I was running late. By the time I arrived, he had found a replacement player to fill my spot. It was a remarkable scene: four players on the court with a combined age of 358 years! Kirk looked young, especially for a 90-year-old. Over lunch, we talked about how playing in their eighties and nineties was different from playing when they were younger. "The guys we play against are thinner these days," one of them told me, and the others agreed—most of their heavier friends had died years ago. I also noticed that all four men had full, thick heads of hair, but I choose to believe that's unrelated to their longevity.

Kirk and his friends are an anomaly for that generation. But they represent the promise of what many in my generation will realize—a vibrant, active, and productive life well into their ninth and tenth decades. The late Robert Fogel, a Nobel laureate at the University of Chicago, told me a few years ago that *average* life span in the developed world will easily exceed 100 within the current century. In fact, it's probable that the first person who will live to be 150 has already been born. There's always seemed to be a natural limit to human life, but with advances in genomics, immunology, stem cells, and organ "printing" and transplants, that limit may be much higher than previously thought.

At a recent Milken Institute Global Conference, Dr. Robert Butler of the Alliance for Health and the Future, pointed out that in terms of health, a 60-year-old woman is equivalent to a 40-year-old in 1960. Today's 80-year-old American man is similar to a 60-year-old as recently as 1975.

To see those numbers come to life, look no further than the Rolling Stones, who recently celebrated their fiftieth anniversary. If you're able to see them in concert, pay attention to the front rows, with attendees in their sixties and seventies dancing like crazed teenagers. This sight is as inspirational for those of us over 60 as it is unsettling for our grandkids.

Advertisers and the media have taken note and updated how they portray older people. (As well they should: By 2017, nearly half the U.S. population will be over 50 and will control 70 percent of disposable income. This is a population that doesn't want to be called "old.") In the late 1980s, LifeCall's commercials featured a capsized woman, next to her walker, moaning: "I've fallen and I can't get up!" Today, Cialis asks the male segment of her age cohort: "When the moment is right, will you be ready?"

Ron Howard's 1985 film *Cocoon* featured Wilford Brimley as the lead actor and part of a group of retirement home residents who were visited by aliens. Brimley was 51 when the movie was released. Imagine a reprisal of that role today by Tom Cruise, Jim Carrey, Steve Carell, or Matthew Broderick—all of whom turned 51 in 2013.

At a conference a few years ago, I estimated the median attendee age was about 35. As a speaker, whatever concern I had about the age gap was allayed when I saw the entertainment: Bob Dylan; Rod Stewart; and Crosby, Stills and Nash. I was the youngest person onstage that night.

The Long View: Never Underestimate Human Ingenuity

The Milken Institute has focused on aging for the past several years. One of my favorite panels remains the 2009 discussion called "Life After 80: Always Looking Forward," featuring five prominent octogenarians. All the panelists were still active in business and philanthropy. Jim Pattison, chairman of the Jim Pattison Group, who was 80 at the time, said, "Retirement is not in the cards." (True to his word, he remains chairman of his company as I write this.) For most of the panelists, social interaction was important, too—they echoed the finding that people with more friends live longer. Diet and exercise were also common themes.

While the benefits of extended life spans are undeniable, developed nations also need to make economic adjustments. When America's Social Security system was introduced in 1935, life expectancy was 61.7 years. It made sense for people to start collecting pension checks as early as age 62. As the program was expanding in the early 1950s, there were 17 workers supporting every beneficiary. By 2012, there were fewer than three workers, and that ratio is expected to drop closer to 2:1 by 2035.

The simplest solution to this challenge is to increase the age at which individuals become eligible for retirement benefits. Ideally, the retirement age should be indexed to average life expectancy. Such a policy shift is inevitable—not for political reasons, but because of simple math. We should summon the will to make this change now, not leave the problem to our children and grandchildren.

Another frequently cited challenge is the cost of health care. With an older global population, it's reasonable to expect that the prevalence and cost of many diseases will increase. As one example, the World Health Organization (WHO) predicts that by 2050 more than 115 million people worldwide will suffer from dementia, up from 36 million in 2012. In addition, WHO predicts that the global cost of dementia, currently $604 billion per year, will rise even faster than the prevalence, suggesting that by midcentury, dementia alone will be a $2 trillion challenge.

That outlook may grossly underestimate the potential of medical breakthroughs. In the 1950s, economists predicted that caring for polio patients in "iron lung hotels" would be economically ruinous. But then came the polio vaccine, which has saved the United States an estimated

$800 billion since 1955. More recently, Oprah Winfrey told her talk show audience in 1987 that AIDS was expected to take the lives of up to one in five Americans by the early 1990s. That, of course, never happened, and researchers have since produced therapies that have transformed that disease from a virtual death sentence into a chronic condition for many patients. An AIDS-free generation may well be within sight.

While the challenges we face today may seem more complicated, the tools we'll use to solve them are also much more powerful and sophisticated. Genomics provides one important example: The original sequencing of the human genome took 13 years and cost $3 billion; today it takes a few hours and the cost is approaching $1,000.

So while it's possible that dementia will cost $2 trillion per year by 2050, advances in medical research and prevention have the potential to render that prediction wildly overstated. Don't underestimate the ingenuity of humankind.

More than Just a Number

John Adams took a dim view of aging. In his personal journal, our second president wrote: "The remainder of my days I shall rather decline, in sense, spirit, and activity. My season for acquiring knowledge is past." He was 36 years old.

Adams had accomplished much as a lawyer by that young age and was well known throughout the colonies. He had already outlived the average global life expectancy, and conventional wisdom told him to retire to his farm for his remaining years. Fortunately, he decided to launch a three-decade encore career in nation building that culminated, at age 61, when he took the presidential oath of office. In fact, he lived to age 90—half a century after signing the Declaration of Independence. Coincidentally, he passed away on July 4, 1826—the same day as Thomas Jefferson, exactly 50 years after they signed the Declaration.

That also happens to be exactly 120 years before the day I was born—July 4, 1946—the first year of the postwar baby boom that lasted until 1964. My generation was the first to be told that one person could change the world, and I'm encouraged by how many of them are doing so.

In fact, many of the contributors to this book are boomers, and their work is influencing policy, creating a better understanding of the social and biological science of aging, and upending outdated stereotypes about what it means to grow older.

As this is written, I'm 67, as active as any time in my life, feeling great, and looking forward to many more years of pursuing my personal and professional goals. But compared with some of my octogenarian and nonagenarian business colleagues, friends, and tennis partners, I'm still just a youngster. Age is more than just a number. It's also about perception. The baby boomers are discovering the truth of the adage that you're only as old as you feel.

Michael Milken
Chairman, The Milken Institute

Preface

Aging and Change—A New Day Is Coming

Paul H. Irving
President, The Milken Institute

In 2009, I was enjoying what many would consider to be the perfect career—a successful senior leadership position in a large law and consulting firm. For many years I had enjoyed my work—and I valued my practice, my clients, and my colleagues. But after three decades as a corporate lawyer, I began to realize that something significant was missing. Approaching 60, I felt called to a different purpose—to something new.

That year, my life changed. I was given the opportunity to spend a year at Harvard University as a fellow in its Advanced Leadership Initiative, which is dedicated to educating and deploying a group of experienced leaders who are interested in addressing national and global challenges.

Harvard is an impressive place to be sure, but equally impressive was a talented cohort of new friends in their fifties, sixties, and seventies—all enthusiastic about learning, changing, risk-taking, and giving back after decades of accomplishment in their primary careers. Here was an older group excited about tackling hard problems, expert at navigating complex environments, skilled at relationship development, and highly collaborative, emotionally intelligent, and thoroughly energized. Life had given us a special opportunity—in which our advancing age and years of experience were recognized as assets.

As I finished my year in Cambridge and faced the next stage of my life, I thought about other older people, and how much the United States and other societies around the world would benefit by capturing and utilizing more of the value that longevity confers. My "encore" career as president of the Milken Institute only furthered my belief in the power and potential of our aging population. And so it was that I began to focus on and talk about the upside of aging.

Many years ago, my generation—the baby boom generation—challenged authority and convention and, in doing so, redefined an age. And the baby boomers are at it again, changing expectations and the way we think about aging.

In the past century, discovery and innovation have enabled longevity that would be unimaginable to our forebears. Increased longevity has contributed to unprecedented global economic growth and new opportunities for personal fulfillment that previous generations could only dream of.

A massive demographic shift across America and the world is accelerating and the possibilities are mind-boggling. Innovations in genomics, precision medicine, digital health tools, and prevention present us and our children with the likelihood of even more time to work, play, learn, give back, and enjoy friends and loved ones.

Let's not kid ourselves. Aging can be really hard. On a personal level, it means aches and pains, memory loss, and a slower step. We're led to believe that our capacity for productivity, creativity, and leadership is diminished. Too many older individuals suffer loneliness and depression, longing for connection, engagement, and continued meaning in their lives. Many worry about whether longevity means their health—and their money—will run out too soon.

At a broader level, increasing age and declining birth rates reveal growing strains on social and financial safety nets and health care systems.

The effects of inadequate retirement savings and the diseases of aging pose seemingly insoluble political, economic, and social challenges.

We segregate older members of society from their communities, civic institutions, and workplaces. We stereotype, discounting their wisdom, judgment, and experience. We dismiss their aspirations and underestimate their potential as workers, entrepreneurs, and consumers. We encourage their retirement, withdrawal, and disengagement during a lengthening period of life in which so much important contribution is possible.

It's a paradox. The miracle of longevity provides such incredible opportunity to individuals and the societies in which we live. Yet today, so much of that potential remains unrealized because we haven't adequately addressed these challenges that hinder older populations from living their later lives in meaningful, productive ways.

While researchers and physicians are successfully extending life, our policies, expectations, and norms reflect a very different set of values. Longevity—possibly the most important development in human history—is considered a burden.

But things are changing, and quickly. Stereotypes and biases are being challenged. Millions of aging individuals across the globe are seeking new ways to remain active, engaged, and contributing members of their societies. Thoughtful leaders are beginning to pay attention, responding to the demographic shift with fresh ideas, practices, and programs. Creative solutions are being discussed. From exciting approaches to disease cure, prevention, wellness and care, to age-friendly housing alternatives and transportation systems, to lifelong learning and encore career opportunities, to travel, entertainment, fashion, and food designed for evolving tastes, to advanced technologies and social networks that engage our aging colleagues, innovations abound.

Knowing that economic growth comes at the intersection of demography and innovation, this older population will move the world forward, driving a new longevity economy as workers, entrepreneurs, and consumers—both through influence and sheer numbers.

We'll age in place—rejecting the model of an isolated life in a distant retirement community with a recreation center, a shuffleboard court, and a cafeteria. Instead, we'll continue, and even increase, active involvement in our communities, educational and arts institutions, civic and charitable organizations, businesses, and places of worship.

Many in this new aging generation will need to continue to work to meet financial goals that are not satisfied by savings, retirement, or social security arrangements. Others will want to move to socially focused encore careers that integrate work and purpose. A surprisingly large group of aging entrepreneurs will start and grow new businesses.

We'll seek products and services that meet our changing needs and, yes, we'll be as interested in high quality, good style, and imaginative design as we ever were. Experience has refined our intelligence and capabilities, and we'll use those faculties as long as we can.

We'll stay connected to families and friends, and we'll be active participants playing visible roles in the fabric of our diverse communities. We'll have examples to set and opportunities to contribute to the lives of younger people—as educators, mentors, advisors, and coaches. Importantly, the upside of aging must not just be for us—the benefits are intergenerational and must be shared.

Increasing longevity is a remarkable accomplishment and a continuing goal. But there's an even more important objective. To capture the full benefits of longer life—to realize the upside of aging—we must rethink the value of longevity, understanding that it's not just about the time we're given, but about the quality and purpose of that time.

Successful aging must become a priority for ourselves, our families, and the communities and societies in which we live. Old and young, rich and poor, of every color and from every community and corner of the globe—if we learn to harness the benefits of longevity, the upside of aging will be realized and the world will be much better for it.

Aging leads to an inevitable end, but older age is not the end. Older age is just another part of life's path—a part of the path with great potential that is just beginning to be understood.

The chapters that follow are the work of prominent experts—dedicated thought leaders in the field—each, in his or her own way, leading the reinvention and reimagining of aging. With very different personal stories, writing styles, areas of specialty and perspectives, they share a strong commitment to improving longevity, each believing that the upside of aging is significant and well within our grasp.

Read, think, enjoy, and join a very big conversation that has critical implications for our future.

Acknowledgments

The Upside of Aging demonstrates the potential for collective action—the notion that people working together for a higher purpose actually can get things done. There are many who play a part in moving mountains. I want to thank some of those movers here.

First, thanks to our chapter authors: Laura Carstensen, Henry Cisneros, Hassy Cohen, Joe Coughlin, Ken Dychtwald, Marc Freedman, Sally Greengross, Freda Lewis-Hall, Jody Heymann, Mike Hodin, Dan Houston, Steve Knapp, Phil Pizzo, Barry Rand, Susan Raymond, and Fernando Torres-Gil. Their thought leadership and commitment to progress gives me great confidence that a new day is coming for our aging population.

I want to express my gratitude to our project editor, Rita Beamish, for her skill, discipline, enthusiasm, and passion for the book's subject matter.

Thanks to the staff at the Milken Institute, who serve our non-profit mission, and work energetically every day to change lives, hearts, and minds. Special thanks to our chairman, Mike Milken, for his many philanthropic achievements; to my research colleague, Anu Chatterjee; and to the members of our team who made such a difference to this project—and to our work on successful aging leading to this project.

To those who've played a part in my own aging journey—the faculty, fellows, and students in Harvard's Advanced Leadership Initiative, my long-time colleagues at the Manatt law firm, and my friends of all ages—my appreciation.

Most importantly, I want to thank my mom, Florence Irving, whose lessons and values motivate me every day; my late dad, Jack Irving, whose passion for scientific discovery and work continued until the very end; my son, Ben, whom I watch with pride and joy as I age; and my wife, Susie Irving—we began as kids, we've been through it all, and there's no one in the world with whom I'd rather be aging.

Paul Irving
Los Angeles, California

Introduction

The Rise of a Mature World: By the Numbers

Paul H. Irving
President, The Milken Institute

Anusuya Chatterjee
Senior Economist, The Milken Institute

Before our authors discuss the upside of aging, let's review some data underscoring key challenges and opportunities presented by the massive demographic shift. Is demography destiny? The numbers begin the story—about the rise of a mature world that will change lives in ways we're just beginning to appreciate.

The Longevity Century

To understand the demographic realities of the twenty-first century's aging population, we must first acknowledge the breathtaking advances of the previous century, namely the scientific and medical innovations that changed human existence. Among the twentieth century's most important contributions was the gift of longevity. In 50 years (1980–2030), global life expectancy is expected to increase by more than 10 years, thanks to new medicines, advanced technologies, and progressive social policies, enabling individual and societal accomplishments unimaginable in earlier generations.

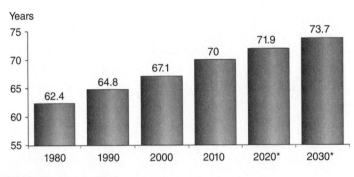

Global Life Expectancy
*Projected.
SOURCES: United Nations; Milken Institute.

U.S. life expectancy is projected to reach 82 by 2030. Remarkably, it was just 47 years in 1900.

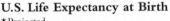
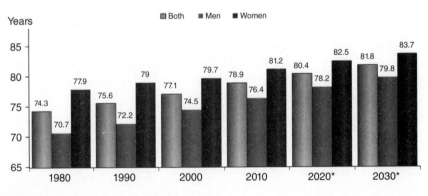

U.S. Life Expectancy at Birth
*Projected.
SOURCES: United Nations; Milken Institute.

Longevity and Birth Rates

As people are living longer, they also are having fewer children, further aging the population. In the United States and Europe, birthrates have fallen for years, due to changing goals and values and access to birth control. The baby boom growth spurt during the 1940s and 1950s put the annual U.S. birthrate at 25 per 1,000. That rate has plunged to 13 per 1,000 at present. Europe's birthrate has dropped dramatically as well, from 21 per 1,000 in the 1950s to 11 per 1,000 today.

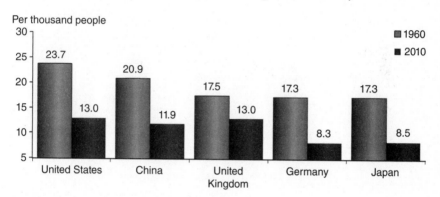

Birthrates, per 1,000 People: 1960, 2010
SOURCES: World Bank; Milken Institute.

Lower birth rates also resulted from government mandates or encouragement of family planning in developing countries, as with China's "one-child policy" and India's encouragement of "two-children"

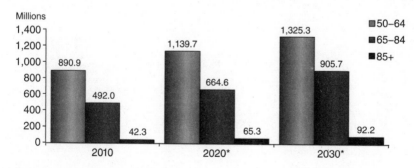

Aging of the World Population
*Projected.
SOURCES: U.S. Census Bureau; Milken Institute.

families in the 1970s. Asia's annual birth rate has declined from 40 per 1,000 in the mid-1950s to 18 per 1,000 today.

The size of the age 50-plus population will be unprecedented by 2030 in virtually all European and Asian nations, and in the United States. More than one in three Americans will be over 50, as will approximately one half of the populations of Germany, Italy and Japan, and 40 percent of China.

Selected Countries, Percentage of Population 50+, 2000–2030

Country	2000	2010	2030*
United States	27	32	36
United Kingdom	33	35	39
Germany	35	40	48
Italy	37	39	49
Russia	28	33	41
Japan	38	44	54
China	18	25	40

*Projected.

SOURCES: U.S. Census Bureau; Milken Institute.

The 65-Plus Group

The traditional "retiree" group, age 65 and older, will continue to grow in the next 20 years, from 0.5 billion globally in 2010, to 0.9 billion by 2030, although, as this book emphasizes, age today does not correlate with retirement as it did in the past.

In the United States, the population age 65 and over will nearly double in a 20-year span, growing from 40 million in 2010 to 73 million

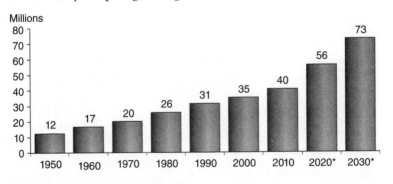

U.S. Over-65 Population, 1950–2030

*Projected.

SOURCES: U.S. Census Bureau; Milken Institute.

in 2030. By the time the last baby boomer turns 65 in 2029, one in five Americans will be age 65 or older.

By 2030, the number of Americans age 65 or older will surpass the number of children under 15.

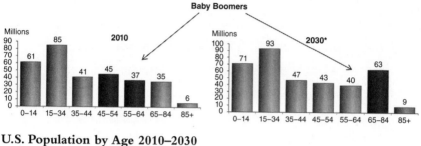

U.S. Population by Age 2010–2030
*Projected.
SOURCES: U.S. Census Bureau; Milken Institute.

The Costs of Aging

The world must address a range of emerging issues as it grows older. The aging population will take a toll in age-related illness, including Alzheimer's, which, without a cure, will afflict 7.8 million Americans by 2030. Nearly 12 million East Asians will suffer from dementia, and India will see a 61-percent increase in diabetes patients by 2030. Medicare spending in the United States is expected to double within a decade.

Workforce growth is slowing. Workforces in many countries are actually shrinking as populations grow older. Today, every 100 people in the traditional U.S. workforce age group—15 to 64—support about

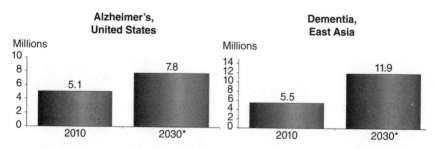

Alzheimer's and Dementia by the Numbers
*Projected.
SOURCES: Alzheimer's Association; Alzheimer's Disease International; Milken Institute.

20 people over 65. By 2030, the same working age group will support 32 people over 65. The ratio is changing even more rapidly in countries like Germany and Japan.

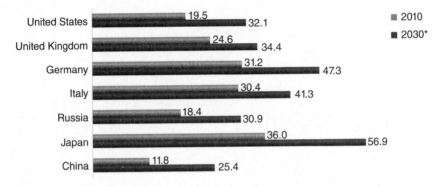

Number of People 65+ Per 100 Working-Age People, 2010, 2030**
*Projected.
**Number of 65+ for every 100 people (15–64 years).
SOURCES: U.S. Census Bureau; Milken Institute.

Mature Workers and Entrepreneurs—Resource for Economic Growth

The aging population, however, has much to offer the world. Thanks to the improved health of older people and the growing recognition of their value, as well as labor shortages in many parts of the world, the 65-and-older group in the global workforce will grow modestly from 20 percent in 1990, to 22 percent by 2020. The United States will see a more dramatic uptick, from 12 percent in 1990, to almost 23 percent in 2020.

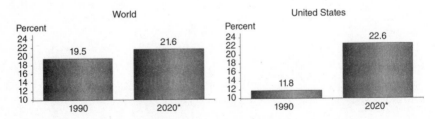

Rise in the Percentage of Workforce Age 65+
*Projected.
SOURCES: Bureau of Labor Statistics; Milken Institute.

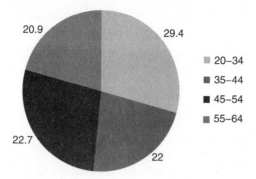

Percentage of New Entrepreneurs, by Age Group
SOURCES: Kauffman Foundation; Milken Institute.

Older people are embracing more entrepreneurial roles, serving as catalysts in innovation, job creation, and economic growth. The Kauffman Foundation found in 2011 that one in five new American entrepreneurs were aged 55 to 64, and almost half of all new entrepreneurs were between the ages of 45 and 64. In Latin America/the Caribbean and in Sub-Saharan Africa, a third of new entrepreneurs fall into the 45 to 64 age range.

In the United States, 9 million baby boomers are already in "encore careers," according to a 2011 study by Metlife Foundation/Encore.org. Research shows that Latin America, the Middle East, and Africa are even more attuned to this trend—focused on both productivity and purpose.

Mature Consumers—The Emergence of the Longevity Economy

Importantly for the world economy, the baby boom generation by its sheer size is a key consumer segment—a market too big to ignore. Those over 50 account for almost half of U.S. disposable income and expenditures. A survey of 3,000 people in 23 countries conducted by A. T. Kearney in 2011, found that people over 60 spent more than $8 trillion in 2010. That number is expected to rise to $15 trillion by 2020. Business leaders, venture capitalists, and other investors are just beginning to understand the magnitude of the opportunity presented by the longevity economy.

And the Internet is an increasingly popular shopping destination for older people. A survey of consumers found that among people over 50, 32 percent of Americans, 30 percent of Germans, and 31 percent of Britons are Internet shoppers.

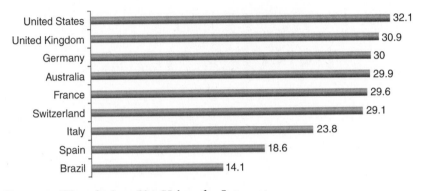

United States	32.1
United Kingdom	30.9
Germany	30
Australia	29.9
France	29.6
Switzerland	29.1
Italy	23.8
Spain	18.6
Brazil	14.1

Percent of People Age 50+ Using the Internet
SOURCES: The Nielsen Company; Milken Institute.

Focus on the Upside

A massive demographic shift is upon us and it's changing our world. We can accept it, embrace it, and capitalize on it—or ignore it at our peril. The following chapters explore how we can reimagine and reinvent the role and place of aging people as a respected, integral part of society. It's time to set aside outdated and outmoded policies and practices, and divisive politics, to enable successful aging and serve the long-term interests of societies and individuals of all ages. The mature world is rising, and it's time to focus on the upside of aging.

Part One

OPPORTUNITIES AND INNOVATIONS

Aging is not lost youth, but a new stage of opportunity and strength.
—Betty Friedan

Chapter 1

Our Aging Population— It May Just Save Us All

Laura L. Carstensen

Director, Stanford Center on Longevity; Professor of Psychology and Fairleigh S. Dickinson Jr. Professor in Public Policy, Stanford University

For the first time ever, a growing resource populates the world—millions of mature people. They are better educated and healthier than prior generations of older people, motivated to make a difference, and knowledgeable and emotionally stable enough to do so.

Emotional stability improves with age. Knowledge grows. Expertise deepens. The brain actually improves in many ways. I was making this case to my dad a while back, about the many positive changes that accompany advanced age, changes that go widely unrecognized in a society centered around the glories of youth. Given the typical characteristics of aging, I said, the presence of millions of older citizens could improve the world significantly.

Not that I needed to convince my father of any of this. He was 92 at the time. His reaction: "Maybe we need to stop talking only about how to save the old folks, and start talking about how they may save us all."

What my father knew, and I also had learned, was that aging has an upside, and that the current aging demographic has much to offer society. For the first time ever, a growing resource populates the world—millions of mature people. They are better educated and healthier than prior generations of older people, motivated to make a difference and knowledgeable and emotionally stable enough to do so. At the same time that we invest in solutions for the very real problems older people face, we must identify and embrace these characteristics and developmental trends that show improvement with age.

A key challenge in the early twenty-first century is to build an infrastructure that taps the important areas of individual growth that improve with age—emotional stability, knowledge, and expertise—for the good of society.

The conversation with my dad about aging actually began some 40 years ago. He was in his fifties, as I am today. I was hospitalized for many weeks, after sustaining multiple broken bones in a car accident, and most of my fellow patients were old women. Orthopedic wards tend to have many older patients, the result of falls and broken bones.

As my pain subsided and boredom set in, my dad, a distinguished researcher and professor at the University of Rochester, suggested that I take a college course. I chose Introductory Psychology, and he offered to attend and tape the classes. He sat in on every lecture and brought the tapes to the hospital. (Little did I know that psychology would one day be my disciplinary expertise. And the fact that older women patients surrounded me as I first delved deeply into human behavior no doubt spurred my interest in aging.)

Despite the fact that my dad at the time was running a large research laboratory filled with graduate students and post-docs, he found time to take an introductory college course purely to benefit his daughter. He is an exceptional man; do not think for a minute that I am suggesting he is typical of any group, old or young. But the tendency with age to prioritize things and people who matter most *is* typical. Moreover, he had reached a stage in life where he had the knowledge and resources to know how to help. The fact that he didn't fall apart emotionally, but felt deeply moved by my situation, also is relevant to what we have learned about the aging brain.

I was trained in both life-span developmental and clinical psychology. Psychological aging offers an excellent example of the gains and losses that occur with age. Most people worry about their aging minds as much (or even more) than their aging bodies. Such fears are not unfounded.

There also are gains, however, and social norms are likely a bigger issue than the physical and mental changes that come with age. For most of that 30-year stretch we label "old age," most people in the United States and the developed world function very well. They live in their homes, and participate in family and community life. They increasingly work, if often part-time. Though there are problems with old age, and the last year or so of life is pretty bleak for many people, that bleakness characterizes the end of life, not old age per se.

Overall, absent significant brain disease, the gains that come with age can functionally offset the declines that typically occur. Indeed, these gains present us with an upside, a resource never before available in human history—tens of millions of older people who are knowledge-able about practical matters of life, who have reared and launched their children, and who care increasingly about investing their time in things that really matter.

Longevity Is Here to Stay

Fears about aging are inherently ironic. Through most of human evolution, life was barely long enough to ensure survival of the species. "Nasty, brutish, and short," is how the seventeenth-century British philosopher Thomas Hobbes described life. Even by 1900, a quarter of babies died before they reached the age of five. Death was common at all ages. Of the babies who survived to 18 years, 20 percent were orphaned in the process.

Women routinely died in childbirth. Romanticized images of multiple generations living together on the homestead were hardly the norm; rather they were exceptions to the rule. The life expectancy at the dawn of the twentieth century was 47 years.

Then, in a single century, we nearly doubled the length of the lives we live, adding almost 30 years to life expectancy for the average person between 1900 and 1999. The increase was spurred by massive cultural shifts that were rooted in medical science and agricultural technologies, large-scale changes that improved sanitation and prevented the spread of disease.

Today, the majority of infants born in the developed world can expect to live into old age. In coming years, families will routinely include four and five generations. Growing old has its share of problems, to be sure, but the opportunity to grow old is very new.

As lives were extended, families had fewer children. The combination of these two phenomena starkly reconfigured population demographics and created aging societies. If people had begun to live longer but fertility had remained high, we wouldn't have aging societies today. The consequences of this aging pattern are clear and enduring, not just a short-term function of the baby boomers aging. The fact that the vast majority of babies born will reach 65 and beyond ensures that the age distribution is here to stay.[1] Short of global plagues that target only the elderly—science fiction–like possibilities—there is every reason to think that these demographic changes will remain into the foreseeable future.[2]

The numbers in Figure 1.1 are for the United States, a youngster when compared to our European counterparts. Western Europeans live longer and have lower fertility rates than Americans. Japan has

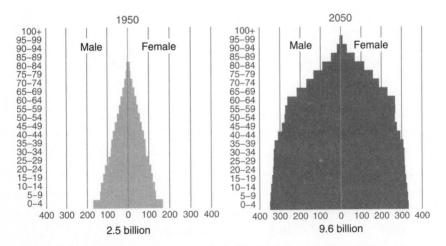

Figure 1.1 World Population by Age and Sex: 1950, 2050 (Projected)
SOURCE: UN World Population Prospects, 2012 Revision.

experienced even starker changes in longevity and fertility, with the longest life expectancies in the world and fertility below replacement levels. One in five Japanese already is over 65.

The fertility declines in the West are expanding to include the developing world, with countries like Brazil, India, and China now aging at an even faster rate than the developed world aged in the last century.

The Future of Aging Societies

In looking at societal aging, I often feel that there are two voices in the public discourse, the doomsayers and the romanticists. The doomsayers are the loudest. They use phrases like the "failure of success" and "gray dawn" to describe older societies. They worry that older societies will be unproductive. They say that large numbers of older citizens will break the bank, create intergenerational strife, and leave children in the dust. We hear their voices regularly on TV news and read their opinions in the newspapers.

The romanticists, on the other hand, equate aging with "sage-ing." They are less prominent in public discourse, but passionate. They depict older people as spending their days pondering life and seeking joy and peace.

The truth, as I see it, lies somewhere in the middle. We should not lightly dismiss those forecasting doom. Golda Meier is famously quoted as saying, "Being seventy is not a sin. It's not a joke either." She was, of course, right. In truth, growing old isn't easy on bodies or minds.

By very advanced age, arthritis, osteoporosis, and hypertension are normative. Muscle strength declines; falls are more common; eyesight, balance, and hearing suffer. Dementia risk doubles with every five years after 65. And because aging occurs in every cell in the body, the older we get, the more likely we are to be injured or become ill, with each health setback taking longer to recover.

However, it is important to recognize that health declines associated with age are a relative issue. In the last 50 years, each birth cohort that has reached old age has been healthier than the one before. Today's 90-year olds are substantially healthier than those who reached 90 just a decade ago.[3] Understand that gains in health may level off and could even fall in light of the tolls taken by obesity and other lifestyle practices, as well as the unhealthful influence of disadvantages associated with race, poverty, and low education. It's hardly time to rest on our laurels. But if we take the long view, there is no question that health in old age has improved profoundly in the last century.

To fully realize the unprecedented opportunities longer lives afford, we need a clear-eyed view of aging. We need to identify fixable problems, find cures for diseases, and develop technologies to address the unfixable ones.

My optimism about aging societies is spurred by the fact that even without scientific advances, aging has its upside. We risk missing the opportunities before us if we focus only on problems and weaknesses associated with advanced age. It is time to carve out new roles for new resources, build technologies that compensate for fragilities, and move forward. In that vein, to begin any serious conversation about the potential of older societies, we need to consider what older individuals may contribute. To start that discussion, we need to consider the aging mind, including evidence supporting the idea that older societies may be wiser societies.

Senior Moments

Cognition refers to the ability to think, reason, process information, remember, and feel. We draw on cognition to comprehend speech, visually perceive and interpret the world around us, calculate probabilities, inhibit thoughts and actions, plan, problem solve, and monitor our behavior. The brain is the organ responsible for cognition, and different regions of the brain are more and less affected by aging.

Most of the research on cognitive aging has focused on what goes wrong, so one doesn't find much comfort in the scientific literature. Until recently, scientists mostly stumbled upon, rather than actively pursued, positive aspects of aging. It's becoming clear that there are lots of preserved areas of function in the aging mind, even some gains, and I'll review them below. But let's put the clear areas of decline on the table first.

Anyone over 50 probably has noticed changes already—forgetting the name of a friend, or words in conversation; lacking concentration when reading the newspaper. These experiences occur for many of us against a backdrop of fear that they may foreshadow dementia, perhaps the most frightening prospect associated with aging. Dementia takes many forms, Alzheimer's disease being the most common. Dementias are horrific diseases. Progressively people lose the ability to remember, and later the ability to dress, walk, and conduct simple activities of daily living.

Scientists once believed that dementia came hand in hand with aging. It is increasingly clear that this is not the case.[4] The (only) good news in this realm is that the majority of people will not get Alzheimer's disease, and that there appears to be less dementia in more recent birth cohorts than earlier historical times.[5] Unfortunately, however, a recent study estimated that as the population ages, so will the number of citizens with dementia. By 2050, the U.S. number is projected to be 13.8 million, up from around 5 million in 2010.[6]

The upside is that we are living at a time when the potentials of science to address illnesses of all kinds are breathtaking. (Of course, we also need to change the way we live. Lives that last 100 years must be paced differently than lives that last 50 years.)

As science looks for a cure to this public health issue, it is important to avoid conflating dementia and normal cognitive aging. Scientists have revealed subtle changes in cognition decades before frank symptoms of dementia appear.[7] So studies of "normal" aging can be skewed because they nearly always include individuals who are in the earliest stages of brain disease.[8]

This fascinating research suggests that the cognitive decline we've considered "normal" may inadvertently include presymptomatic individuals with brain diseases. That is, many years before even a skilled clinician would label the deficits as "symptoms," these folks are scoring at the low end of the normal range. In coming years, we will gain a much clearer picture of "normal" aging, and in all likelihood it will be a more optimistic story than the one we tell today.

The data in Figure 1.2 depict the vastly more robust cognitive trajectory of people without dementia. Still, a vast body of research shows that as normal brains age, the mind is less adept at processing information and innovative thought. Concentration and focus suffer. At the core of these changes is slowing, which inhibits the ability to learn novel

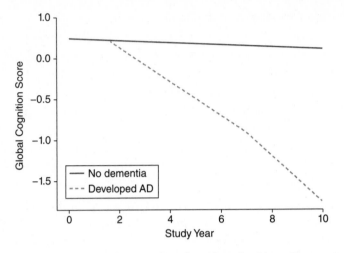

Figure 1.2   Decline in Cognition in People with and without Dementia
Source: R. S. Wilson, S. E. Leurgans, P. A. Boyle, and D. A. Bennett, "Cognitive Decline in Prodromal Alzheimer Disease and Mild Cognitive Impairment," *Archives of Neurology* (2011).

information, and affects attention and inhibition, as well as working, prospective, and episodic memory. Recollection and language are mildly impaired as time goes on.

Most aggravating to many people is the deterioration of memory. The aging brain over time particularly loses working memory—the ability to engage in tasks while mentally holding multiple pieces of information. This type of memory helps us to process and store new information, and to keep in mind the two or three numbers that we are trying to add together.

Older people are all too familiar with the troublesome inability to retrieve the exact word or name that they seek. A full spectrum of comedy relies on jokes in which an old person is asked the name of his old friend across the room. The punch line goes something like, "How soon do you need to know?"

Working memory loss appears inevitable, affecting even the healthiest people as they age. It is well documented across race, sex, educational background, and economic status, beginning, in fact, well before what we consider old age. Effects of slow and steady aging likely are linked to changes in the efficiency of neurotransmission.

The research also brings us good news—specifically, that not all types of memory decline. Procedural memory notably stays intact—governing what psychologists term "automatic" tasks, well-ingrained things that are performed without conscious effort. That could mean anything from using a computer to roller skating. This kind of memory is mostly exempt from the declines of age.

On another positive note, just as physical health has improved over the last century, cognitive decline has lessened. Elizabeth Zelinski and her colleagues studied two birth cohorts, born 15 years apart. As each group reached the age of 74, they were tested. The later-born of the two cohorts scored significantly higher. Indeed, they appeared about 15 years younger than the comparable group born in the earlier time frame.[9] Each group performed more poorly over time but the negative slope in the later-born cohort was less steep.

So, cognitive decline is lessening in the modern era, very likely reflecting more education and better living conditions. As well, while there is ample evidence that aging brings unwanted changes in the speed and efficiency of cognitive processing, the negative slopes are significantly reduced when researchers remove individuals who are in the earliest stages of brain disease.

It's also interesting—and encouraging—that the array of changes do not disrupt functioning in daily life. Although adults slow down, they don't necessarily lose their ability to learn or solve problems in daily life. It's a puzzle that fundamental elements of cognitive processing decline but the logical functional consequences don't follow.

The Power of the Aging Brain

Indeed, why, when asked to name the smartest, most accomplished, effective leaders, do we tend to think of people well into their later years? How does Warren Buffett maintain his legendary reputation as an investor at 83? Why are young scholars so eager to work with professors well into their 60s and 70s? Why do we hear a global sigh of relief when Kofi Annan, at 75, enters into the mix when international conflicts grow heated?

The short answer? Experience. Younger people may learn faster than older people but older people know more. Despite losses in the speed and efficiency of processing new information, learning continues through the most advanced ages. Barring dementia, knowledge continues to build. In the general population, vocabularies are larger and knowledge about the world is greater in the old as compared to the young. It may take older people longer to find words in conversation, but they know more of them.

In highly practiced areas, expertise deepens. Keep in mind that research findings about knowledge surely underestimate domain-specific knowledge because of the idiosyncratic nature of expertise. The general measures researchers use don't tap the deep knowledge that experts have in specialized domains. In one classic study of crossword puzzle champions, psychologist Tim Salthouse found that the older contenders performed better than younger ones, as seen in Figure 1.3.[10] Experts—whether musicians, chess players, or scientists—often reach their peak in advanced years. Especially in areas of expertise, accumulated knowledge compensates well for processing declines.

But it's not a simple matter of accumulating facts and figures. Older people approach problems differently than younger people do. In *The Secret Life of the Grown-Up Brain*, Barbara Strauch, *New York Times* science editor, defied conventional wisdom by maintaining that the aging brain has strengths of its own that hold much opportunity for the betterment

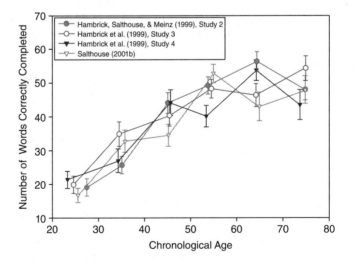

Figure 1.3   Crossword Puzzle Performance by Age

Source: T. Salthouse, "What and When of Cognitive Aging," *Current Directions in Psychological Science* (2004).

of society. The August 2013 issue of *TIME Magazine* carried a large story suggesting that people get more creative as they grow older.

This wouldn't surprise psychologist Lynn Hasher. Hasher and her colleagues have studied disinhibition for many years, documenting in study after study age differences in the ability to suppress irrelevant information—what we might commonly call concentration. When working on a task, young people inhibit extraneous information better than older people. Hasher and her colleagues, however, discovered a potential silver lining. In elegant experiments, she shows that older people access and use the extraneous information when solving problems that arise in subsequent tasks.[11] Younger people are not privileged by the extraneous information. In other words, when your mind wanders while working on one problem, it may be readying itself to solve another.

Neuroscientist Denise Park maintains that high levels of functioning also are facilitated by the nature of our lives.[12] Novel situations become increasingly challenging with age, but older people encounter fewer of them. Instead, we engage increasingly in highly practiced, routine activities—which rely on procedural memory, the memory system that is not affected by age.

We know ourselves better too, what we're good at and where we're lacking. In a study of medication adherence, Park found that older people remembered to take their medication better than middle-aged people whose memories were ostensibly better.[13] Older people, she observed, had established routines that served them better than direct reliance on memory. When you doubt your memory (which is well advised at any age), you rely on strategies that help you compensate.

A stereotype of older people depicts them as fixed in their ways. Park's findings suggest that there is some truth to it. However, daily routines don't extend to rigidity in attitudes or the unwillingness to consider different perspectives. Recent findings suggest that old and young people are relatively open to changing their attitudes. It's middle-aged people who cling to their established views.[14]

Additionally, research on perspective suggests that older people may have a substantial advantage. In a study from my Stanford laboratory, led by Sarah Sullivan, older and younger people were asked to read a story and later recount it from the perspective of the protagonist. In one condition, the protagonist was 25. In the other, she was 75.[15] Otherwise the story was identical. Younger people told both versions the same way. Older people told it as younger people did when recounting the 25-year-old's perspective but differently when told from the perspective of the 75-year-old. It makes sense. We don't lose our younger selves as we grow older. Younger people haven't had the advantage of being old but older people have all experienced youth.

Along the same lines, one of the most reliable findings about aging minds is that they are filled with knowledge about practical matters of life. Increasingly, we find ourselves in situations that have a familiar feeling. We learn from past mistakes. The concept of wisdom has been around for one thousand years, but research on the topic is relatively new.

Some of the most rigorous research was generated by Paul Baltes and his colleagues at the Max Planck Institute for Human Development in Berlin. In a series of studies, they presented older and younger participants with difficult situations and asked how they would address them. Responses were scored based on carefully crafted criteria, including an ability to see things from multiple perspectives, having large stores of practical knowledge, and understanding the relative nature of right and wrong. Reliably, middle-aged and older people scored higher than younger people. The Baltes group observed neither improvements nor declines from middle to old age.

As a rule, researchers have found also that older people seem to appreciate that there are very few pure truths in life. They outperform other age groups in dealing with emotional conflicts that are hotly charged.[16] Richard Nisbett and his colleagues at the University of Michigan have been studying conflict resolution involving cultural and economic disputes over resources. Judges, blind to the age of the participants, reliably score older people's solutions as more even-handed and acceptable than those generated by younger counterparts.[17] Across these studies, higher performance is related to the appreciation of multiple perspectives, willingness to compromise, and recognition of the limits of knowledge.

Motivation, the Aging Brain's Secret Weapon

When it comes to motivation, scientists also find changes across adulthood.[18] In addition to meeting survival basics like hunger and thirst, two general clusters of goals drive much behavior throughout life. One cluster involves exploration and expanding horizons, and includes objectives about learning, risk taking, finding one's place in the world, banking information, and social contacts that may pay off in the long run. The other set of goals centers on emotional satisfaction and emotional meaning.

These two constellations of goals operate throughout life and often compete with one another. When time is perceived as open-ended, as it typically is in youth, exploration usually wins out. Young people persist in struggling to find their place in a crowded world even if that means engaging in activities that don't feel particularly good. When time horizons grow shorter, goals that bring satisfaction and meaning to life win out. For most people, these goals focus on the people and causes that matter the most in life. With age, we tolerate superficial conversations less and value intimate conversations with loved ones more than ever.

And so, with age, we grow more selective about what time we invest and with whom. When time horizons grow short, we see clearly what is important and what isn't. We care less about the trivial matters in life. One elderly woman told me—apologizing because she didn't intend to sound arrogant—that as she gets older she cares less about what others think of her and more about what she thinks of others.

Not surprisingly, these motivational changes are good for mental health. Older people have lower rates of clinical depression, anxiety, and substance abuse.[19] Age is associated with improved emotional experience and emotional stability. Negative emotions are experienced less frequently. We regulate emotions better, avoiding extreme highs and extreme lows.[20]

Brains don't operate like computers, equally reviewing all information. Rather, brains attend to and process information that is relevant to our goals; so our goals determine what we see, hear, and remember. As we grow older and prioritize emotional goals, we come to focus on the good more than the bad in day-to-day life.[21]

So while aging is associated with decline in some aspects of cognitive functioning, and while the incidence of brain disease increases steadily at advanced ages, the majority of people—who will live out their lives without dementia—will find that age also is associated with greater knowledge about the world, deeper expertise in selected domains, and concern for investing in activities and people that really matter.

Tapping a Rich Resource

Many older people today are doing very well, contributing to families, workplaces, and younger generations. To the extent that these mature citizens are physically fit, mentally sharp, and financially secure, societies will thrive. Whether longevity is a benefit or a burden hinges on the status of long-lived people.

Yet humans are creatures of culture. We look to culture to tell us when to get an education, when to marry, work, have children, retire. And the culture that guides us through life today hasn't adjusted to the length of the lives we are living, or to our health and potential for productivity.

Societies need to find creative ways to maximally use older workers and volunteers. We might ask what sorts of societal needs can be best addressed by the well-engrained practical knowledge of older citizens. We have the opportunity to think of new ways to use new available strengths in a new type of citizen.

Instead of proclaiming older societies less productive and innovative, we will do well to begin building an infrastructure that taps this unique resource. The last thing we should be doing is asking older folks to go away and make room for the next generation. While human aging can bring scores of problems, from the physical to societal challenges such as funding retirement systems, populations where people live out their full lives offer unprecedented opportunities.

Aging comes with emotional balance, improved perspective and better mental health—a combination of characteristics that, to many, comprises the very definition of wisdom. Thus, although we must not let up on searches for cures for brain diseases or ignore the less pronounced changes that occur with normal aging, it is critical that we do not overlook the real talent available in a resource never before available in human societies—aging minds.

Notes

1. MacArthur Network on an Aging Society, "Facts and Fictions about an Aging America," *Contexts* 8, no. 4 (Fall 2009): 16–21.
2. Ibid.

3. K. Christensen, M. Thinggaard, A. Oksuzyan, T. Steenstrup, K. Andersen-Ranberg, B. Jeune, and J. W. Vaupel, "Physical and Cognitive Functioning of People Older than 90 Years: A Comparison of Two Danish Cohorts Born 10 Years Apart," *The Lancet* 382 (2013): 1507-1513. doi:10.1016/S0140-6736(13)60777-1.

4. E. Pavlopoulos, S. Jones, S. Kosmidis, M. Close, C. Kim, O. Kovalerchik, S. A. Small, and E. R. Kandel, "Molecular Mechanism for Age-Related Memory Loss: The Histone-Binding Protein RbAp48," *Science Translational Medicine* 5 (2013): 200ra115. doi: 10.1126/scitranslmed.3006373.

5. K. Langa, E. B. Larson, J. H. Karlawish, D. M. Cutler, M. U. Kabeto, S.Y. Kim, and A. B. Rosen, "Trends in the Prevalence and Mortality of Cognitive Impairment in the United States: Is There Evidence of a Compression of Cognitive Morbidity?" *Alzheimer's & Dementia* 4 (2008): 134–144. doi: 10.1016/j.jalz.2008.01.001.

6. L. Hebert, J. Weuve, P. A. Scherr, and D. Evans, "Alzheimer Disease in the United States (2010–2050) Estimated Using the 2010 Census," *Neurology* 80 (2013): 1778–1783. doi: 10.1212/WNL.0b013e31828726f5.

7. R. S. Wilson, S. E. Leurgans, P. A. Boyle, and D. A. Bennett, "Cognitive Decline in Prodromal Alzheimer Disease and Mild Cognitive Impairment," *Archives of Neurology* 68 (2011): 351–356. doi: 10.1001/archneurol.2011.31.

8. M. Albert, Dallas Aging and Cognition Conference (Dallas ACC), January 26–28, 2013.

9. E. M. Zelinski, and R. F. Kennison, "Not Your Parents' Test Scores: Cohort Reduces Psychometric Aging Effects," *Psychology and Aging* 22 (2007): 546–557. doi: 10.1037/0882-7974.22.3.546.

10. D. Z. Hambrick, T. A. Salthouse, and E. J. Meinz, "Predictors of Crossword Puzzle Proficiency and Moderators of Age-Cognition Relations," *Journal of Experimental Psychology: General* 128 (1999): 131–164. doi: 10.1037/0096-3445.128.2.131.

11. R. K. Biss, K. W. J. Ngo, L. Hasher, K. L. Campbell, and G. Rowe. "Distraction Can Reduce Age-Related Forgetting," *Psychological Science* 24 (2013): 448–455. doi: 10.1177/0956797612457386.

12. D. C. Park and A. H. Gutchess, "Cognitive Aging and Everyday Life," in *Aging and Communication*, ed. N. Charness, D. C. Park, and B. Sabel (New York: Springer, 2000), 217–232.

13. D. C. Park, "Aging and the Controlled and Automatic Processing of Medical Information and Medical Intentions," in *Processing of Medical Information in Aging Patients: Cognitive and Human Factors Perspectives*, ed. D. C. Park, R. W. Morrell, and K. Shifren (Mahwah, NJ: Erlbaum, 1999), 3–22.

14. P. S. Visser and J. A. Krosnick, "Development of Attitude Strength over the Life Cycle: Surge and Decline," *Journal of Personality and Social Psychology* 75 (1998): 1389–1410. doi: 10.1037/0022-3514.75.6.1389.

15. S. Sullivan, J. Mikels, and L. L. Carstensen, "You Never Lose the Ages You've Been: Affective Perspective Taking in Older Adults," *Psychology and Aging* 25 (2010): 229–234. doi: 10.1037/a0018383.

16. F. Blanchard-Fields, "Everyday Problem Solving and Emotion: An Adult Developmental Perspective," *Current Directions in Psychological Science* 16 (2007): 26–31. doi: 10.1111/j.1467-8721.2007.00469.x.

17. I. Grossman, J. Na, M. E. W. Varnum, D. C. Park, S. Kitayama, and R. E. Nisbett, "Reasoning about Social Conflicts Improves into Old Age," *Proceedings of the National Academy of Sciences* 107 (2010): 7246–7250. doi: 10.1073/pnas.1001715107.

18. L. L. Carstensen, "The Influence of a Sense of Time on Human Development," *Science* 312 (2006): 1913–1915. doi:10.1126/science.1127488.

19. S. T. Charles and L. L. Carstensen, "Social and Emotional Aging. *Annual Review of Psychology* 61 (2010): 383–409. doi: 10.1146/annurev.psych.093008.100448.

20. L. L. Carstensen, B. Turan, S. Scheibe, N. Ram, H. Ersner-Hershfield, G. Samanez-Larkin, K. Brooks, and J. R. Nesselroade, "Emotional Experience Improves with Age: Evidence Based on over 10 Years of Experience Sampling," *Psychology and Aging* 26 (2011): 21–33. doi: 10.1037/a0021285.

21. A. E. Reed and L. L. Carstensen, "The Theory behind the Age-Related Positivity Effect," *Frontiers in Psychology* 3 (2012): 1–9. doi:10.3389/fpsyg.2012.00339.

Chapter 2

Personalized Aging: One Size Doesn't Fit All

Pinchas Cohen

*Dean, USC Davis School of Gerontology; Executive Director,
Ethel Percy Andrus Gerontology Center; William and
Sylvia Kugel Dean's Chair in Gerontology*

*The upside of aging is personalized aging, based on the idea that no
matter how closely related we are, no two of us travel through the world
or our aging process in the same way.*

When a Scottish grandmother named Ella Bulloch turned 96, she
was asked for her longevity secret. "Chocolate, chocolate, and more
chocolate," she told the *Sun*. "I love it and have never been a fan of
vegetables or fruit. Chocolate keeps me going. I'll have a bit during
breakfast, another bar during lunch, and again during my dinner. That, as
well as what I can get my hands on in between."

When I went to medical school more than 30 years ago, chocolate as the staple of a longevity-assuring, healthy diet certainly never crossed my mind. Neither, for that matter, did anyone at the time seriously propose coffee, olive oil, nuts, or red wine as "health foods."

Since then, however, as my career in teaching and practicing medicine has spanned several continents and institutions—from the Technion in Israel and the Royal Free Hospital in London, to New York University, Stanford University, the University of Pennsylvania, UCLA, and finally the University of Southern California—I have seen evidence-based medicine expanding to explore nontraditional health interventions. I also have recognized that one of my highest responsibilities as a physician and educator is to define for my patients (not to mention myself) what are the "right" things to do and eat.

Thus, while chocolate actually is shown to have health benefits today, it is hardly a food that I, as dean of the USC Davis School of Gerontology, would prescribe as a single remedy for long life. Still, we can't deny that Ella Bulloch did quite well on her chocolate diet, managing to have her cake (chocolate, naturally) and eat it, too. Her story reminds us that while aging may be the most universal of human experiences, its path varies widely with each person.

There is no "one size fits all" when it comes to growing older. Our challenge, in fostering the upside for today's aging world, is to recognize those differences as opportunities for better treatments, solutions, and preventions that are specifically tailored to each individual. I call this revolutionary idea "personalized aging": a new paradigm that recognizes that no two of us are alike when it comes to aging successfully.

Through science, scholarship, and service, we can redefine what it means to age: Aging is not a straight line that we each walk in the same manner, but a unique journey down a path born of our own creation, along with environment and genetics. The upside of aging is personalized aging, based on the idea that no matter how closely related we are, no two of us travel through the world, or our aging process, in the same way. Think of it this way: Few restaurants offer only one meal option. Each diner has different tastes and desires. Why should aging be any different? None of us live it the exact same way.

The old way of thinking about aging and about public health was to divide everything into "good" and "bad" things. The problem was that the distinctions kept changing. The lines kept blurring as science changed its view of what keeps us healthy.

The "one size fits all" mentality, the traditional approach to healthy aging, most certainly won't endure. What it meant to our grandfathers' generation to age "successfully" would not represent the strategies for babies born today, a good thing in many ways. The growing diversity around approaches to aging springs from the activity, enthusiasm, and engagement of many seniors that would astound their own grandparents. This positive trend is only going to expand.

We now think of aging in terms of many "spans." There's the life span, of course, which measures our life expectancy in terms of how many years we live, regardless of their quality. But we hope not to reach 100 only to be miserable, broke, and in dire health. That's where some of the other "spans" come in, most importantly the health span, or the measurement of how many years we remain in good health and manage to avoid the chronic diseases of aging.

Also critically important is the "wealth span," which is the measurement of how many years people remain in financial security. Recently, the first of the baby boomers began turning 65 and reaching retirement age. Never before in history have so many people achieved this age with so much wealth, power, and health—and there's no reason why they shouldn't carry this new attitude into their succeeding decades.

With so many breakthroughs and so many people redefining "old age" as a time of empowerment and excitement, we need to look at the phenomenon of aging in a different way. We know that everyone doesn't age in the same way, but how can we ensure that everyone ages to his or her unique potential?

In my own career, I have been attracted to areas that provide both challenge and hope. I have worked on diverse topics ranging from childhood growth to prostate cancer, but no field has intrigued me more than the science of aging, in which I have immersed myself over the last decade. In particular, I strive to help bring the "genomic revolution" that transformed so many other fields of science to bear directly on each person's ability to healthily age to their individual potential—hence my interest in "personalized aging."

Taking my own family as an example, my wife and I come from completely different gene pools (she is Chinese and I am Jewish). Heart disease is common in my family, cancer in hers. What lifestyle choices should we make as a family? How can our children make their choices? What tools can we use to best capitalize on scientific discoveries that can guide our approaches?

At the Davis School of Gerontology at the University of Southern California, where our faculty regularly study approaches to healthy aging, some of the finest scientists in the field have advanced multiple proposed approaches to these questions over the years. A review of these strategies, which are based on solidly recognized theories of aging and supported by substantial animal, and sometimes human, studies, shows them to be nonredundant and often even contradictory.

Thus, even for my own small, healthy family, it is difficult to confidently recommend a lifestyle to address the enormous variances, including genetic makeup, familial predispositions, and environmental factors, that lead each of us to age in a different fashion.

This failure of gerontology science to come up with a uniform strategy for every aging person is not unique. Many other fields of medicine have struggled for decades with this problem, unable to recommend disease treatments that will be effective in every case, or even the majority of cases.

For example, oncology in the last decade has witnessed an unprecedented avalanche of new treatments that are highly specific to subtypes of diseases (typically identified genetically), representing what is now referred to as "personalized medicine" or "precision medicine." These advances bode well for our aging demographic's ability to sustain longer healthy lives. Unfortunately, this approach so far has focused mostly on the disease rather that the whole individual. In fact, personalized medicine often is geared to identify the "Achilles' heel" of a person's tumor, for instance, rather than identifying the secret weapon the person may possess to fight the tumor.

As a son, a parent, a spouse, and especially as a gerontologist, I want to help usher in a new era of personalized aging in which everyone has access to the unique answers and opportunities of his or her own specific journey. I see this as an exciting time to be alive and aging. To explain why, we can examine how medicine has changed from "herd medicine" to "personalized medicine."

Personalizing Medicine

The medical field has undergone enormous change in which advances in genetics, genomics, molecular biology, and rational drug design have allowed "precision" care for a rapidly growing list of illnesses. This concept is driven by information from genome sequencing and is reinforced by a truth proven time and again through research: People with different genetic makeups respond differently to different treatments. Today, for numerous diseases, we can select appropriate treatments for people based on their genetic capacity to respond. This precision medicine has revolutionized patient treatments—at least in terms of disease.

The challenge now is to look at the broader world of healthy aging and introduce the concepts of personalization and precision in a more integral way. For example, if you were told that your best chances of living a long, healthy life were to subsist on a severely calorically restricted diet, but you died of a heart attack, your heirs might be fairly bitter.

Despite considerable scientific validation of the theory that obese, sedentary people live shorter lives, even here there are clearly exceptions. Both human and animal data show that as a group, most individuals benefit from exercise, but a specific subgroup does not. In addition, it is a fact that most people do not like to exercise. Certainly we'd all like to know if we are in the subgroup of those for whom exercise provides no longevity benefits.

Caloric restriction, the biggest, oldest, and most respected intervention for prolonging life, is similarly limited. In his *Longevity, Senescence, and the Genome*, USC Davis School professor Tuck Finch wrote decades ago, "Caloric restriction is the only known environmental means to alter the acceleration of mortality rate in mammals."[1] However, we now have data, from testing of hundreds of strains of mice, showing that two-thirds lived longer when calorically restricted, but with varying amounts of life extension. About 20 percent don't get any benefit and about 10 percent end up living shorter lives.[2] Clearly, even this classic intervention needs to be individualized by using genetic information that reveals biological differences—a mouse's genes will reveal whether it can live longer with caloric restriction.

Thousands of people in the United States practice this limited-calorie lifestyle today. The Calorie Restriction Society (formally known as the CR Society International) espouses the concept that dramatically limiting food intake will lead to longevity. Most of these practitioners will likely benefit, but which ones? Disappointingly, a two-decade-long study in monkeys, published in the journal *Nature*, showed no benefit of calorie restriction in terms of survival.[3] But this was in an inbred strain of monkeys, underscoring the point that interventions may work in some genetic backgrounds but not others.

Genomics: Sci-Fi No Longer

So how do gerontologists and other scientists determine how we all differ on the genetic level? Right now, scientists use a well-established technique called "genome-wide association studies," or GWAS, to identify certain common genetic factors. This tool involves testing common variations in DNA across the entire genome and comparing their frequency (typically among thousands of subjects) in comparable groups of individuals analyzed against single parameters—for example, having diabetes.

In recent years, this tool has led to discovery of multiple genetic risk factors for diabetes, Alzheimer's, stroke, and cancer. It becomes particularly valuable when a common disease is proven to have dozens of genetic risk factors. Each of these genetic susceptibility markers could be responsive to different interventions—dietary modifications, forms of exercise, or a particular medication. The current challenge is to reliably "couple" a genetic marker with a particular intervention, an endeavor requiring years of expensive research that will be well worth the effort.

One of the major ways in which the world will change to accommodate personalized aging is in the availability of more and more companies to sequence our genomes. The most prominent of these "personal genomics" companies came up with a concept to offer, for under a $100, a service that doesn't *really* sequence your genome—it actually uses markers on the genome.

But soon the technology to completely sequence one's genome and learn every detail about the person's potential genetic modifier will be widely available. This advance will improve the ability of clinical trials to identify response-predicting genetic variants. Soon, commercial companies will actually conduct the sequencing. Identifying the genes that put people at risk for diseases, and the genes that determine their responses to preventive measures, will be a strong incentive for people to employ those preventions and lifestyle choices.

One practical tool now available to help people with lifestyle decisions that could impact healthy aging comes in the output from personal genomic companies. They report genes that put people at risk for melanoma, a finding that might spur use of sunblock and hats. They can identify some genes—unfortunately rather poorly at the moment—that put people at risk for diabetes. Perhaps most accurately, however, they can tell if someone is related to the Queen of England—and the newest prince.

With the rise of more widely available, cheaper, validated data sets, individuals will have more tools to make personalized decisions about healthy aging strategies. How will this impact the public? In crucial areas, as follows.

Nutrition and Genes

We would all like a service that recommends a diet based on genetic testing. This concept, part of a field known as "nutrigenomics,"[4] is still a work in progress, but I see this rapidly emerging science becoming a legitimate industry in the coming years. Once such research is achieved, targeted clinical trials and large randomized clinical studies will be needed to produce results and dietary recommendations.

The aims of nutrigenomics include the ability to demonstrate the effect of bioactive food compounds on maintaining health and achieving longevity. The results should lead to the development of new functional foods that will keep people healthy according to their individual needs.

Nutrients are thought to contribute to the development of multiple cancers, including colon, prostate, and breast cancer. One use for nutrigenomics is to identify gene variants as cancer-susceptibility genes. For example, a gene called N-acetyltransferase, or NAT, is involved in processing amino acids found in heated products, especially well-cooked red meat. Cooking muscle meat at high temperature may activate some amino acids to reactive metabolites, which bind DNA and cause cancers.

People whose blood contains certain variants of the NAT appear to be protected from this reaction while those with other variants are not. Studies have shown that one particular genotype—called NAT2 fast acetylator—was more likely to develop colon cancer in people who consumed relatively large quantities of cooked red meat. Thus, individuals with that genetic variant should be particularly encouraged to minimize red meat consumption.

To Diet or Not?

Diet is an area in which we haven't conducted enough legitimate studies on health effects and weight loss, a fact generally obscured by the string of diet books, websites, and infomercials that barrage our society.

We now know that in mice, and even in worms and yeast, different specimens have different responses to caloric restriction. Some benefit from being starved and some don't. Fortunately for aging baby boomers, diet is perhaps the most important area where personalized aging can be implemented in the relatively near future. A hardcore vegan diet is not for everyone, and thanks to personalized aging, perhaps the people who would not benefit from veganism can discover their tolerances and enjoy that cheeseburger.

Things get particularly confusing when one scans the literature for "healthy diets." Low-fat, low-carb, low-protein, low-calorie, vegetarian, vegan, and many more diets all are touted as having benefits, but rarely have they been put to the test in head-to-head comparisons. Certainly they never have been analyzed properly while considering the genetics, family history, ethnicity, and lifestyles of the people who will choose to follow them. Further complicating conventional wisdom, epidemiological data support a longevity-enhancing effect to coffee and wine, as well as chocolate (yes, chocolate!), but these have not been validated in interventional studies.

One of the most fascinating theories on diet and longevity is that diets have evolved with ethnicities. For example, both the Mediterranean diet of Italy and the Okinawan diet of Japan are famous and frequently touted as longevity boosting. While they have similarities such as being low in animal products, they're also dramatically different. Perhaps we will find they are different because they have evolved empirically based on the different genetic makeups of these two very distinct populations. Perhaps olive oil for the Italians and a lot of green vegetables in the Asian diet serve unique ethno-specific purposes.

A Field in Its Infancy

Nutrigenomics, the scientific study of how genes and nutrition interact, is an exciting branch of personalized aging. Its focus is to study how diet can cause or help prevent disease. But what does this actually mean in terms of personalized aging?

One way to look at the issue of nutrigenomics is to move from population-based nutrition data to individual, or personalized, data—specifically, genetic profile. Health promotion advice is now based largely on data gathered population-wide, revealing what is statistically likely to happen with respect to risk factors and disease outcomes. Nutrigenomics research focuses on tweaking this advice, not replacing it, with an additional level of detail targeted to an individual's genetics. The application would go something like this: You have a blood test to identify specific gene variants. Any particular variant might predict a need for a higher level of one specific vitamin, or may predict whether you could benefit from a specific intervention, like lowering triglycerides. The information from the test allows a person to focus on interventions that actually will help.

As exciting as all this is, it is important to note that nutrigenomics is not ready for immediate translation to the community. We do not yet have the mature tools and the large-scale data from prospective clinical studies to demonstrate beyond doubt the benefits of a particular dietary intervention in individuals with a certain genetic makeup.

My goal, and that of many in the gerontology community, is to build a consensus around the need for such studies, whose results will offer people a chance to customize their diets to their individual genes and family histories.

Such studies will require years, and large amounts of funds. Nonetheless they should become a national priority as important strategies for prevention. Once completed, these large clinical studies can motivate millions of people to change their behaviors, dietary and otherwise, and save the United States alone billions of dollars a year in the cost of care for severe chronic diseases.

Importantly however, despite what we hope is the promise of such research, "clinics" that today already offer nutrigenomics services should be considered as operating outside the boundaries of legitimate medicine, peddling immature and unproven dietary recommendations that have not been clinically validated.

Some have said that "genes are destiny,"[5] suggesting that genetic susceptibility to disease is a fate we cannot escape, but this is not where this field is heading. The coming decades will create new tools for people to make smarter, more informed decisions about diet and lifestyle choices. Our current knowledge base with respect to genetic predispositions is still in its infancy.

Let's Prove It

It is disheartening how little public support and funding exists in the United States for legitimate clinical research into diets designed to prevent disease and promote healthy aging, when the upside of research is so potentially beneficial.

The most cited study was conducted in Spain over six years. It looked at a group of middle-aged people who were randomized to either a standard low-fat diet (commonly recommended for prevention of cardiovascular disease) or to a Mediterranean Diet, rich in vegetables, legumes, whole grains, fruits, and fish, and supplemented with olive oil.[6]

Surprisingly, the Mediterranean Diet was superior to the low-fat diet in terms of prevention of stroke and heart attacks, and there was a hint that it also reduced overall mortality. The study was designed more than a decade ago and unfortunately did not include genomic data, which would have helped create future studies with more individualized design.

Another large European study suggested that a Mediterranean Diet low in simple carbohydrates can reduce the incidence of diabetes. In fact, the latest development of legitimate nutrigenomics has been the demonstration that individuals with certain genetic dispositions for stroke particularly benefited from adhering to a Mediterranean Diet. At the date of this writing, unfortunately, no major dietary study has been launched in the United States.

Another area where a genomic approach could help tailor interventions is the study of centenarians. We are learning that long-lived people frequently have a unique genetic makeup that protects them from environmental insults and enables their remarkable longevity in spite of multiple bad habits that negatively affect most other people. Identifying these genes may accelerate discoveries of agents that will promote healthy aging and longevity.

Clearly, some commonly recommended practices that should enhance aging don't work on everyone. The good news for our aging population is that science has enormous potential to develop more effective and tailored solutions. The public today is more educated than ever about healthy nutrition options, with knowledge that is only increasing. I fully expect nutrigenomics to grow in prominence as our understanding of the enormously important link between nutrition and genetics continues to grow.

To Run or Walk?

No discussion of diet is complete without its close partner, exercise. For decades now, doctors and scientists have pushed the idea that exercise is good. But what is the "right" exercise? And what is the right amount? As with diet, we have seen an extraordinary reimagining of this concept, which has spurred another wave of books, infomercials, and so-called experts, eager to take our money and help us get "buns of steel" and "thinner thighs in 30 days."

Jim Fixx wrote *The Complete Book of Running* in 1977 and helped inspire a generation of Americans to begin jogging and to reconsider physical fitness as an important priority. He quickly became one of the world's foremost experts on exercise. His trim physique proved as much a testament to his methods as his books. Shockingly and dishearteningly to many, however, Fixx died in 1984 of a heart attack at age 52, after a morning jog. His death raised a new set of questions about the benefits of exercise and what should be considered healthy exercise.

We know that some kinds of exercise are more suited to certain people, based on preferences, existing health levels, and access to resources. While swimming may be an ideal exercise for a grandmother who loves the water, we would most likely not suggest it for her granddaughter who is deathly afraid of the water.

It's no surprise that doctors and scientists are unable to reach a universal consensus as to the ideal exercise. Is running better than walking? Are lengthy periods of sustained exercise more beneficial than intense, intermittent bouts? If the goal is to maximize health and life span, what is the ideal exercise over the course of a lifetime and how should it change with age?

It's fascinating to think about how many different ways we have to exercise, but no true guidance on which is the best. Once again, we face open questions that personalized aging can address. The upside for our aging demographic is that science has now confirmed that exercise is beneficial to health and that research is underway to pin down the specifics.

Supplemental Jury Out

An even more controversial area in which we find many questions but few scientifically proven answers is the unregulated "Wild West" of supplements. In health food stores and even supermarkets are literally hundreds of different supplements that claim to have healthy-aging effects. Of these claims, almost none is based on data. In fact, many of these products have been shown to not work, and data shows that some actually have negative effects.

Anecdotal and small studies show that Vitamins E and C and similar supplements don't work in large populations and may even have negative outcomes. However, in smaller populations, they can reveal *positive* health effects. Why? Simply put, certain people may have unique genetics that allow them to benefit from supplements that might not work for their friends.

While the current supplement marketplace may bring to mind the outrageous claims and disappointing (if not downright dangerous) results of medieval miracle elixirs, there is a strong indication that if we could identify the people who would respond positively to the right mixture of supplements, we could serve their health well.

Looking Good, Feeling Good

Personalized aging research at the USC Davis School also looks at what we call the aesthetics of aging. Just as with supplements, hundreds of cosmetics and beauty treatment options are sold to combat the signs of aging. These products vary in quality, efficacy, and safety.

It's easy to dismiss cosmetic concerns as mere vanity, but vanity is certainly a universal quality and one for which we should all show more empathy. It is understandable that people of all ages want to maintain a certain standard of attractiveness that is linked to their feelings of self-worth. Ideally, this standard is not based on a skewed Hollywood image but is tied up with a self-image that derives equal parts of satisfaction in positive relationships, usefulness, and inner beauty.

Besides making people feel better about themselves, the aesthetics of aging can help reveal important health factors. When people look "old" or "young" for their age, it can be a sign of health as well. A 2009 study by the *British Medical Journal* found that people who appear to be more "youthful" tend to live longer than people who look "older" than their years.[7] This may be tied to genetic factors, which suggests that physical appearance may be a marker of health.

Consider how much money is spent on cosmetic fixes for the physical symptoms of aging, whether it is plastic surgery, Botox, or creams and lotions. Although people would welcome sound and safe options to mitigate the physical changes of aging, very few organizations are truly applying twenty-first-century science to address them.

For instance, it boggles the mind to imagine a reliable "prevention strategy" for gray hair or wrinkles, and to think of how we might focus on specific genes. No doubt people would respond if a personalized aging approach could determine their risk for baldness and offer treatments to prevent it—especially since current Food and Drug Administration–approved therapies for baldness help some people, but not others.

Conclusion

The key to personalized aging, I believe, is to accommodate every individual as much as possible to maximize his or her health and happiness. The portrait of "healthy aging" will differ for each person, but this approach provides many opportunities empowering people to make the choices that are best for them, socially and scientifically. By engaging people with modern science, we can continue to rewrite and reimagine what it means to age successfully.

An apropos joke finds a rabbi being asked to mediate an argument between two men. After hearing the first man's side of the story, the rabbi says, "You're right." He then listens to the other man and tells him, "You are right." At that point, the rabbi's wife, who has heard both conversations, asks, "How can you tell one man he is right and then tell the other man he is right as well?" To this, the rabbi says, "You're also right."

Grounded in impeccable research, aging-science can afford all people the opportunity to learn and implement their best health strategies—in effect, every person will have the opportunity to be "right" for his or her own needs. That's at the heart of my vision for personalized aging: arming each person with a unique blueprint for the best chance at maximizing his or her longevity.

With more control over this most universal of human experiences comes peace of mind and the ability to make the most of the time we have. I see the era of personalized aging as nothing short of a revolution in which each of us will be empowered to live our best lives.

I'm reminded that for many years, everyone was forced to choose from a handful of television channels—there were no other options. Today hundreds of cable channels, as well as nontraditional choices ranging from YouTube to Netflix, are tailored for specific audiences and interests—an option for every viewer. Similarly, personalized aging reflects a thrilling prospect: an effective, detailed roadmap specific for each individual's journey through the years.

The era of personalized aging is upon us, and while it may not mean that we can all indulge in "the chocolate diet" favored by Ella Bulloch, it does mean that soon we all will have a much greater say in how we age—how we prepare for and respond to the challenges of aging, which is the greatest opportunity imaginable. Aging well—the greatest adventure any of us will undertake—demands nothing less.

Notes

1. Caleb E. Finch, *Longevity, Senescence, and the Genome* (Chicago: University of Chicago Press, 1994), http://books.google.com/books/about/Longevity_Senescence_and_the_Genome.html?id=_JkMRundeNcC.
2. C. Y. Liao, B. A. Rikke, T. E. Johnson, V. Diaz, and J. F. Nelson, "Genetic Variation in the Murine Lifespan Response to Dietary Restriction: From Life

Extension to Life Shortening," *Aging Cell* 9 (2010): 92–95, www.ncbi.nlm.nih
.gov/pubmed/19878144.

3. J. A. Mattison et al., "Impact of Caloric Restriction on Health and Survival
in Rhesus Monkeys from the NIA Study," *Nature* 489 (September 13, 2012):
318–21, www.ncbi.nlm.nih.gov/pubmed/22932268.

4. M. Grayson, "Nutrigenomics," *Nature* 468, no. 7327 (2010): S1, www.ncbi
.nlm.nih.gov/pubmed/21179075.

5. Mike Bygrave, "False Dawns in the Brave World of New Genetics," *The
Observer*, December 21, 2002, www.theguardian.com/science/2002/dec/22/
genetics.science.

6. R. Estruch et al., "Primary Prevention of Cardiovascular Disease with a Mediterranean Diet," *New England Journal of Medicine* 368 (2013): 1279–90, www
.ncbi.nlm.nih.gov/pubmed/23432189.

7. Kaare Christensen et al., "Perceived Age as Clinically Useful Biomarker of
Ageing: Cohort Study," *BMJ* 339 (2009): b5262, www.bmj.com/content/339/
bmj.b5262.

Chapter 3

The Bold New World of Healthy Aging

Freda Lewis-Hall
Executive Vice President and Chief Medical Officer, Pfizer Inc

Breakthroughs from the world's medical labs will help narrow the gap between our healthiest days and the end of our lives, with a medical trifecta—data and diagnostics, new medicines and vaccines, and a surgery revolution—to help deliver the full promise of healthy aging.

My father, Harvey Lewis, at 95 is sharp and spry. Watching him enjoy life with family and friends brings me immense joy but also reminds me that he's lived nearly twice as long as my mother, Jeannette, who died in her early fifties, cut down by a sudden stroke. The day remains seared in our family's collective memory.

It was a typical Maryland summer's night, hot, and heavy with the Chesapeake damp. I was home from my first year at medical school. One moment she was there, happy about my plans for career and marriage. The next moment, she was gone. My mother's death sent our family reeling into a period of shock and despair that nearly led me to quit medical school.

Today, as a physician and biopharmaceutical executive, I have a ring-side seat to the march of medical progress that is working to unlock the secrets to a long life, like my father's, and understand what cuts some lives, like my mother's, all too short. Thanks to these medical advances and public health successes, members of my generation, the baby boomers, now have a good chance of exceeding the life expectancy predicted for us at birth—most likely by the equivalent of an extra day a week for each week of our lives.

Continued progress means that U.S. babies born today will likely exceed even that eight days a week: One-third of them are projected to live past 100. But longevity begs a pressing question: What of the quality of life? Will we enjoy that eighth day each week, or spend it waiting to die? The upside: Breakthroughs emerging from the world's medical labs will help narrow the gap between our healthiest days and the end of our lives, with a medical trifecta—data and diagnostics, new medicines and vaccines, and a surgery revolution—on track to help deliver the full promise of healthy aging.

Scientists envision developments right out of *Star Wars*: robots doing surgery, 3-D printers churning out transplantable organs, vaccines that stave off Alzheimer's—and much more. However, the biggest upside in aging may not be in the "gee-whiz" developments of the future, but in what we've learned about health care in the here and now. We have it in our power—today—to greatly improve the odds that we will die from old age, and in good health.

The Mother of All Confluences

The front lines of science keep moving relentlessly forward, and I feel safe in saying that the next two decades will be the most productive period ever in biomedical research. Many new therapies will arrive in time to help today's aging generation navigate the shoals of old age. It's very unlikely that we will "cure" aging over the next few decades, but it's a reasonable bet that we will soften many of the hardest edges of getting old.

Medical progress is at the confluence of two massive streams of technology, both rooted in breakthroughs of the postwar baby boom. The invention of the transistor in 1947 set the stage for stunning advances in computing, wireless communications, micro-machines, robotics, and other silicon-chip-based technologies. The 1953 discovery of DNA in double-helix form led in 2000 to the decoding of the Human Genome, arguably humanity's greatest medical achievement.

Thanks to these two enormous technology streams, we've made quantum leaps both in understanding human health and in applying new technology to unmet medical needs. Science is now swamped with new leads—a complete discussion of medicine behind healthy aging is beyond the scope of this book—but the most concrete developments unfolding are in three huge trends that will help transform aging over the next two decades:

1. A revolution in data and diagnosis
2. A new "golden age" in medicines and vaccines
3. A "never too old" movement in surgery

Beyond the next two decades, even more fantastic developments await—suffice it to say that scientists at Stanford University already have pioneered a way to transform our DNA into transistors. It is conceivable that today's millennials will have their own cells constantly reporting on their health.

In the near future, the exciting prospects for progress are tempered by the rising tide of Alzheimer's and other age-related diseases. They may sap our energy, our health care funding, and our best efforts for medical progress. If we can ride out this flood tide, and I believe we can, 75 will be the new 50.

A Data and Diagnosis Revolution

The next two decades promise a revolution in collecting, analyzing, and deploying medical data—with an immense, positive effect on our health, starting with patient-doctor relationships. Soon people's health may be monitored by a host of electronic sentinels communicating directly with us—and our medical professionals. The doctor will always be "in."

At the core of the data revolution is the advent of universal DNA analysis and the global adoption of electronic medical records. Fast and cheap decoding of DNA is a near-certainty in the next several years. By 2020, a person's genetic code will be analyzed in an hour or two, at a cost in line with the price tag for an x-ray. Newborns will get their DNA profiles in the hospital.

Armed with accurate maps of a person's 25,000 genes, patient and doctor will have a sharper picture of the patient's overall strengths and vulnerabilities. The genetic code will help guide medical decision making, and aid health care teams in selecting the safest and most effective medicines, recommending diet and exercise regimens, and predicting chances of setback, from cancer to compulsive disorder.

Along with fast and cheap DNA analysis, the universal use of electronic medical records will reshape the ways people interact with their physicians. Interestingly, this new technology may bring back into style the "hands-on" doctoring that marked an earlier age.

When I was a kid growing up in Washington, D.C., our community physician, Dr. Settles, who inspired me to be a doctor, knew every one of his patients and their medical histories. A visit with Dr. Settles was anything but curt and clinical. He connected your symptoms to what he knew about you. We all know that's changed. For most of us, interactions with our doctors begin with a clipboard thrust through a waiting room window, and end with an invoice handed through that same window. In between is usually a short, rushed consult.

Electronic health records will, almost counter-intuitively, help humanize the partnerships between people and their doctors, first by enriching the information doctors have about their patients, and then by maximizing the benefit of the time physicians spend with their patients.

Such records also will provide a common language for all the medical experts engaged in a person's care. The patient will be the gatekeeper, admitting an inner circle to obtain a complete picture of his or her health. No longer will the individual's health depend on the skill of one health professional in reading another's handwriting. Electronic health records should make health care more personal, more efficient and far less hazardous, considering that more than 210,000 U.S. patients die prematurely each year from preventable harm in the hospital, according to an estimate by Dr. John T. James of Patient Safety America.[1]

Converting medical records to bits and bytes also will open new vistas for biomedical research. Stripped of personal details, a person's health information will be incorporated into large pools of computer-analyzed data—the result of advances in what is now called "Big Data."

Backed by computing power in the quadrillions of calculations per second, medical researchers will be able to see patterns of disease in subpopulations, and predict how well a new therapy might work for a patient in that subpopulation. Such predictions will lead to the best therapy from the start, eliminating the need to try therapy after therapy in search of what works.

Big Data will illuminate global patterns of health and disease, and guide predictions of individuals' chances for cancer and other life-threatening diseases, and even risks for suicide and addiction. Big Data will be at the front lines of our defense against epidemics, not only to predict and track them, but also to swiftly evaluate how to slow or defeat a new pathogen.

Our New Guardian Angels

In the mid-1990s, Japan's TOTO company introduced the first "intel-ligent toilet"—with health-monitoring devices integrated into it. The toilet automatically analyzed urine, tracked blood pressure, and weighed users, transmitting results to home computers or doctors. The toilet also included a bidet, a drying feature, and a pneumatic seat that returned to the "down" position.

TOTO was in the vanguard of a diagnostic revolution. Within 10 years, and mostly through successors of smartphones, we will be surrounded by an army of tiny but relentless sentinels. They will not only monitor many dimensions of our health, but will also help us optimize our diets, medication, and exercise regimens.

The first such devices are here. Former U.S. Senator Bill Frist of Tennessee, once a practicing heart surgeon and now a speaker on health issues, is always quick to show off a surprisingly affordable smartphone app and case that when pressed to the chest offers up an instant electro-cardiogram. It's possible to envision such an app as one of many health-status monitors, and that phone case as a wireless-enabled, dime-sized monitor stuck discreetly to a person's skin, or even woven into cloth-ing. And this smart device could be always in touch with even smarter computers, programmed to signal a health issue well before it becomes a crisis.

Over the next decade, "lab on a chip" technology will advance to the point where smartphones will be able to analyze a blood or saliva sample accurately enough to diagnose the origin of many infections or even to test for chronic diseases such as diabetes. Dr. Eric J. Topol, editor-in-chief of *Medscape*, believes that the emerging global networks of smartphones, smartwatches, and smart glasses, connected with the supercomputers of the future, will change the paradigm for diagnosis, and along the way, make health care much more efficient,[2] given that up to 30 percent of U.S. health care costs can be traced to unnecessary doctor visits and treatments.[3]

The rule in diagnosis is that the earlier a serious health issue can be identified, the better the chances of a positive patient outcome. Advances in remote monitoring may, within a decade, eliminate one of our worst fears: sudden, unexpected health trauma, leading to death, such as the "bolt from the blue" stroke that claimed my mother's life.

We are now learning that many of these seemingly unpredictable events are preceded by subtle changes in body functioning or chemistry. As an upside in aging over the coming years, we will gain the upper hand over these sudden events and their dramatic, devastating effects.

"Smart" devices, bristling with diagnostic sensors, will detect the often-unnoticed and even transient dysfunctions that precede a full-blown health crisis. The most important mobile phone call you may get 10 years from now is one advising that you or a loved one is in imminent danger of heart attack or stroke. Researchers at the Stroke Program at the University of Texas believe that such early detection systems will yield vast changes in stroke treatment, possibly including a new definition of the "golden hour" of emergency treatment—from intervention within the first 60 minutes after onset of symptoms of an event, to the interception of such an event in the days or hours *before* it happens.

Smart devices may also liberate aging people from the pain and trauma of falls and fractures. Technologists in a number of institutions, including the Norwegian Informational Security Laboratory, have already demonstrated that accelerometers in smartphones can identify a person by his or her gait, and can distinguish changes in gait. It's not a stretch to envision that such accelerometers can be deployed to signal danger of falling. Should a person begin to topple, engineered cloth-ing, using variants of automotive airbag technology and connected to accelerometers, could deploy in an eye blink to protect the wearer from serious injury.

Since 2008, a Japanese company, Prop, has marketed such an air-bag system for people at extreme danger of serious injury from falling. Preventing trauma from falls would be no small victory. An estimated 250,000 Americans over age 65 suffered hip fractures last year, beginning for many of them their loss of independence and decline into death.[4]

This vanguard of microelectronic sentinels will be able to help monitor and improve health without any extra effort, running in the background of an individual's daily routine. At MIT's Media Lab, Professor Alex "Sandy" Pentland is already using the sensors on a typical smartphone to demonstrate how changes in its owner's daily routine can indicate a range of health problems, from depressive episodes to the onset of schizophrenia.

At the doctor's office, patients will encounter a host of sophisticated assistive devices that amplify the physician's ability to make accurate diagnoses. For example, late in 2011, the Food and Drug Administration approved a scanning device, the MelaFind, which combines a handheld wand with a computer program to analyze skin lesions and determine if they should be investigated as melanomas, the deadliest form of skin cancer. Clinical studies indicate that MelaFind's assessments are as accu-rate as those of doctors as a whole.[5]

Doctors themselves will have new office mates keeping patients healthy. Within 10 years, medical computers based on IBM's Watson technology, the computer that defeated human opponents on the *Jeopardy!* quiz show, are expected to be in common use. In a second, it can crunch the information in millions of books, and use it to develop a "most probable" answer.

In 2012, Watson was dispatched to several academic medical cent-ers, including The Cleveland Clinic and Columbia University, to be crammed with health and medical information, beginning a multiyear experiment that may refashion the idea of a "physician's assistant."

By 2020, next-generation Watsons will proliferate, helping doctors keep up with the explosion of medical knowledge, now doubling every five years. "Assistive" computers will then move into direct diagnosis—understanding the language you speak, knowing your health history and current health status, and doing what doctors do—serving up a highly informed theory on what ails you, according to IBM's Watson technology team. Unlike the doctor, Watson will be able to keep up with every medical breakthrough and the latest clinical studies. Within a decade, Watson-type computers may be the first "practitioners" a patient sees, either in the doctor's office, or through a remote "house call."

The revolution in diagnosis ultimately means that older people will have a set of personal sentinels keeping constant watch over their health and safety. These sentinels will only become less expensive and better over time, as they collect, analyze, and compare greater amounts of data about what's really going on inside the body, and tell that story to health care professionals who are increasingly well armed to heal people.

A Golden Age of Medicines

The next 20 years will see a golden age of medicines, with a substantially larger set of pharmaceuticals and biologicals at the ready for physicians. Many of these new therapies will be precisely tuned to each person's DNA, RNA, proteins, and metabolites. Many will treat a disease. Others will prevent it. A few therapies may do both.

Medical futurists have long discussed "personalized" medicines—the idea of formulations fitted to each patient. This may eventually happen, but in the meantime we will see the fast rise of "precision medicines" designed to address a specific genetic malfunction or protein expression triggering a disease.

The precision approach is taking hold in oncology, where it is understood that large diagnostic categories, such as breast cancer, are actually collections of dozens of diseases, many of them attributable to a narrow variation in gene sequence or tiny malfunction. In a dramatic treatment shift for large categories of cancers, doctors will rely on advanced diagnostics to find the "fingerprints" of the cancer's cause, and prescribe a treatment that "smart-bombs" that cause.

This precision approach will give new hope to people suffering from rare diseases, which collectively are not rare at all. It's estimated that 1 person in 10 globally has a rare disease, 80 percent of which are genetic. About 7,000 rare diseases have been identified. Only 500 have approved treatments.

Hundreds of rare diseases, such as lupus and multiple sclerosis, present in adulthood. Precision medicine should yield many more candidates for therapies over the coming decade, and may be able to get those therapies into doctors' hands more cheaply and more quickly than is possible now.

The New World of Vaccines

The revolution in medicines will extend to vaccines. Vaccines will move beyond their role in preventing disease to a new role in treatment—and they eventually may be deployed not only for people at threat of infection, but also for people suffering from chronic conditions such as Alzheimer's, diabetes, and nicotine addiction.

To understand where vaccines are going, we need to understand how they have evolved and their value to both patients and society. The best-known preventive vaccines, such as Salk's polio vaccine, were humanity's first effective defenses against viral infections. Such vaccines work by exposing the patient to a killed or weakened form of the virus, enabling the patient's own immune system to recognize the virus and fight off a full-scale infection. Vaccines against bacterial infection, such as diphtheria, pertussis, and tetanus, work by inactivating the toxins produced by the bacteria.

The vaccines broadly recommended for children under six have been devastatingly effective against diseases that once killed or disabled millions each year. I lived with an uncle who contracted polio and spent a lifetime dealing with the painful realities of paralyzed legs. Some of my earliest family memories are of him imprisoned in a whole body cast. Polio is now nearly eradicated. Diphtheria, once a common cause of death among children, is down to a handful of yearly cases in the United States.

The next generation of vaccines will tackle even more insidious infections. The Holy Grail is a vaccine effective against HIV, the virus that causes AIDS. Having eluded efforts at a therapeutic or preventive vaccine for more than 25 years, HIV's time as an in-body marauder may soon be up.

New antibodies effective against HIV have been isolated, and, as of this writing, more than three dozen HIV vaccine clinical trials are underway, leading to hopes for a vaccine within a decade.[6] The next ten years also likely will yield vaccines effective not only against other viral and bacterial infections, but also fungal and parasitic ones. A vaccine against malaria, for example, could save a million lives, mostly those of the very young and very old, each year.

Especially promising for the nation's aging demographic, the next 10 years will see the rise of a new category of vaccines—therapeutic vaccines—effective against age-related, noncommunicable, chronic diseases. Arguably the first such vaccine, Dendreon's PROVENGE, was approved by the FDA in 2010 to treat certain kinds of late-stage prostate cancer. This vaccine takes a body's own immune cells and, in a sense, reprograms them to hunt down a specific antigen found on prostate cancer cells.

Today a range of chronic diseases, including nicotine addiction, diabetes, hypertension, and Parkinson's disease, are targets for future vaccines. These vaccines generally will use pieces of a harmless virus to trick the body's cells into making antibodies that keep a disease from taking hold. Within the lifetimes of baby boomers, we even may be able to immunize people against Alzheimer's disease, a breakthrough that can't come a moment too soon.

Never Too Old—For Surgery

My father survived a world war, the Depression and a dozen recessions. He's been a Pullman porter, a store owner, and a limo driver. He grew up among freed slaves and lived long enough to meet, face to face, America's first African American president. He runs rings around people half his age.

But, at 95, he would have a serious decision to make if he needed surgery to preserve his quality of life. The risks of death from serious complications of surgery tend to rise dramatically with age. Surgery is tough on the heart, lungs, and brain. Enormous breakthroughs in surgical technology, post-surgical recovery, and pain and infection control are making surgical decisions a lot easier. There are barriers to successful surgery, but increasingly, age won't be one of them. Minimally invasive techniques have greatly lessened the severe strains the body once endured in surgery, making even the oldest people surgery candidates in the next 20 years.

In the decade to come, skilled surgeons increasingly will turn to robots to amplify their talents and efforts. Robot-enabled surgery isn't new—Intuitive Surgical's four-armed da Vinci system, already used in 2,000 operating rooms,[7] was introduced in 1999. It enhances a surgeon's abilities by giving him much more hand range and dexterity, and much sharper vision.

The surgeon works seated, at a console, alleviating much of the strain that can degrade performance. We can envision next-generation robotic systems becoming smaller, smarter, and much more user friendly. Systems like da Vinci may weigh a half-ton and often dominate an operating room. Smaller systems could conceivably move surgical procedures into stand-alone systems that are cheaper to run and would enable faster surgical interventions. Within two decades, it's likely that first responders will be equipped with robotic systems that will initiate surgery on route to the hospital.

Smarter surgical systems also are coming. Advances in voice recognition, visualization, and artificial intelligence will allow robotic systems and human surgeons to work as a team. The newest robotics systems feature "shared control," in which the surgeon marks out areas for incision, along with off-limit areas. The robot never lets the surgeon stray into the wrong places.

The next two decades also will bring many "smart" devices for implantation, including artificial limbs that respond to thought patterns. The state of the art here is moving rapidly.

In 2012, the journal *Nature* reported that a 58-year-old paralyzed woman, using a new technology called BrainGate, expressed a thought in her mind that was translated into movement by a robotic arm. For the first time in three decades, she was able to get a drink of water without assistance.[8] This technology will blossom in coming years, to the benefit of people facing diminished loss of movement or mobility from trauma, disease, or old age.

Is That My Liver on the Printer?

Today, in Tokyo's FabCafe, visitors can have their heads replicated in chocolate through a three-dimensional printer. Unlike a standard printer, which can lay down just a few layers of ink, 3-D printers work by laying down successive layers of material, so what emerges has height, depth, width, and weight. Within 10 years, 3-D printers will be as common as home computers, and such printers may eventually "print" replacement hips and knees. Right now, though, scientific teams are tackling an amazing "what-if?" What if we could program 3-D printers to replicate new body parts, ready for immediate transplant, from a patient's own cells?

In an example of early success, doctors from the University of Michigan replicated part of a baby's trachea on a 3-D printer. Over time, the bioplastic material of the artificial trachea dissolves, replaced by the baby's own tissue. It's likely that within 10 years, organs such as bladders will be routinely created through 3-D processes. Within 20 years, a range of organs should be available, and 3-D transplantation will be as common as joint replacement is today.

The Wild Card: Tackling Alzheimer's

As mentioned earlier, realizing the fullest potential of healthy aging faces numerous challenges. The biggest comes from Alzheimer's and other age-related dementias. In the past, most people didn't live long enough to be affected by these dementias, which experts once viewed as a normal part of aging. Now with longer life spans, millions of people are crossing each year into the danger zone for Alzheimer's, which begins around age 65.

At their current pace, Alzheimer's and other age-related dementias will strike more than 115 million people globally by 2050[9]—1 person in 85 with dementia, overwhelmingly Alzheimer's. Push that ratio much further, and there may not be a health care system in the world that can afford the costs of Alzheimer's and age-related dementias.

Alzheimer's presents a huge challenge because it is almost the "perfect" disease. It plays out in the body's most mysterious and least accessible organ, the brain. It runs its course over many years. It is hard to diagnose—until recently, the only absolutely positive diagnosis came with autopsy. It is hard to design a clinical trial to test therapies. And it is difficult to determine when we should begin treatment. There is still considerable disagreement as to the actual mechanism of action of the disease. Is it caused by a toxic load of beta-amyloid in the brain? Or does the disease begin with the tangles of tau protein?

Current research is largely aimed at slowing down the progression of the disease. Just postponing the onset of serious dementia by five years could reduce the number of patients by 43 percent and save more than $440 billion in caregiving costs, in the United States alone, according to estimates by the RAND Center for the Study of Aging.[10]

Currently the world's research-based biopharmaceutical companies are developing about 80 new therapies for Alzheimer's disease, often in collaborations with other companies, major universities, foundations, and governments. Concepts under development include gene therapies that deliver natural growth factors to the brain, intranasal therapies that boost the brain's ability to protect itself, and vaccines that induce the body to rally against beta-amyloid proteins that clog the brain. There's reason to be cautiously optimistic, but even greater reason to put more concerted, collaborative effort into defeating the impending Alzheimer's epidemic. To put it simply: We've got to bring Alzheimer's to its knees, because it can bring us to ours.

We Have Met the Solution, and It Is Us

As exciting as it may be to look a decade or two down the road in health care, we don't have to wait to significantly improve our chances for a longer, higher-quality life. Relatively modest changes in lifestyle, along with access to good health care, can significantly lengthen our quality time on earth. It's astounding to think that new organs may someday be printed on a 3-D device, but better to think of ways to preserve and extend the useful life of our natural organs.

The biggest threat to our quality of life comes in the form of disabling chronic diseases. Half of Americans over 50 now have a chronic disease that puts them at risk for disability, the U.S. Centers for Disease Control reports. Many of these diseases, such as diabetes, hypertension, and high cholesterol, are preventable or readily treatable. The most impactful individual and collective action to assure an upside to aging is an intensified attack on chronic diseases.

According to the World Health Organization, eliminating just three risk factors—poor diet, lack of exercise, and tobacco use—could prevent 80 percent of heart disease and stroke, 80 percent of adult-onset diabetes, and 40 percent of cancers.[11] Altering lifelong habits isn't easy, but clearly, healthier lifestyles now could extend lives, increase productivity, and decrease health care costs. Even modest gains against heart disease and cancer can translate into trillions of dollars in global productivity during our collective lifetimes.

None of this is new, but it's all worth repeating. Each of us should consider how we want to grow old, and confront the threats to healthy aging. We need to be alarmed that chronic diseases are growing and that some of them, notably diabetes, are increasingly affecting people younger than 40. Compassionate care, farsighted thinking about aging, and a new sense of personal responsibility can help us meet a wave of chronic diseases that will, if left unchecked, drive hundreds of millions of people around the world into a state of premature disability.

Eight Days a Week—Only the Start

When the Beatles sang about a week with eight days, they didn't have in mind a literal week extender that would put more time in our lives. But the catchy lyrics by the musical icons of a generation unknowingly foretold a reality that would come true for the baby boomers singing along. Now, we can push this happy reality even further ahead for generations to come.

Notes

1. John T. James, "A New, Evidence-Based Estimate of Patient Harms Associated with Hospital Care," *Journal of Patient Safety*, September 2013.
2. Eric Topol, "Topol on the Creative Destruction of Medicine," *Medscape*, May 15, 2013.
3. Congressional Budget Office, "The Overuse, Underuse and Misuse of Medical Care," July 17, 2008.
4. National Hospital Discharge Survey (NHDS), National Center for Health Statistics, Centers for Disease Control, 2010 results.
5. "MelaFind for Melanoma Disorders: Will It Change Practice?" *Medscape* Multispecialty, January 9, 2012, www.medscape.com/viewarticle/756436.
6. Scripps Research Institute, News release, "AIDS Researchers Isolate New Potent and Broadly Effective Antibodies Against HIV," August 17, 2011. International HIV Vaccine Initiative Database, 2013.

7. Intuitive Surgical website, www.intuitivesurgical.com/company/faqs.html#23.

8. Leigh Hochberg et al., "Reach and Grasp by People with Tetraplegia Using a Neurally Controlled Robotic Arm, *Nature*, May 17, 2012.

9. "Alzheimer's Association Annual Report and Year in Review, 2012," www.alz.org/annual_report/overview.asp.

10. Michael D. Hurd et al., "Monetary Costs of Dementia in the United States," *New England Journal of Medicine*, April 4, 2013.

11. World Health Organization, "Widespread Misunderstandings About Chronic Disease—and the Realities," WHO Global Report, 2005.

Chapter 4

Disruptive Demography: The New Business of Old Age

Joseph F. Coughlin
Founder and Director, Massachusetts Institute of Technology AgeLab

To succeed in a shifting demographic landscape, innovators must under-stand the features of the new terrain—a generation that will demand a better old age, the revenue sources that will pay for them to experience it, and the organizations that will deliver it.

Ralph, Clarence, and Shorty were my childhood best friends. Aged somewhere between 70 and 80-something, they taught me, an only child, everything that could possibly interest a boy—sports, fishing, shooting, repairing boats, hiking, reading the sky for bad weather, what happened during the "war," and yes, more than a few vulgar jokes. But these friends—my neighbor Ralph, and Clarence and Shorty, who let me hang around and later work at their fishing shop near our New York vacation home—taught me something more: learning, living, and

51

laughing did not have to stop at any age. My interest in aging as an academic pursuit came later, when I was old enough to realize that my friends were, in societal terms, "old men." The example of their spirited lives inspired me to combine my love of technology with institutional engineering to build a career devoted to living not only longer, but better.

Now, we need that vision to come true, because the world is growing old at an unprecedented rate. Although we're still far from fully understanding how disruptive demographic change will affect society, the aging trend itself is perhaps the most predictable large phenomenon in the world. As described throughout this book, most countries are aging in a way that the world has never seen. People over 50 are the fastest-growing population in the industrialized world, and in some nations, those over age 85 are the fastest-growing cohort. More life per person, emphatically, is a good thing. But the question of how to realize the dividend of longer life while managing both the economic and social challenges of an aging society remains unanswered.

Ironically, the greatest current beneficiary of longer life is the cottage industry of doomsayers—thinkers and organizations who decry a "gray dawn," "the perfect storm," or a "seismic shift" toward an older society that will bankrupt economies, stifle innovation, and devastate health care systems.

These dire forecasts are indeed likely if we view future aging as an amplified replay of our grandparents' "old age." However, there is another face to aging. I fully believe that longevity is a gift, not a curse—but that we can only take advantage of it if growing old becomes something new: if we heed aging as a call to innovate.

To succeed in a shifting demographic landscape, innovators must understand the features of the new terrain—a generation that will demand a better old age, the revenue sources that will pay for them to experience it, and the organizations that will deliver it.

Demographic Transition and the New Face of Old Age

In 1900, the average person born in the United States could expect to live to 47, while today, most people that age are just hitting their strides professionally and personally. Longevity is perhaps humankind's greatest success.

As improved health, declining birthrates, and aging baby boomers transform predominantly young populations into old ones, we're already seeing economic effects. In 2011, for instance, adult diapers began to outsell baby diapers in Japan.[1] But does this demographic transition simply mean more older people? Not at all. The reality is far more complicated.

The new face of old age is increasingly healthier, wealthier, and more educated. It is also female. Future retirees will include a far higher proportion of empowered women who are better educated than their mothers and have at some point participated at least part-time in the workforce.

The postwar baby boomers also represent a generation inspired by technology. From television to mobile phones, they have more experience than any previous age group with the capacity of technology to improve life. These are more than characteristics of a generation; they are factors that create markets and feed expectations to live not just longer, but better.

A healthier older adult will anticipate active living well into old age. A wealthier older consumer will demand products that respond to his or her life-stage needs. An educated older citizen will seek trusted information to help navigate market choices in pensions, nutrition, health, housing, and more. An older, educated, professional woman, with few or no children, will seek new policies, products, and services to maintain her quality of life as she ages. A tech-savvy retiree will expect the next "new, new" thing to be cheaper, faster, and easier to use, in addition to being responsive to her daily needs. Finally, the generation that redefined the institutional and infrastructural landscape of the United States and elsewhere will seek to leave a legacy for the next generation, reinforcing core values in government, business, and society.

These expectations of today's aging generation present immediate opportunities for innovation by both business and government alike.

Mapping New Markets in an Aging Society

How can businesses design and deliver products and services to meet the needs of all age groups, while simultaneously exciting and delighting the new older consumer? What roles will government and the nonprofit sector play in enabling and delivering these innovations?

The private and public sectors and academia have conducted considerable research and product development to respond to the needs of an aging society. The resultant technologies, combined with the boomer demand for a better old age, have the potential to change aging as we know it, and exactly when we need it.

What has been less clear is how these technologies will make their way into common usage. How will they be delivered, and by whom? Who will pay for such innovations? How will people who need these services, either for themselves or their loved ones, learn that they are available? How will new products and services be integrated into existing infrastructure and institutions? Aging, in part, is a problem of organizational capacity.

Delivery of innovations to support the needs and wants of older adults will vary with government policies, business investment, and the role of the nonprofit sector. Figure 4.1, though far from exhaustive, presents an organizational map of selected private and public sector opportunities stemming from the demands of a new aging generation.[2] It identifies who might assume the costs and who is likely to deliver these products, services, and policies.

Each of these opportunities benefits older people and their families— and will provide new markets for business, and new prospects for nonprofits and government to improve lives. The categories in Figure 4.1, visualizing the delivery and cost roles of the private, public, and nonprofit sectors, are here for convenience, although inevitably there is significant overlap among these efforts.

The horizontal axis of Figure 4.1 represents a continuum of organizations that deliver products and services to older adults —"Who delivers?"— beginning with "Private Institutions," a category that includes businesses, individuals, and family. The continuum extends through public-private partnerships to government-funded and -operated programs. Public-private partnerships are more than work shared between government and industry—they include nonprofit organizations that are often the most knowledgeable about aging services, such as Age Concern in the United Kingdom, or AARP in the United States, as well as countless faith-based service groups.

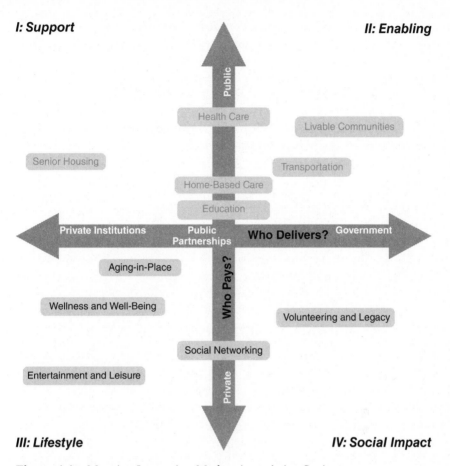

I: Support   *II: Enabling*

III: Lifestyle   *IV: Social Impact*

Figure 4.1   Mapping Innovation Markets in an Aging Society

The vertical axis—"Who pays?"—identifies the possible revenue sources for the markets and services. Private revenue sources include individual households or private firms: for instance, a family that purchases mobile phone services for an elderly parent, or a business investing in workforce training. Other financial support comes from individuals, businesses, or governments, co-investing to create markets to improve quality of life or productivity, or to shoulder the public costs of necessities such as health care and pensions.

As shown in Figure 4.1, four markets emerge from the new demography: *Support, Enabling, Lifestyle,* and *Social Impact.* The markets are not necessarily independent. Rather, they show a likely clustering of products, services, and policies that might share organization and delivery models.

Supporting People as They Age

Support is the traditional aging market, emphasizing formal caregiving and services such as nutrition services, health care, and care for the chronically ill and disabled. The *Support* market relies financially on the nonprofit or voluntary sector, some private funding (such as families), but most important, long-standing public agencies to ensure that the most frail or isolated receive care.

Significant R&D is underway to build solutions for the *Support* market, partly due to growing levels of need. However, many innovators also focus on this quadrant because it fits the traditional image of aging: that growing old is tantamount to disability and diminished health.

Prominent R&D efforts include the creation of ambient intelligence and "smart" technologies in the home for elderly, isolated individuals. Often, such technologies are designed to monitor, manage, and motivate healthy behaviors and well-being—for instance by monitoring an older adult's movement and adherence to diet and medications. Similar systems, such as telehealth, make it possible to better manage the allocation of physician and nursing resources, identifying and triaging those patients who most require a visit. Such technologies can remotely monitor body weight, glucose levels, and other factors, which allows caregivers to focus on people with more problematic needs.

In most developed countries, the *Support* market is funded mainly by public providers who try to improve health outcomes and reduce costs. These costs are accrued during emergency room visits, hospitalization, chronic disease, and premature nursing home placement, due in part to the fact that fewer adult children are available to care for aging parents. Examples of organizations pursuing this area include Spain's Telefonica and University of Rochester's delivery of Parkinson's teletherapy to rural upstate New York.

The introduction of such e-health services in the home is likely to be tied closely to government reimbursements of the costs. Private sector actors, such as Turnstall in the United Kingdom, Senior Watch in France, and Philips Lifeline in the United States, may be limited to developing the devices, installing systems in the home, and operating call centers. The nonprofit sector, trusted by many older adults, may become a highly sought channel for information about publicly and privately provided services.

Adult children of the elderly contribute to a *Support* market that is still developing. Financial services providers, such as Italy's Generali insurance, now are offering home-health aide services in France, an example of how aging-related services can be horizontally integrated. Even U.S.-based Wells Fargo Bank is providing administrative support to elderly parents of affluent clients who find it increasingly difficult to assist their parents while balancing competing work and family demands, often over increasing geographic distances.

Enabling Independence

Enabling refers to the physical "infrastructure" of an aging society, including community design, transportation services, and housing. These services and facilities investments, which are government funded or subject to public planning processes, are essential to independent and healthy living for older people.

One of the greatest risks of aging is reduced connectivity with family, friends, and community, making "livable communities" ever more important as the population ages. Many older cities with comprehensive public transit systems have emphasized "livability" for decades, enabling residents to age in place, staying independent yet socially connected for as long as possible. Developing newer communities with these characteristics will not only support older adults, but will promote economic growth by attracting new residents.

In the *Enabling* market, government is most likely to set standards and finance infrastructure and public transportation. The nonprofit sector also is contributing innovations to home and community design and integrated services. These efforts include neighborhood co-op associations that identify, vet, and deliver services, such as the Village to Village Network that began in Boston and now has spread throughout the world. In the private housing sector, new modular technologies and innovative financing will promote the emergence of larger multinational developers of "ageless" and "age-friendly" housing.

Transportation poses a major challenge to enabling social connectivity among older adults, but great strides are being made. The automobile industry has invested in ensuring personal "automobility." Most companies know that the older consumer typically purchases their most profitable cars, and Daimler has conducted research on safety restraint systems with an older, frailer occupant in mind. Likewise, Ford has young design engineers wear its "Third Age Suit" to simulate how products affect those with reduced vision, dexterity, and strength. Renault, meanwhile, was pleasantly surprised to discover that its Spartan-designed Twingo—marketed initially to younger car buyers—was also popular with older French drivers who found both its simplicity and low price attractive.

A new opportunity that will enable older adult independence and financial security is education throughout the life span, as detailed elsewhere in this book. Today, education is still considered the realm of young people. But education throughout the life span is poised to become the new norm, with aging adults in the United States and many other nations planning to continue working into their traditional retirement years.

Continuing education programs will allow workers to remain sharp in the skills and technology of their professions, already routine in medicine, law, and finance. However, the dizzying pace of technology advancement and knowledge growth may make this a requirement to remain productive and competitive in most careers at 35, 45, and beyond. Similarly, education will facilitate career changes for those who seek new fields at age 50 or even 60, after decades in one profession.

The new business of education may be financed and provided by the government as an extension of existing schools and training centers. Or, it may evolve into a new form of lifelong learning—financed by individuals, unions, and employers—on the Internet or in schools yet to be developed. The rise of massive open online courses (MOOCs) such as MIT's edX may evolve into a new expectation for midlife skills updates.

New Lifestyles of the Mature Adult

Lifestyle products and services represent a rapidly emerging market. The *Lifestyle* market focuses on an enjoyable vision of older age that is now changing as the desirability of "retirement" shifts. This market includes pursuing fun, travel, and wellness, and proactively managing the impacts of age. Consequently, it is funded almost entirely by personal discretionary income.

Fun is not often equated with aging, but that is changing. Nintendo's success with its Wii console has shown that older adults enjoy consumer electronics and games as much as their grandchildren. For some applications of consumer electronics (e.g., Wii Fit), the promise of a tangible benefit such as exercise can make what was traditionally the domain of children or adolescents into a lucrative product for the entire life span. A new market of toys and games that appeals across the generations is waiting to be developed—especially online games that foster interpersonal relationships without the impediment of transportation challenges.

If fun is not traditionally associated with aging, neither is work. Aging has been synonymous with full retirement from work in much of the developed world for decades or more, but that is quickly changing. The new older lifestyle is a working life—at least part-time—for pay or fulfillment. In the United States, the most frequently stated reason for working into older age is that it's preferable to not working. This feeling is especially strong among college-educated workers.[3]

Another pivotal aspect of improved lifestyle is wellness, which already is emerging as a metaphor for the health-conscious middle- and older-age consumer. Wellness is a holistic approach to self-improvement, self-care, and the desire to achieve optimal performance at any age. Perhaps one of the fastest growing markets worldwide, it touches nearly every industry and is fueled by the aging of the boomers, now entering chronic disease prime time and experiencing the aches and pains of older age.

Food is merging with travel, leisure, and health under the banner of wellness. The food industry already is finding a rich market for purposeful foods and nutraceuticals. Mars developed Cocoa Via, a dark chocolate treat designed to provide the benefits of healthy phenyls found in chocolate. Because many people aged 50-plus complain of fatigue and suffer from dehydration, PepsiCo and Coca-Cola are shifting towards energy drinks and waters to power an older demographic.

Housing modifications also are intimately connected to *Lifestyle*. Most older adults indicate that they would like to "age in place": that is, stay in their longtime homes and communities, a difficult goal with families becoming smaller and more geographically dispersed. The next generation of older adults will seek products and services to help them age in place in lieu of familial help, such as easy-to-use appliances that include age-friendly safety features.

Whirlpool, Bosch, and other manufacturers have designed appliances that are easy to access, reducing stress on sore backs—an innovation equally likely to be appreciated by a grandmother with reduced flexibility and a young mother with a child in her arms. Meanwhile, LG and other firms have added "intelligence" to their appliances, creating a home network that will report refrigerator and medicine and kitchen cabinet contents, among other factors.

Demand for home modification is likely to increase as middle-aged and older customers consider improvements to help them age in place. However, this trend also will evolve into an opportunity for manufacturers and contractors to build houses that are age-ready from the start, with features such as:

- Easy-to-reach bathroom fixtures, kitchen cabinets, and countertops that enable the occupant to sit while preparing a meal.
- Fashionable lighting that compensates for lost night vision and contrast sensitivity.
- Floor coverings that add style, but reduce the possibility or mitigate the effects of a fall.

In addition to home modifications, demand for assistance with home maintenance will grow. At age 80-plus, changing a light bulb on a high ladder becomes an extreme sport. Along with simple cleaning and repair, home maintenance services will extend to remote monitoring of major appliances such as hot water tanks, furnaces, ventilation, and air conditioning.

The *Lifestyle* market will be the most dynamic of the four quadrants, and introduce some of the most creative products and services. In many ways, the older adult market will become the lifestyle leader for a new way of living across the life span.

It's likely that only the affluent will be able to afford the first wave of *Lifestyle* innovations. However, as markets have seen with personal computers, mobile phones, and other electronics, products tend to rapidly drop in price and become widely available to all once they are introduced. Governments may subsidize *Lifestyle* products, services, and delivery strategies for the less affluent, and these purchases in large quantity then will affect price and availability for all.

The Boomers' Social Impact

The emerging *Social Impact* market represents the investment of private time, money, and passion by people who want to "make a difference." Although primarily related to older adults' desire to leave a legacy, the *Social Impact* market has great potential to impact the future of business and public policy in areas well beyond aging. The nonprofit and activist community may find in this market its greatest growth opportunity since the baby boomers were in their teens and twenties, as membership rosters swell with newly energetic older adults. As the *Social Impact* market grows, businesses and government will find that it wields outsize influence on their operations and policy decisions. For instance, as boomers gray, they may also become more green, not only demanding sustainable products but making green behaviors their legacy. A 2011 Del Webb survey found that 54 percent of boomers expressed interest in purchasing an electric vehicle, and 87 percent said they considered it important to invest in green technology to reduce their utility bills.[4]

In another example of how the *Social Impact* market will affect society, age discrimination and ageist policies will become increasingly unacceptable. As the population becomes older, any organization seen as discriminating based upon age may find itself with a damaged reputation and lost market share, sometimes overnight. Age discrimination will no longer be defined as bias against a once-stealth minority, but prejudice against a vocal third of the population.

Finally, the lasting social impact of the next generation of older people may be due simply to their renewed activism—that is, "old" becomes synonymous with re-engagement, not retirement, as civic engagement in older age becomes the new standard. And as older adults form a new core of activist groups, many will achieve amplified societal effects online, thanks to the increasing numbers of older people using the Internet.

Conclusion

The implications and opportunities of demographic aging are profound. Longevity is to be celebrated, embraced, and invented. Older adults in nearly all industrialized countries will form a new "disruptive" force that demands a rethinking of what aging is, and what is needed to meet an aging population's needs and expectations. As tomorrow's markets take shape, individuals and businesses can best position themselves to benefit from disruptive demographic change by understanding who will be paying for the new expectations, and who will be delivering in the emerging markets of an aging world:

- *Support* markets to serve the frail, disabled, and their families.
- *Enabling* markets to create the infrastructure of living longer and living better.
- *Lifestyle* markets to define the infinite possibilities of nearly a third of a person's life.
- *Social Impact* markets, where older people will leave their legacies for their families and society.

These are not exhaustive market classifications, nor complete in terms of the multitude of innovations that will touch every aspect of daily life in the future. But they serve to map possibilities and to identify the stakeholders who can play important roles in translating global aging into global opportunity for the good of individuals, their communities, and the world.

Notes

1. Yuki Yamaguchi, "Elderly at Record Spurs Japan Stores Chase $1.4 Trillion," *Bloomberg News*, May 9, 2012, www.bloomberg.com/news/2012-05-09/elderly-at-record-spurs-japan-stores-chase-1-4-trillion.html.
2. MIT AgeLab, "Demographic Transition, Innovation & Mapping the New Business of Old Age," MIT AgeLab white paper, 2009.
3. Barry P. Bosworth and Kathleen Burke, *Changing Sources of Income Among the Aged Population* (Chestnut Hill, MA: Center for Retirement Research at Boston College, 2012).
4. "Del Webb Research Shows Boomers Willing to Invest More in Green Technology; Teams With Chevrolet to Showcase Volt Electric Vehicle in Chicago," PR Newswire, www.prnewswire.com/news-releases/del-webb-research-shows-boomers-willing-to-invest-more-in-green-technology-teams-with-chevrolet-to-showcase-volt-electric-vehicle-in-chicago-130777593.html.

Chapter 5

A Longevity Market Emerges

Ken Dychtwald
President and Chief Executive Officer, Age Wave

Historians will no doubt wonder why American industry worked for so long to sell to the youth market when it was their parents and grandparents who had both the money and the clout. Boomers create huge opportunities for companies—whether financial, interpersonal, or recreational.

Working with older people initially was not my cup of tea. Or so I thought. I had moved to Berkeley, California, in 1974, to work with a new human-potential training program that involved concepts like biofeedback and tai chi, nutrition and dream therapy. When it struck the program's creator, Dr. Gay Luce, that nobody in our youth-centered culture was using these innovative therapeutic techniques to focus on the potential of the elderly, she asked me to help her create such a program. I hesitated. I was in my early twenties and I liked being with people my own age and working with those in their thirties and forties. I told Dr. Luce that I would help launch the project and then move on.

Instead, I got hooked and have remained hooked for 40 years. I became fascinated with aging, longevity, and older people. Looking past their clothing and sometimes-grizzled appearance, I saw towering figures, seasoned men and women with a vast perspective on life and intriguing home-grown wisdom. I grew increasingly intrigued by the journey of aging itself—our individual choices that make us healthy and engaged, or ill and disconnected. I realized that this aging demographic would dramatically transform the global marketplace, business world, society at large, and the quality of life we enjoy. The business potential was enormous.

The coming impact of this "age wave" was underscored by a congressional Office of Technology Assessment panel, on which I served in 1982. It forecast the radical transformation of early twenty-first century America as 78 million baby boomers moved into their fifties and sixties.

I saw that we had shaped our world in every way around the form and fit of what we had always been—which was young. I foresaw a world in which typefaces would be too small, the change time for traffic lights would be too quick, and the auditory range on our telephones and TVs would be out of sync with aging ears.

I thought, "What's going to happen to the pharmaceutical industry? What about people who will want to reinvent their careers? What will become of retirement? What new maturity-oriented businesses will be needed?" If the business world, and society at large, met the challenges and opportunities presented by this aging demographic, the potential for seniors' quality of life and their contributions to society were indeed vast.

That flood of ideas led me in 1986, with my wife Maddy, to form Age Wave, the world's first think tank and consultancy focused on the emerging needs of maturing men and women. I'm proud to say that in the past quarter century, our clients have included more than half the Fortune 500.[1] Much of what I relate here comes from what I've learned in working with these clients, and on broader issues of aging.

The Age Wave Marketplace

Until now, most businesspeople have operated on the belief that the youth market is expanding with growing numbers of free-spending consumers, and that anyone over the age of 50 is staid, crusty, and tight with what little money he or she has. But the Age Wave is beginning to pull the marketplace in new directions. The national economic picture is shifting. The 98 million Americans already over 50 turn out to be the most powerful and affluent consumer group in history.[2] Decades from now, historians will no doubt wonder why American industry worked for so long to sell to the youth market when it was their parents and grandparents who had both the money and the clout.

A key driver of the maturing marketplace is the aging of the boomer generation. The size of this cohort means that at any stage of life, boomers create huge opportunities for companies that can meet their needs—whether financial, interpersonal, or recreational. Boomers didn't just eat food—they transformed the snack, restaurant, and supermarket industries; they didn't just wear clothes—they transformed the fashion industry; they didn't just go to work—they transformed the workplace; they didn't just go to the doctor—they transformed health care; and they won't just grow old—they will transform aging itself and the marketplace that serves it.

This metamorphosis has already begun. Representing 32 percent of the total U.S. population, Americans over 50 now have a combined annual personal income of over $3.9 trillion and control 77 percent of the total net worth of U.S. households—nearly $46 trillion of wealth.[3]

Members of the 50-plus population own: 85 percent of certificates of deposits, 79 percent each of bonds and stocks, 63 percent of retirement accounts, and 72 percent of all financial assets, according to a Federal Reserve survey.[4] In addition, they:

- Purchase 49 percent of all new domestic cars and 48 percent of all luxury cars.
- Spend more money on travel and recreation than any other age group, and purchase 60 percent of all luxury travel.
- Spend more on health and personal care products than any other age group.
- Spend more per capita in the grocery store than any other age group, and purchase 51 percent of all alcoholic beverages.
- Gamble and watch TV more than any other age group.

- Spend more on quality clothing for their grandchildren than the children's parents do.
- Account for 48 percent of total customer demand.

Madison Avenue constructed a smoke screen of myths about the older consumer that for a long time steered businesses away from the opportunities in this potentially powerful market segment: We have been told that older people are too poor to purchase new products or services, that they are fanatically loyal to their brands, and too set in their ways for advertisers to bother marketing to them.

In fact, a vast market awaits. But businesses and industry first will have to learn about the needs of the over-50 population. This section explores six key consumption-oriented characteristics of the mature consumer. They don't like to be thought of as old, and seek ways to postpone physical aging. They are more interested in purchasing experiences than things. They consider security and safety in their buying decisions, and seek products that accommodate the physical changes of aging. And, unlike earlier generations of older men and women, they definitely like trying new things. By understanding this purchasing profile, we can glimpse the broad range of product and service needs for a mass global older population.

What, Me—Old?

Marketers often lump everyone over 50 into one amorphous group. That's a mistake. Lifestyle, life stage, and mind-set are more potent drivers of consumption than age. But, for our purposes here, I will segment the 50-plus consumer into three separate age groups, understanding also that each group contains nonconforming exceptions.

50–64: Middle Adulthood (Middlescence)

People in this group, with their children usually grown and their mortgage mostly paid, have the highest disposable income of any demographic group. They are better educated and more affluent than their parents were at the same age.

Since they can expect to live longer on average than any previous generation, their major issues are health, self-fulfillment, social activities, comfort, and how to spend their increasing free time. They are an excellent market for financial services, health promotion, wellness and nutrition products and services, luxury travel and tours, personal-care products, adult education, second homes, and recreational products and services.

They spend money on themselves as child-rearing financial burdens recede, and as new grandparents they buy for their grandchildren. At the same time, many seek products and services to help care for their aging parents.

65–79: Late Adulthood

Today, most people in this age group live active and independent lifestyles. They are not yet "old" and they share many of the social, health, and leisure activities of those aged 50 to 64. But they have greater concern for health and growing fear of serious illness. Their use of medical and long-term health care services rises dramatically, as does their reliance on family and friends for assistance with daily living. Like 50-to-64-year-olds, they are a strong market for finance and estate services, health and fitness products, education, travel, personal-care products, and second homes.

Many in this group, no longer working, are sensitive about being excluded from society. They most definitely do not want to be "put out to pasture." They often have active social networks and remain involved in the community. At this stage in life, the number of female-headed households begins to climb.

80+: Old Age

With the average life expectancy now in the late seventies for both men and women, the over-80 group is smaller than other 50-plus groups. By now, many have lost a good deal of their health and personal independence. Only 5 percent of 80-plus-year-olds are working, compared with 23 percent in the 65 to 79 age range and 64 percent of those 55 to 64.[5] They also have the highest poverty levels of any age group in America.

Although some 80-plus men and women remain active in the community, most have retreated to a life of daily self-care and contact with a small group of family and friends. Approximately two-thirds of the 80-plus population is female.

This group has the most difficulty shopping and moving around. Loss of physical vigor and independence makes this group an eager market for services like finance management, medicine, home care, gardening, housecleaning, cooking, and driving.

I Am Not My Age

Perhaps it's a reflection of our cultural gerontophobia that many older people prefer not to be referred to by age at all. This poses a challenge to marketers—how to target products to a mature population that shies away from being identified as older. Two solutions can work: first, targeting the self-perceived "cognitive age," and second, bypassing age altogether and instead targeting lifestyle "affinities" that are both common and important to the older consumer.

Targeting Self-Perception

Studies have consistently shown that once people pass their fiftieth birthdays, they tend to feel 10 to 15 years younger than their actual age. Thus, companies that pitch straight to the age of their target audience will find themselves missing the market.

Years ago, Johnson & Johnson designed a shampoo for over-40 hair called Affinity. And that's exactly how they marketed it. It struggled in the marketplace for several years, until finally Johnson & Johnson eliminated all age references from the ads. As one ad executive told me, "How many women want to walk into a drugstore and say, 'Do you have that shampoo for women over 40?' None."

To bypass age altogether, the marketer should focus on some issue, need, or "affinity" of older people that is likely to get their attention and draw them to the product. Quaker Oats used a simple and direct tack, for instance, when it launched a national campaign to promote its cereals to older people: "Quaker Oats is nutritious, low in sodium, has no cholesterol, and is good for digestion." Since heart disease and good digestion are likely concerns for a mature man or woman, the ad hit its mark. Similarly, by promoting aspirin products for their prophylactic effect against second heart attacks, as Bayer does, an affinity is immediately created with the 50-plus population, which is at risk for heart disease.

Another way to create consumer affinity is by tying a product to a celebrity familiar to the target generation. A few years ago I was watching a football game with my elderly father, when a Michelob beer commercial featured rock-guitar legend Eric Clapton. A Clapton fan, I turned to my dad and said, "Can you believe Michelob was able to get Eric Clapton to appear in their ad?" My father replied, "Who's Eric Clapton?" On the other hand, had the commercial featured an entertainer from my dad's era, the conversation would likely have been reversed.

By targeting self-perceived cognitive age or lifestyle affinities, savvy marketers can appeal to older consumers while avoiding their feelings about chronological age.

Show Them Something New

Historically we have lived according to what I call the *linear life plan*: first you learn; then you work intensely for three or four decades; and then, if you're fortunate enough to have a bit of longevity, you have time to rest and relax a bit before you die. Learn, work, rest, die—more longevity simply means stretching out the "rest" part.

But that's not what people do now. During the traditional "rest" interval, they are going back to school, or quitting their jobs and starting whole new careers. Widowed or divorced at 60 or 65, they're thinking it may not be too late to fall in love again. Or they see the chance to rebuild their health and realize several satisfying years after surviving a cancer battle.

So we're starting to think in terms of a *cyclic* life plan, with continual rebirth and reinvention, as seen in Figure 5.1. For many of us, hanging up our cleats and "retiring" just isn't enough. Too often, our twentieth-century version of maturity left out the crucial element of *purpose.* We want to keep our minds stimulated and maybe continue earning an income—but we also want to be engaged in something that feels meaningful, that has purpose, that allows us to feel lit up and turned on.

The cyclic life also means openness to new kinds of spending (see Figure 5.1). Men and women over 50 now spend disproportionately to their numbers. Yet, much of the multibillion-dollar advertising world has historically targeted young consumers with the increasingly obsolete notion that lifetime brand loyalty is fixed between the ages of 15 and 25. After that, it was believed, people were so set in their ways that there wasn't much value in advertising to them. However, while most TV programming focuses on the youth demographic, it's the 50-plus viewer that has both the money and the desire to buy new things. And "brand loyalty" may in fact be simply the seasoned consumer's good judgment and concern for quality.

Older consumers are less inclined to follow fads or buy on impulse than the young. A woman who has purchased 10 cars has a more critical eye than a first-time buyer, and is likely to look for things not evident to the novice. As well, older people pay attention to price, but are more willing than young people to pay for quality and service.

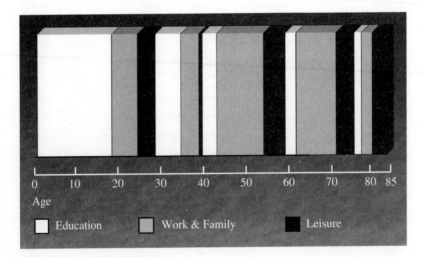

Figure 5.1   Cyclic Lifeplan

The New Look of Longevity

Older people are sensitive to being portrayed negatively. Years ago, many older people were insulted when Wendy's fast-food chain featured Clara Peller in its "Where's the beef?" ad campaign. "We don't look or act like that," they angrily responded. They felt that Peller's performance fostered images of older people as silly, cranky, and funny looking. More recently, a Taco Bell ad showed seniors breaking out of their old age home for a night of sex, drugs, and rock and roll—generally portraying them as buffoons. Ageism (like racism or sexism) isn't funny, and it's not smart marketing.

The advertising industry is swiftly moving to a more positive image of aging, using older Americans in commercials as authority figures, lovable grandparents, and people who have their own full, rich lives. Ads today show attractive and vital people of all ages. A middle-aged man in a bran commercial does aerobics while his wife cheers him on. A mature beauty in an Oil of Olay commercial says, "I'm about to wash a whole day's worth of aging away." A glamorous mature model touts Cover Girl's Replenish for "changing" skins, and asks, "Who says you ever have to stop being a cover girl?"

Of course, as the boomers age, they'll fight to stay as young as possible. They want products and services that will make them feel and look better physically, mentally, and socially. Tens of millions will seek the near impossible: trying to extend their youth. Perhaps the greatest concern pertaining to youthful appearance is skin that loses elasticity. In coming years, the aging of the boomers will drive continued, likely unprecedented, growth in the cosmetics industry. Beyond topical formulas, cosmetic surgery is among the fastest-growing U.S. medical specialties. Trendy *Los Angeles* magazine routinely runs dozens of cosmetic surgery ads. Figure 5.2 shows a stunning 98-percent increase in procedures from 2000 to 2012, according to the American Society of Plastic Surgeons. Botox injections rose 680 percent.

Aging and Experiences: Doing, Not Owning

We think of consumers as wanting "things"—but there are only so many things people can buy before they fill their homes. Instead, maturing

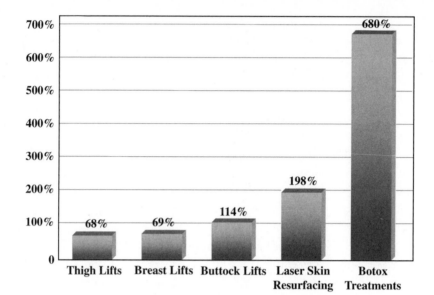

Figure 5.2   Increase in Plastic Surgery Procedures 2000–2012
SOURCE: American Society of Plastic Surgeons

men and women are drawn to products or services that create a desirable experience.

Having the money and time to travel, to learn, and to explore new areas of their lives, mature consumers pursue goals of personal well-being and self-fulfillment. While previous generations were relatively conservative in their appetite for leisure, boomers are barreling toward their retirement years with a bigger sense of wonder about the world and its people, and about the value of time spent in faraway places.

Another sector primed for age-related transformation is the food and beverage industry, which will see revolutionary changes as it adapts to older bodies. The average 30-year-old has 245 taste buds on each little bump (papilla) on the tongue. By the time that person reaches 80, he or she will have only 88—a decrease that makes it harder to discriminate among sweet, bitter, sour, and salty. Older people who don't feel like eating may not be depressed or ill, but perhaps simply uninterested because food doesn't taste the way it used to. They often add more spices or sweeteners to their food in an attempt to recapture tastes they remember from their youth.

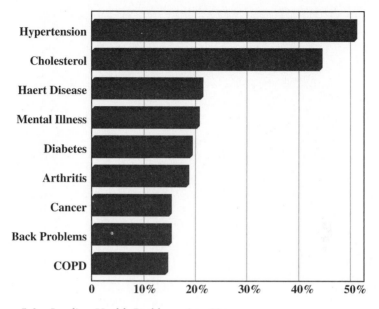

Figure 5.3 Leading Health Problems, Age 50+
DATA SOURCE: AARP Public Policy Institute, "Chronic Condition Prevalence in the 50+ US Population," 2011.

As food manufacturers and restaurants meet these age-related challenges, seniors will find more enjoyable dining experiences. The market is ripe for the emergence of specialty foods designed to appeal to their palates while at the same time meeting their nutritional needs. Since 83 percent of people over 65 have at least one chronic degenerative disease[6] (see Figure 5.3 for health problems in the over-50 age group), the market will have to adjust with age-related dietary revolutions in the ways we grow, manufacture, flavor, and distribute food.

Comfort Matters

As we age, we become more interested in physical and psychological comfort—as manifested by the growing interstate "gray migration." Knowing why and where people move provides a useful insight into the quest for comfort. Half of all Americans over 65 who relocate are leaving familiar neighborhoods to move south and west for warm weather and comfort.

1)	Florida	21%
2)	Arizona	18%
3)	South Carolina	10%
4)	North Carolina	10%
5)	Tennessee	9%
6)	Colorado	7%
7)	Virginia	7%
8)	Texas	7%
9)	New Mexico	6%
10)	California	6%

Figure 5.4   Top Ten Relocation States for Older Americans
DATA SOURCE: 2010 Del Webb Baby Boomer Survey.

The Sun Belt migration is easy to understand since the inconveniences of winter—shoveling snow, driving on icy roads, and being housebound much of the time—all weigh more heavily on the old. Sun Belt states thus are highly sought destinations for them (see Figure 5.4). Together, Florida, California, Arizona, and Texas account for nearly half of all older Americans who move to new states.[7]

The desire to be comfortable goes far beyond a warmer climate. As we age, we come to feel that we've had enough hassles. We are less inclined to conform to products that were not designed for ease of use. Older Americans can expect more convenient products as savvy developers become more attentive to age-related physical changes.

Next time you're at a traffic light, ask yourself how we decided on the number of seconds needed for pedestrians to cross the street. How was the font for newspaper typeface determined to be the right size? How do we decide on the colors for a cereal box, on the brightness of images on a computer monitor, on how much strength it should take to open a bottle of soda, or how high bus steps should be?

We have woven a physical world that is as suited to our needs and activities as a beehive is for its bees. But it revolves around an ideal in the form and physiology of youth. Margaret Wylde, president of ProMatura, a market research firm specializing in senior consumers, observes, "The average five-foot, eight-inch tall, able-bodied male is the nemesis of everyone who *isn't* an average five-foot, eight-inch-tall, able-bodied male, since products designed around this 'Everyman' don't take individual differences into account."[8]

The physical changes of aging cause thousands of mismatches in the way we interact with the world around us. Older people can expect the mismatches to diminish as the huge aging demographic continues to make itself known.

Studies have highlighted many ways in which the standard physical environment is ill-suited to older people who want to remain in independent living situations. What manufacturers may not take into account in designing products is that seniors often have trouble with everyday tasks like opening packages and reading product labels, fastening buttons and zippers, using tools, cleaning bathrooms, moving around the house without falling, and reaching high things.

These inconveniences that make life difficult as we age are born of poor product or environmental design. As the marketplace ages, products and environments will need to be redesigned for our changing needs, promising a life of enhanced comfort, safety, and self-reliance for older people.

The Psychology of Security and Safety

Older men and women tend to seek security in two ways: through products and services that directly protect them from harm, or those that make them *feel* more secure. As we age, we tend to feel more physically and socially vulnerable, as evidenced by the commanding presence of external walls, alarm systems, guards, and passkeys.

New technology now enables older people to feel more psychologically secure in their homes. The pioneer in this category was Dr. Andrew Dibner, a Boston University psychology professor who researched the psychological concerns of older Boston-area residents living alone. One of their greatest fears was falling or needing help without being able to call out or reach the telephone. They enjoyed living independently in their own homes, but this particular anxiety had many of them terrified.

Dibner developed an ingenious piece of equipment that he called Lifeline. It connects directly to a standard telephone and is controlled by a tiny wireless transmitter that can be worn on the wrist or around the neck, or placed in a pocket or purse. Some systems also include touch pads or pull chords on the walls of frequently used rooms. To summon help, a person need only press the button on the transmitter or wall pad. It signals the telephone to dial for help. Today, more than 7 million people have purchased Lifeline to facilitate independent living.[9]

Accommodating the Aging Body

To envision how products will be redesigned for maximum independence and well-being, it is essential to understand some of the bodily changes that occur with aging.

Vision

Our eyes begin to change when we are still in our mid-forties. The lens hardens and thickens, the pupil becomes smaller, and the open-and-close muscle is slower to respond. Because a smaller pupil lets in less light, a person over 80 may need three times more light than a 20-year-old to see clearly. Color perception changes, and shades may become difficult to differentiate. An advertisement, web page, or container that appears striking to a young designer might miss the mark completely with the older people it targets.

Older people, having difficulty seeing in low light and a narrower range of vision than young people, may not be as quick to see landmarks, items on high shelves, or freeway signs. In the future, brightly lit public environments, enlarged signs for easy reading, and simplified lettering will address those needs.

Manual Dexterity

Another challenge comes from stiffness and loss of finger dexterity, a constant problem for many older people. More than half of those over 65 have some arthritis in the finger joints. That means that medicine bottles, food packaging, cutlery, computer keyboards, appliance controls, and purse clasps will likely be redesigned for older hands. Similarly, clothing manufacturers will use more Velcro tabs and larger buttons, eliminating the small fasteners that are difficult for older hands to manipulate.

Mobility limitations, also restricting some older adults, range from minor (like mild arthritis), to severe (like stroke recovery). Mobility problems can stem from changes in the brain and central nervous system, especially in coordination of organs, senses, limbs, or functions. Declining speed of nerve impulse transmission causes slower reaction and performance on tasks like driving and using a computer.

Also deteriorating with age is the kinesthetic sense, or the awareness of the body's position and location in space. Decline of this inner ear–related sense causes older people to lose balance and become increasingly prone to falls. One-third of America's elderly fall each year.[10] In the coming years, bathtubs and kitchens will have nonskid surfaces. Just as over the past decade, most doorknobs have been replaced by more ergonomically friendly door levers, we can expect increasingly to see chairs with higher seats and arms that are long enough to provide support for getting up or sitting down.

The Age Wave Marketplace: What's Next?

A wide range of opportunities awaits companies and individuals who anticipate the emerging needs and interests of the new silver market. The upside of aging is massive. To imagine the future, consider the following major marketplace changes and product/service/business ideas brought on by the emerging avalanche of 50-plus consumers.

Technology
- Internet-based, personal "intelligent agents" that would build in-depth profiles of their elder "clients" to anticipate their needs and desires, and recommend what to buy.
- Furby-like personal robots programmed to talk, react to their owners' thoughts, and even discuss current events. Conceivably they could take any shape—dog, robot, butler—or be "virtual" companions in a computer.

- Microsensory maximizers to replace eyeglasses, and hearing aids that boost neurosensory functioning.
- High-tech exercise gear and equipment programmed to precisely "train" users to build stronger, healthier bodies, or expedite the rehabilitation of stroke and trauma patients.
- Smart clothes that adjust temperature in different body zones depending on the circulatory needs of the older wearer.

Anti-Aging, Human Enhancement

- Nutraceuticals—appetizing food, drink, and supplements engineered with macro- and micronutrients to fight aging and safely promote energy, relaxation, sexuality, mental alertness, endurance, recuperation, and wellness.
- "Cosmeceutical" rejuvenation therapies from pharmaceuticals, botanicals, minerals, and vitamins that will keep the skin and hair youthful longer.
- Customized youth-extending hormone therapeutics to retard aging processes.
- Brain enhancement herbs, vitamins, drugs, acupuncture, software, and mind exercises aimed at promoting memory and stalling dementia.
- Bio-implants that will continually monitor biomarkers and deliver anti-aging nutrients and hormones on an as-needed basis.
- Anti-aging spas with revitalization programs ranging from toxin purging to nervous system tune-ups.

Health Care

- A new science of "human biomarkers," using genomics as key indicators of a person's health, mental vitality, and potential for longevity.
- Specialty diagnosis and treatment centers for particular body parts, such as the eyes, ears, muscles, bones, or nervous system. Each center would have the capability of re-engineering any defects or problems, orchestrated by an integrated human/computer Internet-based medical system.
- Cloned kidneys, livers, lungs, hearts, skin, blood, and bones for replacements.
- Homecare nurses and aides (both human and robotic) to help individuals with chronic health problems maintain their independence at home.

Financial Services

- Longevity insurance that, rather than paying an individual's family in case of early death, provides financial support for people who live very long.
- Investment insurance that provides security for people's retirement funds.
- Estate and trust services to help families manage the $10 trillion inheritance cascade that is about to occur, while minimizing taxes and family duress.
- Equity-release, reverse mortgages to help older adults who find themselves cash-poor but "brick-rich" draw cash out of their homes.

Lifestyle Support

- "Lifelong learning" at colleges, churches, community centers, and on the Internet, which includes vocational training and enrichment classes for seniors.
- "Retirement Zone" stores featuring items for older adults, such as sports equipment, musical instruments, software, and speedboats.
- Lifestyle support managers for time-consuming functions such as laundry, transportation, shopping, and waiting in line for tickets.
- Mature escorts and companions for people who want someone to accompany them to the movies, the doctor, or vacation.
- Transportation services to take older adults who are unable to drive to the doctor, the airport, the beauty salon, the bank.

Housing / Independent Living

- Ergonomic home elements—door levers instead of doorknobs, easy-open drawers and windows, slip-resistant flooring.
- "Foot mops" that slip over a shoe to clean up spills without bending over. Lightweight, motorized scrubbers for pots and pans.
- Large or contoured-handle eating utensils for easier gripping.
- Senior roommate finders to link older adults with compatible housemates.
- Assorted forms of retirement housing, from longevity communities for health-minded elders, to high-tech complexes for "wired" seniors, to university-based retirement communities for elders who desire lifelong learning.

Death and Dying

- Hospice caregivers, psychotherapists, and spiritual counselors trained to help people die with dignity and comfort.
- High-tech funeral enterprises and Internet-based gravesites—complete with the deceased's photos and favorite literature, music, and television shows—so that future generations can "visit" the lives of their ancestors.
- Theme-oriented dying retreats, where people can select the mood and atmosphere they prefer for their customized death experience.

Fitting the New Form

Many of us envision the future as a world created by and for the young, a world in which we will not fit. This concern provokes our fear that, like Gulliver, we will become physiological outcasts in our homes and communities, as well as in our own bodies. But the Age Wave will change things profoundly, and as more of us grow older, we will force the marketplace to bend in our direction.

We will strike down the obstacles that could prevent us from living independent, fully vigorous lives. We will construct a new, more mature blueprint of psychological, physical, and lifestyle values and preferences. From our needs and wishes, a wide range of life-supporting products, services, technologies, and environments will be constructed. The economic bonanza from these products will support new and retooled businesses and industries. The Age Wave is coming, with an upside for all of us.

Notes

1. "AgeWave Homepage," www.AgeWave.com.
2. "Statistical Abstract of the United States: 2012, 131st edition" (U.S. Census Bureau: Washington, D.C., 2011), www.census.gov/compendia/statab.
3. Bureau of Labor Statistics, "Consumer Expenditures Survey 2012," www.bls.gov/cex/faq.htm.
4. U.S. Government, "Federal Reserve Survey of Consumer Finances, 2010," www.federalreserve.gov/pubs/bulletin/2012/pdf/scf12.pdf.
5. Bureau of Labor Statistics, "Current Population Survey, 2013."

6. Centers for Disease Control and Prevention and The Merck Company Foundation, "The State of Aging and Health in America," 2007.

7. Del Webb, "2010 Del Webb Baby Boomer Survey," http://dwboomersurvey.com.

8. Margaret Wylde, interview with Age Wave staff, 1990.

9. "Why Choose Philips Lifeline?" www.lifelinesys.com/content/lifeline-products/how-lifeline-works/why-choose-lifeline.

10. J. M. Hausdorff, D. A. Rios, and H. K. Edelber, "Gait Variability and Fall Risk in Community-Living Older Adults: A 1-Year Prospective Study," *Archives of Physical Medicine and Rehabilitation* 82, no. 8 (2001): 1050–1056.

Chapter 6

The New Global Economy, through an Aging Lens

Michael W. Hodin

Executive Director, Global Coalition on Aging;
Managing Partner, High Lantern Group

Through a new perspective on a "life course" of aging—one that is commensurate with twenty-first-century longevity, marked by ongoing social and economic participation—the upside of the aging population will be economic growth and wealth creation.

Like many young Americans growing up in the 1960s, I absorbed a daily diet of national and international politics. From the struggle for equality and the civil rights movement to the debates over America's role in Southeast Asia and the world, I developed a passion for—and an understanding of—how ideas could be the intellectual pathway to political solutions.

So perhaps it is unsurprising that I was attracted to Senator Daniel Patrick Moynihan of New York—one of the unique politicians of the time. More than any other, Senator Moynihan fused ideas and public policy to create a better America that was built on the finest liberal democratic principles. In addition, he had a particular intellectual curiosity about how large demographic trends would influence America's future, including its engagement in international relations. Moynihan taught—and I would like to believe I learned—that, with the right elements of political economy informed by the best of liberal democracy, we could continue to produce wealth and prosperity, and generate a better place for all to live.

This optimism became decisive for me in the 1990s when I was working for Pfizer's European Business and was first exposed to the challenges brought by population aging. Through survey research and policy analysis that I had helped create, the incompatibility between twentieth-century policy and institutions and twenty-first-century demography became apparent. But, remembering Senator Moynihan's insights and beliefs about demography and the impact of liberal democratic principles, I believed that population aging could become a source for better social, economic, and political outcomes. All we would need were the right pathways to get us there.

Peril or Promise?

It is well recognized that the twenty-first century will be defined by the aging of the global population, a profound transformation as birthrates drop, lives extend, and the post–World War II baby boomers reach their senior years. The United Nations Population Division projects that by midcentury those over 60 will outnumber those under 14.[1]

Never before has the world seen more "old" than "young." The implications for health, work, education, and all other facets of society are immense. A new kind of population structure is emerging throughout all societies across the globe, prompting a new reality that demands a rethinking and reimagining of how we organize ourselves in the twenty-first century.

To many commentators, this means trouble. Economic growth and fiscal stability are seen to be at peril. A *New York Times* headline claims,

"Slower Growth Seen in Graying World."[2] The sober-minded *Economist* warns that aging "will cast a pall over growth."[3] And the *Huffington Post* offers a sensational editorial[4] on a report by Fitch Ratings, citing the agency's claim that, "Whilst a successful resolution of the current fiscal crisis remains the most important driver for many advanced-economy ratings, without further reform to address the impact of long-term ageing these economies face a second, longer-term fiscal shock."

The implication is clear: Aging equals economic demise. Yet it is Standard & Poor's that gets it right in its 2010 *Global Aging* report, stating, "No other force is likely to shape the future of national economic health, public finances, and policymaking as the irreversible rate at which the world's population is aging."[5] They're precisely correct about the extent to which aging will shape economies, and they're also right to withhold verdict about the outcomes.

As the World Economic Forum's 2012 text notes, global population aging can lead to "peril" or "promise." Indeed, *Global Population Ageing: Peril or Promise* demonstrates the potential "upside" to aging—socially, politically, economically, and individually—if we can move beyond the twentieth-century model of aging that is shaped by dependency and disability. Through a new perspective on a "life course" of aging—one that is commensurate with twenty-first-century longevity, one that is marked by ongoing social and economic participation—the upside of the aging population will be economic growth and wealth creation.

Today we are the lucky recipients of miraculous achievements in advances of public health. This is true not only in the developed world, but also in emerging economies and even poorer parts of the developing world. Now it is time to realize the potential of these miracles by rethinking what it means to age and reconsidering how aging can be a time of extended contribution to families, businesses, and societies at large.

Forward-looking organizations are blazing the trail to turn population aging into a great story of success. And many of those organizations—large public companies across every sector of economic activity—are embedding the demographic shift into their core operations. Increasingly, the business community is recognizing that future success is predicated on the market opportunities of population aging.

Global Strides Toward Aging's Upside

To harness the potential of the aging population, leadership will be required from both public and private sectors. It will take both dedicated, progressive public policies and innovative business solutions to drive growth in an aging world. In the public sector, a number of positive developments are underway that are building the basis for sound public policy strategies.

The leading global institutions have been especially prominent in this regard:

- The United Nations convened an historic General Assembly High-Level Meeting in September 2011 to discuss strategies against the global rise of noncommunicable diseases such as diabetes, cardiovascular disease, cancer, and Alzheimer's and other dementias. All are exploding as the global population ages, and each presents serious challenges to be solved if the full promise of aging is to be realized. According to estimates, the global number of Alzheimer's cases will skyrocket from 35 million today to 66 million by 2030 and 115 million by midcentury.[6]

- The World Health Organization dedicated 2012's World Health Day to healthy and active aging. In addition to its core work on promoting health and offering guidance on how to prevent disease, WHO's Department of Aging and Life Course has become a global leader in aging advocacy. Its pioneering efforts around Age-Friendly Cities—communities that enhance the ability of people of all ages to participate in society—are most notable. Already, the growing network has more than 130 global cities as members that are creating infrastructure and establishing commissions to guide age-friendly policies.[7]

- The European Union, which is "older" than any other region in the world, has embraced age-friendly approaches to economic and social policy. With nearly one-quarter of its population projected to be over 60 by 2015 and one-third by midcentury, it has taken population aging as a top policy priority, dedicating 2012 as the Year for Active Ageing and Solidarity Between Generations.

- In 2011, high-ranking officials from the Asia-Pacific Economic Cooperation nations met with private-sector leaders in Washington to discuss how APEC member economies "will benefit from collaboration in health care and technology, regulatory harmonization, and ongoing reduction in trade and investment barriers." APEC representatives took the insights back to their home countries to influence policy.

- In 2013, the Organization for Economic Cooperation and Development convened with Oxford University and the Global Coalition on Aging to discuss how "big data" can be leveraged for better treatments and prevention of Alzheimer's disease. Big data enables researchers to see correlations in disease patterns, thus opening up entirely new paths of discovery. The OECD plans to continue this work in 2014 in order to spur aging populations as new sources of economic growth.
- The G8 is focused on how population aging can drive economic growth. During the United Kingdom's 2013 presidency of the G8, British prime minister David Cameron encouraged a global effort to defeat Alzheimer's.
- The World Economic Forum's Global Agenda Council on Aging is leading a private-sector effort to bring a set of business principles to global companies. These principles, which articulate how businesses can leverage population aging to fuel business growth, aim to parallel efforts in environment conservation, anticorruption, and transparency.

Yet, for all of this momentum, there remains critical work to be done by the private sector. A number of businesses are leading the way and setting models for others to follow. Some of these changes have been developed in response to an aging consumer and customer base, while others have incorporated an older, multigenerational workforce. A view of these changes by sector reveals the promise emerging from the private sector.

It's Just Good Business

As soon as 2020, 1 billion people will be older than age 60, according to UN projections.[8] From the perspective of business planning and strategy, this creates a market of substantial opportunity. These billion "customers" will have unique tastes and preferences, and their needs will be different than any "senior" demographic that preceded them. Companies already are adapting to meet this marketplace need, creating jobs, products, and services for a population that is seeking healthier, more productive courses of aging. Across industries, companies are adapting to meet the unique social, economic and health needs of this century's new demographics—and proving that it's simply good business.

Long-Term Care

For the past century, long-term care has been costly, impersonal, and overly institutionalized. With the over-80 demographic growing faster than any other, the industry is poised for innovation and transformation. For both social and fiscal reasons, more people are choosing to "age in place"—thus creating market demand for home-based care. Family caregivers will provide some services, but the rapid growth of the home-care industry illustrates the growing need for supplementary services—ranging from companionship to errand running to help with daily tasks.

This burgeoning market is evidenced by the rapid growth of Home Instead Senior Care, a global network of franchises that has pioneered the model of providing a wide range of home-based, nonmedical services. The company already has more than 900 franchises in 17 markets, with more than 65,000 trained caregivers. By filling the gap between familial caregiving and traditional institutionalized caregiving, the Home Instead model is a new solution for twenty-first-century demographics. By employing many older people as caregivers, it also creates new work opportunities for this demographic. As the ratio of old-to-young continues to tilt, this kind of home-based, nonmedicalized care has the potential to transform the way that we have traditionally delivered care.

Simultaneously, technological innovation is revolutionizing home-based care, with cutting-edge digital solutions for more effective, compassionate, and efficient care. Intel, for example, is working on innovations that monitor health data and communicate directly with health care professionals in real time. As care-management technologies move from "passive" to "active" functionality, the potential for the nonmedical home-care model is expanding, enabling the irreplaceable personalization of care.

Pharmaceuticals

The incredible leaps in human longevity are partly due to the past century's pharmaceutical innovations. The twenty-first century may prove equally fruitful. The pharmaceutical industry is engaged in cutting-edge advances in diagnostics, prevention, and treatment, and each branch of innovation holds a key to unlocking healthier, more active aging. For health needs that range from Alzheimer's to vision to nutrition, pharmaceuticals are creating new opportunities.

Diagnostics

One of the greatest challenges with solving Alzheimer's—a disease that can only be considered the greatest health and economic threat of the twenty-first century—is the development of effective diagnostic tools. One promising development comes from Eli Lilly and Company, which is developing new imaging technologies to take photographic images of brain plaque. Such images would open new doors for diagnostic abilities and overcome some of the greatest barriers in research and clinical trials. With no broadly effective treatment on the market for Alzheimer's, better diagnosis is a critical first step to better treatment and prevention.

Treatment

A range of innovative work is under way to slow the progression of disease as well as mitigate the effects. The consequences are vast. For example, for the first time in human history vision loss is not an unavoidable consequence of aging. New medicines by companies like Bayer are prolonging visual capabilities to extents that were recently unimaginable. The personal, social, and economic consequences are profound, as are the long-term health implications for both individuals and communities. Eighty percent of vision loss is preventable, and early treatments are driving this rate down and improving life in the later years.

Immunotherapies for Alzheimer's—which act much like a vaccine—also are being developed to slow disease progression. Novartis is developing one immunotherapy that, if successful, will revolutionize how people can live after receiving an Alzheimer's diagnosis. Moreover, it will free families from caregiver responsibilities, prevent the overconsumption of health care resources, and enable affected adults to continue active, engaged lives.

Medical nutrition is an exciting new branch of treatment. For a range of age-related diseases—from Alzheimer's to diabetes to renal failure and sarcopenia—specialized nutritional interventions to complement drug therapy are in the works. The science of nutrition is one of the most dynamic, rapidly developing fields in all of health care, and the future of healthy aging will likely hinge on nutrition far more than we understand today.

Prevention

The old chestnut—that an ounce of prevention is worth a pound of cure—has become a truism for a reason. And as the population ages, it's becoming a critical economic principle. Several noteworthy preventions are coming to market.

A life course approach to immunization, stressing vaccines in the adult years, for example, is a cost-effective tool for enabling healthy aging. Just as childhood immunization led to one of the twentieth century's greatest health advancements, adult immunization holds that potential for the twenty-first century. Pfizer has developed a vaccine to protect older adults from pneumococcal disease. Greater awareness and uptake among patients, physicians, and other health care providers would lead to reductions in preventable disease—with commensurate capacity for societal contributions by the aging population.

Galderma, which makes skincare products, has launched a global initiative around adult dermatology to provide preventative products and services. It ultimately will save substantial sums in health care costs, by preventing non-melanoma skin cancer, promoting skin hydration, and preserving senior mobility through healthy nails. These innovations are good for both individuals and health systems, as they prevent future costs—an especially important goal for global health systems becoming increasingly pressed by fiscal constraints.

Johnson and Johnson also is driving prevention by encouraging individual "ownership" of health through a Digital Health Scorecard, an interactive, personalized digital version of each person's health record. By enabling users to create, update, and interact with their personal health records by either computer or mobile device, Digital Health Scorecards empower and motivate individual prevention efforts.

Travel and Transportation

While travel has long been a "retirement" goal, the industry has begun to recognize that travel can promote healthy aging, which results in customers who will travel for more years. For decades, we assumed that if you aged in good health, then you would be able to travel later in life. Now, it is understood that travel later in life is associated with behaviors that promote good health. It's a tremendous insight for an industry that is an engine of the American and global economy. The travel industry alone generates $124 billion in taxes[9] annually and supports one in nine nonfarm jobs in the United States directly or indirectly, according to the U.S. Travel Association.[10]

Further, companies are tailoring modes of transportation for older users. Harley Davidson, for instance, is redesigning its products for the physical needs of aging consumers. Most notably, it has introduced the Tri Glide, a three-wheeled version of its legendary motorcycles, which was designed in recognition that older riders have trouble mounting and balancing heavy two-wheeled motorcycles.

Financial Matters

As lives stretch routinely into the eighties and nineties, a new model and philosophy of financial planning is required. The European-based insurance and asset management company Aegon is leading this effort as it seeks to "change the face of retirement." At a time when people are not prepared to "retire" as they have in times past—and when such a course makes little sense with today's demographic and fiscal realities—Aegon is creating new opportunities and strategies for retirement, offering solutions that many others are reluctant to address, like re-approaching the entire notion of "retirement age."

Along similar lines, Bank of America Merrill Lynch is offering new courses of work in the later stages of life through its notion of the "Second Act"—a productive, fulfilling alternative to traditional retirement. The Second Act encourages people to find interesting, entrepreneurial alternatives to retirement that enable them to do both well and good. This Second Act program, like Aegon's "changing face of retirement" campaign, introduces new ways to think about work throughout the life course.

Creating Age-Friendly Workplaces

In addition to products and services, companies are transforming internally for an aging workforce. The "promise" of an older workforce is real. Evidence shows the fallacy of believing that older workers are bad for the overall job market—and would, ostensibly, prevent younger workers from entering the workforce or climbing the career ladder. Global companies are showing this belief to be incorrect and rooted in a static view of economic growth and development.

The arguments against older workers today parallel the opposition to the economic integration of women in the mid-twentieth century when some men argued that women would "take our jobs." Their flawed view of the economy, in metaphorical terms, assumed that the economic pie would have to be cut into more, and smaller, slices. But the unique contribution of women to the economy enlarged the pie, resulting in more for everyone.

Such is the situation with older workers today. Organizations that become age friendly will gain distinct competitive advantages, both in attracting and retaining top talent, and in shaping products and services for aging consumers. Yet few global businesses are making the necessary preparations. So what is an age-friendly workplace?

A recent global survey by Deloitte Consulting reveals that new frictions are emerging in the multigenerational workplace. Younger workers are frustrated by the purported "gray ceiling" created by older workers who are delaying retirement, and older workers are frustrated with company leadership, feeling that their "loyalty and hard work has been neither recognized nor rewarded."[11] As the Deloitte report suggests, these attitudes can create barriers to business growth.

The age-friendly business creates programs and policies that foster cooperation and teamwork across generations. It designs retention incentives that are generationally appropriate, and provides training on effective intergenerational cooperation. The age-friendly workplace enables younger workers to plan for longer careers that do not follow the traditional "career ladder." The "once-and-done" model of aging—one degree, one career, one direction—is no longer relevant, according to Jeff Schwartz, partner at Deloitte and expert in human capital. What is more relevant today, Schwartz contends, is "serial mastery"—the cross-discipline competency that enables people to remain flexible and open to new, unexpected change.

The age-friendly workplace also recognizes that employees of all ages may need increased flexibility for family caregiving duties. The National Alliance for Caregiving estimates there are over 65 million unpaid caregivers in the United States. The workplace implications are vast. Of these 65 million, nearly three-in-four are still in the workforce while acting as caregivers, and 70 percent claim that their workplace performance is affected, either through tardiness, absenteeism, or early retirement.[12]

These U.S. numbers may be far lower than in other parts of the world, given the level of U.S. long-term care and in-home professional caregiving services. In China, for example, which lacks such professional caregiving infrastructure, the impact of caregiving on workplace production is likely to be significantly higher.

Businesses are increasingly recognizing that employees who are caregivers require policies and programs to support their multiple obligations. An exemplary program is the employer coalition ReACT (Respect a Caregivers Time), which builds business environments to support and recognize the challenges employees face as they juggle their professional and caregiving duties.

ReACT's membership includes some of the world's most significant businesses. It is working with leading caregiving organizations to build out national caregiving knowledge and awareness. For businesses of all sizes, ReACT's insights can help develop a company culture that enables caregivers to balance their dual responsibilities.

Age-friendly workplaces also facilitate older workers who must extend their careers and move beyond old models of retirement, education, and savings. In 2007, German automaker BMW recognized that within the decade the average age of its workforce in one manufacturing facility would jump from 39 to 47, consistent with the aging of the region's population as a whole. BMW created a taskforce to discover how the older workers were performing, and learned that they performed more slowly than their younger counterparts. Management held workshops with some of the older workers, and they collaborated to establish a list of simple changes—brighter lights, padded floors, rest areas, more ergonomic workstations, and the like—that could improve their health.

Over a short period, this older set of workers became the plant's most productive overall team. The older workers themselves were enthusiastic about the workshops and the changes. They didn't want to be less productive; their decline was simply the consequence of a working environment designed for younger bodies. The BMW lesson is clear: Quick, low-cost, and sustainable initiatives can create an age-friendly workplace that improves employee wellness and productivity, for not only older workers but also their young counterparts. We can anticipate that many other companies will recognize the upside of such changes that accommodate senior workers.

Embracing the Window of Opportunity

Over the last century, a long, ugly line of global catastrophes has been prophesized but failed to materialize. One can look back to midcentury and the "zero population growth" scare mongering, for example, to see one of the greatest flops of doom prophesizing (perhaps China can comment on how that worked out). Recent years have seen the telling of an especially vibrant host of near-cataclysmic fortunes: from Y2K to bird flu to the ozone layer. Now, add population aging to the list.

Aging, to the contrary, holds endless opportunity. Yet, like all opportunities, the window is small and fleeting. Public and private organizations must continue to step up to the leadership challenge, to create forward-looking policies and programs that are fit for twenty-first-century longevity. Given the number of exemplary trailblazers in the public sector, and the growing changes among businesses, there's reason to believe that we will indeed capture the upside of aging for individuals and for societies all over the world.

Notes

1. United Nations Department of Economic and Social Affairs, Population Division, "World Population Prospects: The 2012 Revision."

2. Floyd Norris, "Slower Growth Seen in a Graying World," *New York Times*, November 9, 2012.

3. "Working-Age Shift, Growth Will Suffer as Workers Dwindle," *The Economist*, January 26, 2013.

4. "Fitch: Aging Population Putting Economies at Risk of 'Fiscal Shock,'" *Huffington Post*, January 22, 2013, www.huffingtonpost.com/2013/01/22/fitch-aging -population_n_2522198.html.

5. "Global Aging 2010: An Irreversible Truth," Standard & Poor's Global Credit Portal, October 7, 2010, www.apapr.ro/images/stories/materiale/ COMUNICATE/2010/2010%2031%20attach.pdf.

6. BrightFocus Foundation, "Alzheimer's Facts and Statistics," August 21, 2013, www.brightfocus.org/alzheimers/about/understanding/facts.html.

7. Age-Friendly World, a website created by International Federation on Aging with the assistance of the World Health Organization, www.agefriendlyworld .org/cities-and-communities.

8. U.N. Population Division, "World Population Prospects."

9. "US Travel Answer Sheet," January 2013, www.ustravel.org/sites/default/files/ page/2009/09/US_Travel_Answer_Sheet_Jan2013.pdf.

10. "Travel and Tourism Works for America," June 2010, www.visithersheyharrisburg .org/uploads/files/tourism-works-for-america.pdf.

11. Deloitte Development LLC, "Talent Edge 2020, Building the Recovery Together—What Talent Expects and How Leaders Are Responding," April 2011, www.deloitte.com/assets/Dcom-UnitedKingdom/Local%20Assets/Documents/ Services/Consulting/UK_Consulting_Buildingtherecovery.pdf.

12. National Alliance for Caregiving, http://caregiveraction.org/statistics.

Part Two

A CHANGING LANDSCAPE

If you associate enough with older people who enjoy their lives, who are not stored away in any golden ghetto, you will gain a sense of continuity and of the possibility for a full life.

—Margaret Mead

Chapter 7

Encore: Mapping the Route to Second Acts

Marc Freedman
Founder and Chief Executive Officer, Encore.org

The upside of aging amounts to a human capital windfall, capable of turning dependency ratios into a new source of abundance—not just the opportunity for more fulfilling lives but the key to solving many of the social problems that ail us as a nation.

Crossing my personal midcentury mark, I found myself face-to-face with an unexpected, and uncomfortable, reality. Here I was, someone who for more than a decade had headed a nonprofit organization to help people aged 50 and over move on to new, productive chapters in their lives. Yet when I hit the milestone myself, I found myself leaning out, not in. In short, I needed a break from that very work. I still cared deeply about it—and knew how lucky I was to have a job in the moribund economy of 2008—but I was starting to flag, even unsure about what should come next.

I was approaching traditional retirement age, but I had a young family, with two sons who eventually would be joined by a third. Simple math made it clear I'd be working for decades to come. As I found my personal and professional concerns converging in ways that caught me by surprise, I decided to cobble together a three-month sabbatical, to reconnect with the sense of mission that had carried me to this point, and get a much-needed breather.

In a previous generation, this might have been a prelude to retirement, or even an early foray into retirement itself. My dad had retired at 57 having seen me through college by the time he was 50, with my sister soon to follow. And after a quarter-century of postemployment, his retirement has stretched nearly as long as his earlier career.

Not so for me—or for millions of my aging baby boomer peers who represent a demographic transition that is one of the defining phenomena of the twenty-first century. I came to see with increasing clarity that I was remarkably typical, and like the people my organization counseled, I was nowhere near ready, or able, to head to the sidelines.

In light of that baby boomer outlook, the upside of aging amounts to a human capital windfall, capable of turning dependency ratios into a new source of abundance—not just the opportunity for more fulfilling lives but the key to solving many of the social problems that ail us as a nation.

Rethinking the Patio Life

The confusion I (and others of my generation) have faced is due in large part to an outmoded concept of what a working life looks like, and more broadly the woeful inadequacy of our social and cultural maps for life after 50. They are dangerously short on useful guidance, premised on realities that no longer hold.

Those approaching retirement now regard the "golden years" in a much different way than their parents and grandparents did. Golf, fishing, knitting, a condo in Sun City—these were the images conjured by the words "when I retire." To some boomers, that still sounds fun, to be sure. But, I suspect even they wonder—as golden years become golden decades—can fishing and golfing and sitting around the patio sustain them physically, emotionally, intellectually? Will that lifestyle satisfy the soul? And will it sustain the coffers?

Healthier and more energetic than their predecessors, many of those moving beyond the middle years today want continued purpose in life. They want engagement, stimulation, and challenges. Many want to help.

They also want continued income, often out of necessity. And, by dint of their hard-won sagacity, their contributions to the workplace and to society at large might be even more relevant and meaningful than ever. Taking advantage of this resource—a ready, able, and substantial graying population—can benefit societies in countless ways.

But the aging transition isn't easy. Psychological inertia, financial risk, health issues, and the needs of family members (whether parents or kids)—such stressors further complicate an already freighted time. The vast wave of baby boomers now moving into these largely uncharted waters between midlife and old age represents just the beginning of the surge. Research suggests that children the age of my own kids, in the developed world, may have a 50 percent chance of seeing their one-hundredth birthdays. Longer lives are the new normal, not an aberration.

Given the scale of this shift, it is clearly not sustainable—at either a personal or societal level—to follow an outdated map that finds retirement beginning at 65, or 60, or even earlier. Nor is it desirable. But what's the alternative?

Over the years since I first started thinking about what's next in my own life and took my sabbatical, I've considered these issues not only in the context of my personal situation, but also in the context of the broader trends unfolding. I've come to the conviction that we need to do more than solve these challenges one at a time with individual improvisation. We need to rearrange society to help the graying population find its footing as it surges into uncharted territory—and to do so in a way that will not only serve boomers, but all the succeeding generations. That challenge entails the invention not only of a new stage of life, but one of work, what I've taken to calling an encore career, a second act at the intersection of passion, purpose, and a paycheck.

I feel more convinced than ever that these needed social innovations can transform an unsustainable situation into one both sustainable and attainable, and that can produce an enduring payoff.

A New Stage of Life

Over the past century, we have slowly and fitfully begun to recognize that the stage between midlife and old age is a distinct and uniquely valuable one. As long ago as the early 1920s, the psychologist

G. Stanley Hall—who had previously written the definitive text on adolescence as a distinct life stage—described the period preceding old age as a glorious "Indian summer," combining the perspective that comes from experience with the capacity to act on those insights. Similarly, the demographic historian Peter Laslett described what he called "the third age" as a time of continued productivity and learning, with a particular responsibility to the well-being of future generations. More recently, the Harvard sociologist Sara Lawrence-Lightfoot has written powerfully about the emergence of a generative "third chapter."

But despite these glimmerings, the stage between midlife and old age is still awash in confusion and contradictory messages. As Lawrence-Lightfoot puts it, we live amidst "deeply ambivalent, shifting societal expectations, institutional norms, and cultural presumptions about the 'normal' developmental trajectories of aging."[1]

Such perplexity is hardly surprising, given that the entire field of adult development, premised on the understanding that adults, as well as children, change over time in predictable ways, is a relatively new one. As recently as 1978, the pioneering psychologist Daniel J. Levinson could write: "The basic developmental principles of adult life remain an enigma."

In fact, life stages are a form of fiction, although they're often seen as fixtures: They are social construction projects. There's nothing natural or determined about them. We create new stages deliberately in order to solve problems, to bring more sense to the world, to reflect our deepest values. In Levinson's words, "Each phase in the life cycle has its own virtues and limitations. To realize its potential value, we must know and accept its terms and create our lives within it accordingly."[2] He might have said *define our terms*.

So how do we turn this nascent and still murky stage of life from one that is all too often characterized by identity void, economic disengagement, and societal confusion into one that has a shot at being the new crown of life?

How do we ensure that the best thing that ever happened to us as individuals—the prospect of extended and healthier lives—is a boon to the broader community, now and into the future?

How do we transform cultural assumptions, replacing what Lawrence-Lightfoot describes as "the still prevailing and anachronistic images of aging," with true-to-life images of contribution and growth?

It's a daunting assignment, creating a life stage and rewriting the map of life. Fortunately, we don't have to start from scratch. We have past experience as a guide, through obvious examples like the invention of retirement and the creation of childhood and adolescence. And the models don't stop with the existing stages of life. Concepts such as parenthood also offer useful lessons.

Parenthood itself was a social invention, and a relatively recent one at that, according to Jill Lepore, a professor of American history at Harvard. At first glance, that seems like an odd idea—how can one conceive of human beings without parenthood? But Lepore notes that for much of our history, children were born to very young parents, who kept having babies until they had produced 10 or 12 children, several of whom would likely suffer an early death. In eighteenth- and nineteenth-century America, Lepore says, "to be an adult was to be a parent."[3]

By the turn of the twentieth century, smaller households, increasingly longer lives, and more childless adults started to change the picture. A life phase emerged in which the kids became adults with their parents still alive. Parenthood became a distinct category—and with it a wave of parenting experts, advice literature, niche parenting magazines, and pediatrics as a specialty. Parenthood became an indelible feature of the social landscape.

As this example attests, the remapping of life's categories is rarely an orderly, or linear, process. There is no reason to think that this new life stage will be any different.

That process entails a messy break from old patterns of thinking that compromise our ability to reimagine the period between midlife and old age. That means resisting the temptation to see this time as a version of something else—whether that's endless midlife or reinvented retirement. That means 60 is not the new 40, any more than it's the old 80; 60 is the new 60.

Once we break free of old ideas, we need to replace them with something else. That means launching the new stage with a new dream for this period, a new definition of "success," and new language and branding to establish the integrity and weight of this time of life.

We are still just beginning to appreciate both the gifts and the opportunities of this new stage. What I describe below in broad outlines is intended as a start—a set of measures that might begin to carry us into new territory, even as we continue to devote our energies to better understanding it. And the place to begin is with the shift from midlife to the stage that has yet to even acquire a name.

A Gap Year for Grown-Ups

Entering this new life stage is an enormous transition, one commensurate to the shift from employment to retirement, though altogether different. Rather than preparing to leave the workforce, the shift into the years stretching out between midlife and anything resembling traditional retirement or old age entails a period of preparation for a new stage of personal meaning and productive contribution.

One strategy to aid this transition is a "gap year" specifically tailored to this stage of life, much as a growing number of young people take a gap year between high school and college, an opportunity on their journey to adulthood to gain the new perspective needed to make the most of what's next.

While transitions always entail discomfort, there are ways to ease this pain. William Bridges, who has written widely on the topic, urges those in the midst of such changes to avoid the temptation to act quickly simply for the sake of taking action—to recognize that transitions, by their very nature, simply take time. "Transitions clear the ground for new growth," he writes. "They drop the curtain so that the stage can be set for a new scene. What is it, at this point in your life, that is waiting quietly backstage for an entrance cue? What new growth is ready to germinate in this season of your life?"[4]

A gap period—perhaps a year, perhaps some longer or shorter length of time—would offer the time to ponder such questions, providing the kind of pause or foundation needed to launch a new stage of life. Indeed, many approaching this juncture are already intuitively responding to the need for time off, though absent widespread acceptance of the gap-year model, they often opt for the existing, if ill-fitting, vehicle of retirement.

A study from the RAND Corporation shows that a sizable portion of the U.S. population first retires and then "unretires," an act researchers find is primarily by design and not the result of unexpected

circumstances.[5] In other words, many may be using the cover of retirement, followed by unretirement, as a kind of de facto gap year.

There are countless possible permutations of the gap-year model.
For some, the best option might be a kind of stealth gap year, along the
lines of an executive education program—one that uses holidays, week-
ends, and vacation time to fly beneath an employer's radar.

Such a version might include trying a "vocation vacation" (pioneered by the entrepreneur Brian Kurth) that provides weeklong internships in a potentially appealing second career, like working on animal
welfare or in a bakery. That week could be combined over a period of
months with an academic course, life and career coaching, volunteering, and perhaps some adventure travel to create a stimulating period of
renewal and reevaluation.

Highest Education

Just as a young person's gap year is typically followed by college, an
adult's gap period may well precede further education. The education
suited to this stage of life is likely to combine vocational preparation,
personal transformation, and intellectual stimulation, all with the goal of
paving the way to a new stage of productive contribution.

The Advanced Leadership Initiative at Harvard is one shining star
in this new arena, as are the dozens of community colleges around the
country beginning to create transition programs focused on helping
those over 50 navigate the often bumpy path to purpose. Increasingly,
alumni associations and continuing education programs are also leading
the way.

We must do all we can to build on such beginnings. The old model
simply doesn't make sense for a 100-year life span. Why invest all our
higher-education time and most of our higher-education dollars in the
18-to-25-year-old sector when people are going to live for 60 or 75
more years? Moreover, it's impossible to know at 20 what you'll want to
do at 50 or 60—or even what jobs will exist then.

One possible model for this approach is a network of "EncoreU"
schools that would likely provide transitional help to their alumni
seeking greater purpose in the middle years and beyond, and become

spearheads for community members to find second acts through continuing education. They could also help their own faculty and staff navigate the passage to ongoing purpose.

As Harvard's Rosabeth Moss Kanter has argued, "third-stage education"—her term for this new stage of training beyond the middle years—would "give higher education a transformational concept and a catalytic innovation" for its own next chapter.[6]

Paying for the Encore

Of course, most Americans are hardly in the position to self-fund a gap year or foot the bill for their own tuition even as, in many cases, they are still putting their children through school. However, this should not—and does not have to—stand as an absolute barrier. We need to get creative, to develop the public- and private-sector solutions that will help those entering the encore years as they regroup for a productive new stage. In particular, I suggest two possible strategies: Individual Purpose Accounts and an "Encore Bill" akin to the post–World War II G.I. Bill.

Individual Purpose Accounts (and More)

When they were created in 1974, Individual Retirement Accounts (IRAs) were intended to supplement pensions or other traditional retirement vehicles, all premised on the notion of a life map that no longer applies. Why should we save all our money for an extended period of not working when we really need savings to cover the costs of more transition periods in life? We should be saving for this shift, given the cost of going back to school or living without a full salary during a gap year or fellowship.

Since society has so much at stake in such a large segment of the population finding their footing post-midlife, we should be creating tax-advantaged vehicles like the IRA to help fund this transition. What about an IPA—an Individual Purpose Account aimed at the transition or transitions in one's fifties and sixties?

Financial institutions are well placed to offer IPAs that integrate, streamline, and automate the processes for taking advantage of tax treatments, employer matches, investment options, loan programs, and other incentives. A side benefit: If the financial-services companies are involved in developing these products, their marketing muscle will be applied to putting the new stage on the map.

Another proposal that's been floated—lifelong learning accounts, or LiLAs—also might help workers save for the future education needed to jump-start encore careers. Modeled on a program already in place at IBM, tax-exempt LiLAs would pay for certain educational expenses, including tuition, fees, books, supplies, and information technology devices. LiLAs would provide individuals with a tax credit for cash contributions to their own LiLA accounts, and allow employers a tax credit for contributions they make to the LiLAs of their employees.

Finally, educational financial-aid policies should be revamped. Existing financial aid disadvantages part-time students, including those with family obligations or full-time jobs. Micro Pell Grants should be available to those who want to take perhaps one encore career–related course per semester or earn an occupational certificate.

An Encore Bill

The G.I. Bill is credited as a central force behind the decades of prosperity that followed World War II. Millions of soldiers were returning home, facing a harsh transition to a postwar future in a changing civilian landscape at home. The G.I. Bill was created to honor the veterans' sacrifice and service, and to ease the entry of this large influx of workers into postwar employment. Although the social forces today are different, tens of millions of people are now undergoing a great midlife migration and, like those returning G.I.s, their happiness and society's well-being are both at stake.

Yet at this point in history, no coherent policy agenda exists to help those millions develop their human capital, transition into new roles, or handle financial challenges. No incentives have been created to channel their skills to where they are needed most. No wonder this shift so far has remained largely a do-it-yourself undertaking.

There are positive signs. The Troops to Teachers program, for example, proves that skills developed in midlife military careers translate well into encore careers as public school teachers. Just as important, Troops to Teachers demonstrates how this midlife juncture can offer a second chance—an opportunity not only for new fulfillment, but also for social mobility, a chance to move up a ladder that wasn't available to many when they first started out.

Still, such efforts are just a beginning—a hint at what is needed, which notably includes far-reaching reforms of Social Security. Making Social Security more like an annuity, with flexible options that can be adjusted in light of an individual's situation, would allow for drawing down extra benefits during career transitions or for extraordinary expenses and topping them back up when earnings are higher.

For example, individuals could begin taking Social Security at 62, and use it to subsidize a period of renewal or a gap year. Then they could stop the benefits as they return to the workforce, in a way that actuarially adjusted their later payments to be revenue neutral.

An even more radical approach would let individuals take a year or two of Social Security before 62, say at 50 or 55, to underwrite a transition year, with the understanding that they would begin getting full benefits later (again in an actuarially neutral way).

The Freedom to Work

There is confusion about what work should look like in this period. In my view, encore careers—second acts over 50 at the confluence of money, meaning, and social impact—are an enormously promising approach to addressing the profound demographic and social changes of our age. Most older people need or want to work longer, but they don't want to keep doing the same thing they've been doing. Many don't have the option of staying the midlife course. They need income, but they thirst for new work that channels their experience into improving their communities and the world.

Encore careers already have drawn an enthusiastic following. One study shows that nearly 9 million boomers have moved into second careers in areas like education, the environment, health, and social services. Some 31 million more say that it's an attractive option for their post-midlife years.[7]

What leisure was to retirement, encore careers potentially are to the emerging stage between the middle years and anything resembling retirement or old age. Only 5 to 10 percent of the older population ever moved to places like Leisure World and Sun City. Yet these individuals, planting themselves in age-segregated, golf course communities, came to represent a new definition of success for later life. I believe that the millions flooding into encore careers, and the many millions more aspiring to the same dream, might well play a similar role in once again redefining the good life. In doing so they stand to replace the old goal of the *freedom from* work, with a new one that might be characterized as the *freedom to* work—in ways not only personally meaningful but with merit to society as well.

We need to strike a new deal around longer working lives that is as powerful as what was crafted to sustain shorter working lives a half-century ago. That requires a shift in thinking—taking the emphasis from "you have to work longer," and putting it on "there's important work for you to do." With that shift we can once again make virtue out of necessity, transforming a perceived burden into an extraordinary asset.

Even as we devise ways to make the transition to an encore career financially feasible, we need to expand the pathways for channeling passion into purpose. National service programs—most notably the Peace Corps—were designed for young people. Now the very people the Peace Corps was created to engage are themselves at the new stage. And many of them seek a new round of service with the same motivations that spur young people: to give back, to have an adventure, to acquire experience, and to gain the credentials and credibility to launch a new chapter of life and work.

Along with new pathways, we need new "encore friendly" employment policies. Some are simple and obvious. These include flextime to care for aging parents, children, or other family members; part-time or part-year jobs; on-the-job skills training; and, of course, an end to subtle and not-so-subtle age discrimination in hiring. Other policies and practices are more complex and involve helping employees make the transition to encore careers and related pursuits.

IBM was one company to respond early to these needs, creating the Transition to Teaching program to help its employees shift to teaching jobs in math and science. The company has since launched similar vehicles to help employees transition to jobs in government and the nonprofit sector.

Meanwhile, the former math teacher and Paramount Pictures CEO Sherry Lansing has created the EnCorps Teachers Program in California. It involves companies helping former engineering and high-tech workers move into new chapters teaching math and science in public schools.

A more recent effort is the Encore Fellowship program, launched initially with Hewlett-Packard in a key role piloting the first fellowships in Silicon Valley. Now a range of other major corporations have joined in helping retiring employees move toward a new stage, with the fellowships serving as a bridge to their encore careers after leaving their companies. Intel announced in 2012 that it would cover the stipend and health insurance of any retirement-eligible employee who is placed in an Encore Fellowship in a nonprofit organization.

Capitalizing on the Upside

There's no question all of this requires a sizeable investment, along with a big change in thinking—not only by individuals, but by business, government, and other institutions as the new reality of longer lives and all its implications upends the social landscape. Just think of the imagination we mustered in the last half of the twentieth century, transforming retirement from a dreaded destination to a centerpiece of the American dream. In a short stretch we concocted senior centers and retirement communities, the Older Americans Act and Medicare, AARP and lifelong learning, to name just a few advances. The accomplishments were groundbreaking and breathtaking.

Will our leaders recognize the need for comparable innovation in social infrastructure and public policies to address the challenges as millions move toward a new stage of life—and not simply to avert the potential downsides, but to capitalize on the vast upside? My suspicion is that none of this will happen without a social movement driven by those with the most to gain from the change, all of those over 50 who can enjoy a second chance at meaning and impact. We'll need to roll up our sleeves, tell our stories, tap the spirit of innovation, and get to the hard and exciting work of forging a new map of life.

We can do this work animated by much more than self-interest; by the sure knowledge that we're creating a new vision and a transformed landscape for all those millions of young people who will reach the same juncture, faster than they ever imagined.

Notes

1. Sara Lawrence-Lightfoot, *The Third Chapter: Passion, Risk, and Adventure in the 25 Years After 50* (New York: Farrar, Straus, and Giroux, 2009).

2. Daniel J. Levinson, *The Seasons of a Man's Life* (New York: Ballantine Books, 1986).

3. Jill Lepore, *The Mansion of Happiness: A History of Life and Death* (New York: Knopf, 2012).

4. William Bridges, *Transitions: Making Sense of Life's Changes* (New York: Perseus Books, 1980).

5. Nicole Maestas, "Back to Work: Expectations and Realizations of Work after Retirement," Rand Corporation working paper, 2007.

6. Rosabeth Moss Kanter, Rakesh Khurana, and Nitin Nohria, "Moving Higher Education to Its Next Stage: A New Set of Societal Challenges, a New Stage of Life, and a Call to Action for Universities," working paper, Harvard Business School, 2005.

7. MetLife Foundation, "Encore Career Choices: Purpose, Passion and a Paycheck in a Tough Economy," 2011, www.encore.org/files/EncoreCareerChoices.pdf.

Chapter 8

The Mature Workforce: Profiting from All Abilities

Jody Heymann

Dean, UCLA Jonathan and Karin Fielding School of Public Health;
Founding Director, WORLD Policy Analysis Center

Companies can benefit from the expertise of older workers; fellow employees reap the advantages of mentorship, and enjoy better working conditions as employers improve training, workplace flexibility, and career opportunities across the life course.

Barbara Rosenkrantz was a brilliant Harvard professor, and I was extraordinarily fortunate to have her as one of my PhD thesis advisors. She brought an unmatched depth of knowledge about the history of public health, insights into decisions on how to address tuberculosis—based on her years of immersion in the field—and a highly honed ability to be both demanding of and patient with her doctoral students.

113

She was 69 years old when she served as my advisor. The next year, students weren't so lucky—not because her abilities were any less sharp, her commitment less deep, or her inquiry less energetic—but because at that time Harvard still had a mandatory retirement age. At 70, Professor Rosenkrantz saw the options vaporize needlessly for her and her graduate students.

Many people value work for more than what they earn and, no matter what their age, continue to contribute to the community through unpaid work. Like Dr. Rosenkrantz, my grandfather, Sydney Heymann, was not ready to stop working at an arbitrarily designated age. He'd worked since his teen years, when he signed on with a translator for immigrants making insurance claims. He became the primary support of his family when his own father lost work during the Great Depression, He took great pride in ensuring that his progeny would have the educational, work, and life opportunities he never did. He finally retired from paid work at age 77. But income was never the only reason he worked—what kept his life rich had always been his connection to people with whom he worked. He knew he had to replace his paid work, and well into his late eighties, he regularly sang to the residents at a local nursing home and volunteered to prepare older immigrants for their U.S. citizenship exams.

A Shaky Foundation

When it comes to aging, national and global attention has focused overwhelmingly on how we can ensure that older people do not need to work, and that they do not live in poverty while not working. Concern about poverty in old age is certainly critical, as are policies that ensure older adults who are not in the labor force can lead full lives—but this is only part of the puzzle.

Next to nothing has been done to ensure that older men and women who want to work have that opportunity. Little has been done to prevent hiring and workplace discrimination, or to facilitate ongoing fruitful work lives. Nor does society do much to benefit from the skills of older workers or support the quality of their engagement in civic life once they leave the paid labor force.

These omissions are to the detriment of the economy and society as a whole, and to each of us as well, as we and our family members age. Companies can benefit from the expertise and skills of older workers. Fellow employees can reap the advantages of mentorship, and enjoy better working conditions as employers improve training, workplace flexibility, and career opportunities across the life course. Additionally, all employees can share in the economic gains related to mature workers' productivity.

Even the information that is collected about older citizens reflects the lopsided approach that we've taken thus far. Countries measure the size of pensions, who receives them, how they are provided, and whether they are economically sustainable—all crucial questions. They far less commonly examine how many older adults would like to or can continue to work, what bias and needless obstacles they face, whether they have opportunities for training or to advance their careers, or whether they have opportunities to contribute to civil society. Global organizations monitor policies such as how many countries offer pensions, but not how many bar age-based work discrimination. They focus on whether countries charge tuition for schoolchildren, but not whether adult education is available.

In the 20 years that I have worked with policymakers (nationally and globally) on working conditions, leaders and the public have always assumed that work has inherent value. Whether in the U.S. Congress or the International Labour Organization, leaders have widely viewed the chance to work, and to have an adequate income, as essential. When policymakers address the needs of parents, the goal is to ensure that they can care for their children *as well as* work in the paid labor force if they need or choose to—a philosophy that underlies protections such as maternity, paternity, and sick leave.

When decision makers examine social supports for people with disabilities, their goals are to ensure that disabled adults are not living in poverty, to support their ability to work, and to avoid disincentives to work.

The only exception has been older people. Like parents of young children, older adults may or may not choose to work. Like persons with disabilities, they may need workplace adaptations. Like all adults, older people deserve the chance to participate to their fullest capacity.

Revisiting Perceptions and Biases

Discriminatory preconceptions about older people are rampant in the working world. They typically are presumed to be less productive, less trainable, and less promotable.[1] People assume that cognition is impaired when a reply does not match the question—even when it is only hearing that is impaired, and the query simply was not heard. When physical mobility becomes more limited, people assume that the mind has slowed as well. When health conditions impair the ability of an employee to do his or her former job, employers do not imagine other abilities the employee could bring to different positions.

However, individual studies and meta-analyses of the research reach no consistent finding that age leads to lower performance.[2] In fact, the research shows that older adults suffer when supervisors evaluate them by subjective means, but that objective assessments do not find the same age-related variations. As a result, researchers, policymakers and others began calling more than 25 years ago for nondiscriminatory measures to accurately evaluate performance (and replace the poor proxy of age).

While age and employee productivity are not directly linked, factors that do affect productivity include:

- Experience and knowledge, which typically increase with age.
- Motivation and disposition, which are influenced by incentive structures within the organization and have no clear relationship with age.
- A working environment adapted to employee needs and characterized by support from colleagues and supervisors, access to training opportunities, and other factors, which can be designed to support employees across the life course.
- Some health problems that increase in likelihood as people age, the extent mediated by how well the workplace addresses employees' different needs; many new-onset limitations can be readily accommodated.

Clearly, bias plays an important role in the reason that older adults are treated differently than other demographics. Studies confirm the prevalence of age-based workplace discrimination. In Boston and St. Petersburg, Florida, researchers found that younger job applicants were 40 percent more likely to be selected for interviews than older workers.[3] Nearly two-thirds of older workers surveyed by AARP reported seeing or experiencing age discrimination in the workplace.[4]

In fact, there is no group against which greater bias has been measured. Project Implicit, one of the largest studies of implicit bias, has examined the extent to which positive and negative words are associated with characteristics like age, disability, ethnicity, and others. Individuals of every age demonstrated marked bias toward older age groups, the tests found.[5] Overall, 35 percent of respondents demonstrated a strong automatic preference for young people over older people. The only comparable bias was a 35 percent automatic preference among respondents for able-bodied people over the disabled.

For other groups commonly identified as experiencing significant discrimination, respondents also expressed bias, but at a lower level than for older adults: for example, 28 percent based on sexual orientation, 27 percent based on race/ethnicity, 25 percent against the obese, and 12 percent against Arab Muslims.[6]

Deflating Age Discrimination

Many tools already are at hand to transform the world of work from one with few options for older people to one of opportunities equal to their capacity and commitment. The following steps have a proven track record of success for some worker populations in the public and private sectors—the change would be to apply them across the life course. Firms need to:

- Take simple steps to reduce discrimination in hiring and promotion. As they have done for other groups subject to bias and discrimination, employers should demonstrate and serve as role models for nondiscriminatory hiring and promotion practices. They should teach supervisors about the cost of bias and the benefits of hiring from a fully qualified pool, and remove requirements that only facilitate discrimination. For example, applications contain many questions that do little more than make it easy to discriminate based on age, such as date of birth or years since high school or college graduation, while offering no meaningful information on skills, expertise, or productivity. Once hired, teams should be integrated across age groups.

• Develop effective measures of employee productivity.

All employers need effective ways to assess employees' productivity. Age (including mandatory retirement) is often used as a blunt instrument in pursuit of this goal, but is a poor correlate. Removing mandatory retirement ages and opening up opportunities for older adults must be accompanied by methods to ensure that they—and employees at every age—are productive. As just one example, when universities in the United States eliminated the mandatory retirement age, it became increasingly important to be able to assess the contributions and productivity of faculty members who had tenure. While this demanded new criteria for assessment, these measures are as vital to ensuring the productivity of tenured 48-year-olds as of 68-year-olds. Incentives for productivity should apply across the working life.

A number of initiatives that have sought to retain and promote employees based on accurate productivity measures could be useful in this endeavor, For instance, a strategy called Results-Only Work Environment uses results-oriented, flexible working conditions and focuses on output rather than on specific times and locations of work. When employers used this framework, employees were found to have less work-family conflict, better health and well-being, and higher job satisfaction and commitment.[7] Employers benefited by directly rewarding productivity, and also from lower turnover rates.[8]

• Make training and transitions into new roles available at all ages.

The majority of training opportunities are provided to young people at early stages of their careers. Training and job transition opportunities matter at all ages. Older workers who can no longer carry out physical labor required of previous positions still can bring their skills, knowledge, and experience to firms. As just one example, Baptist Health increased its retention of older employees by cross-training nurses in different skills so that they could switch roles when the physical demands of their jobs became too great.[9] Retraining affords employers the continued expertise of these older employees. As technologies change, it is often assumed that older men and women are too out of date to be effective while younger people are presumed to have more current skills. In fact, this has much more to do with retraining than it does with age.

Access to training also ensures that older adults can continue their career growth, which is an important motivator for all workers.[10] Dow Chemical, for example, encourages company-wide training opportunities for employees of all ages and all levels.[11] Motivation comes in part from productivity incentives, as discussed in the previous section, but also from the chance to continually transition into roles that strongly match skills, expertise, and interest.

- Recognize the need for flexible workplaces at all stages of life.

Substantial evidence shows that companies can benefit from flexible work schedules and locations. Flexibility for working parents has allowed firms to lower job turnover, increase retention of top employees, lower recruitment and retraining costs, and increase employee loyalty at little or no expense.[12] This same flexibility has yet to be fully applied to older employees. In cases where firms have applied flexible scheduling across the life course, the benefits to employee and employer have been great.

Laying the Foundation

The private sector can do a great deal to enable older people to work to their full capacity. But companies are unlikely to succeed alone. The public sector needs to:

- Create a legal foundation prohibiting discrimination.

Governments should bring the same commitment that they have applied to issues of gender, race, ethnicity, and religion to preventing discrimination based on age; national laws should clearly prohibit discrimination. This does not mean that older workers cannot be let go, or must be hired over younger workers. Rather, it means that older workers, like every other group, should be evaluated based on performance.

- Support training across the life course.

Government programs that support education and training should apply to all ages—to students completing university or vocational training for the first time as well as those seeking training opportunities following changes in the workplace or in their own lives.

- Remove financial penalties for older adults who choose to work.

Governments should ensure that policies allow older people to retire without falling into poverty, and that they can continue to work without financial penalty. Here again, policies relating to disabilities provide great lessons. Workforce participation among the disabled has been found to be very low in countries where they could only qualify for financial support while unemployed. Their participation increased when countries corrected these disincentives by allowing benefits for disabled people who worked but needed the extra resources to meet their needs. Similarly, pension policies should provide that older citizens who choose to retire do not have to worry about falling into poverty; and those who choose to work should not have to risk access to their own retirement savings or Social Security benefits when they do retire.

- Develop and implement public policies that facilitate part-time work and flexibility.

Many older people want to transition from full-time to part-time work, as opposed to not working at all. This viewpoint applies to many caregivers—be they parents of young children or caregivers for sick adults—who need work-schedule flexibility to attend to driving chores, medical appointments, or in-home care. The workplace flexibility accorded to young parents also can apply to older employees.

In addition to the role that employers play in determining policies on leave, schedule flexibility, and working conditions, national laws also are important to guarantee access to flexibility. The United Kingdom, for example, has laws giving workers the right to request flexible schedules, while leaving employers the right to deny the request if financially justified; this approach has proven very successful.[13]

On another important issue, part-time workers should have access to the same working conditions and protections that are guaranteed to full-time employees. Part-time parity is a simple but important concept. If a full-time employee receives 20 vacation days a year, then a half-time employee receives 10 days. Every benefit—sick leave, pensions, and the like—is similarly proportioned. While this seems obvious, part-timers in fact frequently receive disproportionately less access to workplace protections and benefits than their full-time counterparts. Guaranteeing part-time parity at a national level is critical to ensure that older adults, who disproportionately work part-time, experience equal treatment in the workplace.

Reaping the Economic Gains

None of these are pie-in-the-sky ideas. Measuring productivity, providing productivity incentives, and ensuring adequate training and correct job placement are core to human capital management in all firms. Companies succeed when they can hire the best employees and when they can maximize the contributions of the employees they have; increasing opportunities for older men and women will advance both of these areas.

When companies are prevented from discriminating among applicants based on age they will be hiring from a larger pool of workers. By ensuring training opportunities and rewarding productivity without regard to age, public and private sector employers will experience a deeper talent pool of people remaining at the company. Workplaces will be able to go from institutions that are often impoverished in terms of mentors, to ones that have ample numbers of mentors with expertise. Companies will have more long-term expertise to draw on when making decisions, when brainstorming new possibilities, and when making innovations to improve performance and efficiency. Deutsche Bank and John Deer & Co. are just two examples of companies that have realized benefits from the mutual learning that occurs in teams that are intentionally multigenerational.[14]

Also significant is the role this approach can play in filling numerical gaps in the workforce. Employers around the world already experience shortages of skilled workers. In a survey of 1,258 CEOs in 60 countries, PricewaterhouseCoopers found that one-quarter had been "unable to pursue a market opportunity or had to cancel or delay a strategic initiative due to talent constraints."[15] Manpower surveyed more than 38,000 employers in 42 countries in 2013, and found that 35 percent had difficulty filling job openings because of talent shortages. This reality doesn't just affect the market for professionals—shortages were most often in skilled trades. Some of the greatest shortages were in Japan (85 percent) and Brazil (68 percent).[16]

Well-accomplished changes result in financial benefits from both increased productivity and lowered costs. BMW, the car manufacturer, increased productivity by paying attention to ergonomics, physical strength, and production line equipment that affected all employees but older people to a greater degree.[17] ARO, Inc., a business process outsourcer, created flexible worksites, enabling more employees to work off-site. This approach was attractive to workers across the life course while creating a particularly strong draw for older employees. Productivity increased 15 percent while turnover dropped.[18]

Firms also reap economic rewards from the readier match of employees to staffing needs. Companies that benefit from specialized skills, like the Aerospace Corporation and Monsanto, have found they can build on their existing scientific talent pool by allowing older workers to consult or provide services part-time. Not only does the company benefit from the expertise of older workers, but it also can meet fluctuating personnel needs by calling on retirees to work part-time. In addition, the program facilitates the transfer of expertise from older employees who are retiring to other workers.[19]

For companies like CVS Pharmacy, whose business can grow and shrink seasonally and geographically, the flexibility of older employees is often helpful. CVS has hired older workers in northern states during the summer, while employing them in the southern states when they travel to warmer climates in the winter.[20] These approaches provide older workers with part-time and temporary work options and give employers access to a pool of experienced workers, saving training and recruitment costs.

A Zero-Sum Game or an Intergenerational Win?

Whether dealing with work opportunities for seniors or the extent to which countries will invest in pensions, the debate often is framed as pitting the interest of older generations against youth. If we gave older citizens the chance to be as productive as they are ready to be, would they take the jobs that the young need and crowd them out of the workforce? Would there be economic damage? Although we hear the argument that older workers will push younger people out, the evidence does not support the idea of a "fixed pie" of jobs and wages in an economy. It shows that this pie can expand or contract.

The debate is not new. Similar fears were expressed when women entered the labor force. In the nineteenth century and continuing into the twentieth, working men and labor unions argued against women in the workforce. Chief among their objections was the belief that women would push men out of jobs, particularly because women earned lower wages than men.[21] In 1836, the U.S. National Trades' Union Committee on Female Labor stated that "the female in a short time becomes so expert as entirely to supercede the necessity of the male; and . . . when the females are found capable of performing duty generally performed by the men, as a natural consequence, from the cheapness of their habits and dependent situation, they will acquire complete control of that particular branch of labor."[22]

Nonetheless, women flocked to the workforce in the twentieth century.[23] Labor force participation rates for women aged 16 and older shot up from 34 percent in 1950 to 60 percent in 1998. The most substantial increases were among women between the ages of 25 and 54, whose participation rates grew by as much as 42 percentage points, depending on age group, over this period. Nothing even close to a corresponding decrease materialized in the employment of males in the parallel age groups. Their participation declined by between 3 and 8 percentage points, depending on their age. The significant change was in the subgroups of men aged 55 to 64 (a decline of 18.8 percentage points), and over 65 (down 29.3 percentage points).[24] The declining rates of men working since the 1950s, largely in the older cohorts, has been attributed to the introduction of Social Security and other pension and insurance systems.[25]

In the long run, the employment of young and middle-aged working adults is unlikely to suffer from the increased labor force participation of older workers. When older people work, they spend more money; the economy grows and more jobs are created. Moreover, young and middle-aged workers are likely to benefit from this participation, as the need to contribute to social security programs and retirement systems to support retirees is spread over a greater number of working adults, and the dependency ratio is decreased.

Older people also typically transfer income to children and grand-children, providing households as a whole with more purchasing power to invest in the economy. Studies in the United States, and 40 countries across Asia, the Americas, Europe, and Africa, all show that financial transfers flow predominantly from older generations to younger ones.[26]

A Rejuvenated Workforce

The many direct individual benefits of work are clear—from a sense of purpose and accomplishment to social engagement. Research in many nations shows significantly higher life satisfaction among mature adults who are working, whether in paid or volunteer positions.[27]

Equally as profound are the health benefits of work as we age. Older adults who are physically and mentally active are less likely to develop chronic conditions, and more likely to lead longer, disability-free lives. Those who already suffer from a physical or mental health condition are likely to do better if they stay active and intellectually engaged.

A longitudinal study in the United States demonstrated that work even for as few as 100 hours per year had a protective effect on health for older adults.[28] A study in Singapore found that older adults who continued to work had significantly higher cognitive performance, less depression, and higher overall mental well-being than nonworkers.[29] Meanwhile, older workers who experience involuntary job loss have higher rates of subsequent physical and mental morbidity.[30] This is all before we get to the higher income provided by employment. Public and private pensions replace income to an important degree but rarely match what could be earned in the labor force, particularly for those whose retirement lasts for decades.

Some argue that the right to work for older people is left unad-dressed out of concern that it will somehow compromise the retirement opportunities for people who need to or want to leave the labor force. However, these two objectives need not conflict. To ensure that people can choose to retire or to work, all workplaces should be fully accessible to people as they age and none should discriminate; rather they should hire, retain, and promote employees based on ability and contribution, leaving those who want to retire the freedom to do so with the benefit of a public or private pension. This is far from the current case, but it is well within our reach.

The Space-Program Effect

The desire for opportunities in life is not unique to any age. Just as millions of parents want the chance to choose between staying home to care for a child or returning to paid work, and just as young adults want the option of higher education or entering the workforce—as well as the chance to return to school later in their careers—so too do older people value the chance to choose how they balance paid work, civic engagement, caring for family members, learning opportunities, leisure time, and other activities.

When the United States set the goal of humans landing on the moon, it had to invest heavily in scientific innovation. Far less innovation will be needed to make the workplace truly accessible to older men and women, but these two initiatives would share something in common. The space program yielded many benefits that went far beyond the program itself; scientific advancements that provided widespread benefits to society. The same will be true of programs to make the workplace more accommodating.

Employees at every age who have a physical limitation—be it in vision, hearing, mobility, or other—will benefit from universal design measures taken by companies to make work accessible to the older employees who face these limitations. Any employee seeking flexibility or part-time work—whether due to age, the need to care for young children or older family members, or the desire to spend time volunteering—will benefit when companies become more skilled at offering these options.

This chapter was made possible by the invaluable research contributions of Megan Arthur, Tina Assi, Nicolas de Guzman, Isabel Latz, and Parama Sigurdsen and the extraordinary editorial skills of Kristen McNeill.

Notes

1. A. B. Diekman and L. Hirnisey, "The Effect of Context on the Silvery Ceiling: A Role Congruity Perspective on Prejudiced Responses," *Personality and Social Psychology Bulletin* 33 (2007): 1353–1366.

J. McGregor and O. L. Gray, "Stereotypes and Older Workers: The New Zealand Experience," *Social Policy Journal of New Zealand* 18 (2002): 163–177.

P. Shah and B. Kleiner, "New Developments Concerning Age Discrimination in the Workplace," *Equal Opportunities International* 24 (2005): 14–23.

P. Taylor and A. Walker, "The Ageing Workforce: Employer's Attitudes towards Older People," *Work, Employment and Society* 8 (1994): 569–591.

S. Steinhauser, "Age Bias: Is Your Corporate Culture in Need of an Overhaul?" *HR Magazine* 43 (1998): 86–90.

J. Lahey, (2006). "Do Older Workers Face Discrimination? New Evidence," presented at the session, Boomers' Work and Retirement Plans, at Older and Out of Work: Jobs and Social Insurance for a Changing Economy, the 18th Annual Conference of the National Academy of Social Insurance, January 19–20, 2006.

J. A. McMullin, W. M. Victo, "Ageism, Age Relations, and Garment Industry Work in Montreal," *The Gerontologist* 41, no. 1 (2001): 111–122.

M. Wilson and J. Kan, "Barriers to Entry for the Older Worker," Auckland, New Zealand, The University of Auckland Business School, 2006.

E. L. Perry, C. T. Kulik, A. C. Bourhis, "Moderating Effects of Personal and Contextual Factors in Age Discrimination," *Journal of Applied Psychology* 81, no. 6 (1996): 628–647.

F. Frerichs and G. Naegele, "Discrimination of Older Workers in Germany: Obstacles and Options for the Integration into Employment," *Journal of Aging & Social Policy* 9, no. 1 (1997).

M. Wilson and J. Kan, "Barriers to Entry for the Older Worker," Auckland, New Zealand, The University of Auckland Business School, 2006.

2. G. McEvoy and W. Cascio, "Cumulative Evidence of the Relationship between Employee Age and Job Performance," *Journal of Applied Psychology* 74, no. 1 (1989): 11–17.

S. Czaja, "Aging and Work Performance," *Review of Public Personnel Administration* 15, no. 2 (1995): 46–61.

T. Ng and D. Feldman, "The Relationship of Age to Ten Dimensions of Job Performance," *Journal of Applied Psychology* 93, no. 2 (2008): 392–423.

S. Rhodes, "Age-Related Differences in Work Attitudes and Behavior: A Review and Conceptual Analysis," *Psychological Bulletin* 93, no. 2 (1983): 328–367.

M. Sturman, "Searching for the Inverted U-Shaped Relationship between Time and Performance: Meta-Analyses of the Experience/Performance, Tenure/Performance, and Age/Performance Relationships," *Journal of Management* 29 (2003): 609–640.

D. Waldman and B. Avolio, "A Meta-Analysis of Age Differences in Job Performance," *Journal of Applied Psychology* 71, no. 1 (1986): 33–38.

V. Skirbekk, "Age and Productivity Capacity: Descriptions, Causes and Policy Options," *Ageing Horizons* 8 (2008): 4–12.

U. Backes-Gellner, M. Schneider, and S. Veen, "Effect of Workforce Age Quantitative and Qualitative Organizational Performance: Conceptual Framework and Case Study Evidence," *Organization Studies* 32, no. 8 (2011):1103–1121.

C. Göbel and T. Zwick, "Age and Productivity—Evidence from Linked Employer-Employee Data," ZEW Discussion Paper No. 09-020, 2009.

C. Göbel and T. Zwick, "Age and Productivity: Sector Differences," *De Economist* 160 (2012): 35–57.

A. Sharpe, "Is Ageing a Drag on Productivity Growth? A Review Article on *Ageing, Health and Productivity: The Economics of Increased Life Expectancy*," *International Productivity Monitor* 21 (2011): 82–94.

G. van Zyl, "The Relative Labour Productivity Contribution of Different Age-Skill Categories for a Developing Economy," *SA Journal of Human Resource Management / SA* Tydskrif vir Menslikehulpbronbestuur 11, no. 1 (2013): 1–8.

3. J. Lahey, "Do Older Workers Face Discrimination? New Evidence," paper presented at the Boomers' Work and Retirement Plans session at Older and Out of Work: Jobs and Social Insurance for a Changing Economy, the 18th Annual Conference of the National Academy of Social Insurance, January 19–20, 2006.

4. AARP. *Staying Ahead of the Curve 2013: AARP Multicultural Work and Career Study. Perceptions of Age Discrimination in the Workplace—Ages 45–74* (Washington, DC: AARP, 2013).

5. B. R. Levy and M. R. Banaji, "Implicit Ageism," in *Ageism: Stereotyping and Prejudice against Older Persons*, ed. T. D. Nelson (Cambridge, MA: The MIT Press, 2002).

6. Project Implicit. "Implicit Social Cognition: Investigating the Gap between Intentions and Actions," www.projectimplicit.net/index.html.

7. R. Hill, E. Tranby, E. Kelly, and P. Moen, "Relieving the Time Squeeze? Effects of a White-Collar Workplace Change on Parents," *Journal of Marriage and Family* 75 (2013): 1014–1029.

R. Hill, E. Tranby, E. Kelly, and P. Moen, "Making Changes or Feeling like You Can: Parents' Time and Control over Work Time in a Changing Workplace," report: University of Minnesota, January 2010.

P. Moen, E. Kelly, J. Lam, "Healthy Work Revisited: Do Changes in Time Strain Predict Well-Being?" *Journal of Occupational Health Psychology* 18, no. 2 (2013): 157–172.

P. Moen and E. Kelly, "Flexible Work and Well-Being Study," Final Report, University of Minnesota, Fall 2007.

8. P. Moen, E. Kelly, and R. Hill, "Does Enhancing Work-Time Control and Flexibility Reduce Turnover? A Naturally Occurring Experiment," *Social Problems* 58, no. 1 (2011): 69–98.

9. L. Morton, L. Foster, and J. Sedlar, *Managing the Mature Workforce.* Research Report 1369 (New York: The Conference Board, 2005).

10. R. Strack, J. Baier and A. Fahlander, "Managing Demographic Risk," *Harvard Business Journal* 86, no. 2 (2008): 119–28, 138.

11. K. Dychtwald, T. Erickson, and B. Morison, "It's Time to Retire Retirement," *Harvard Business Review* 82, no. 3 (2004): 48–57, 126.

12. J. Heymann and A. Earle. *Raising the Global Floor: Dismantling the Myth that We Can't Afford Good Working Conditions for Everyone* (Stanford, CA: Stanford University Press, 2010).

13. A. Hegewisch and J. C. Gornick. *Statutory Routes to Workplace Flexibility in Cross-National Perspective* (Washington, DC: Institute for Women's Policy Research, 2008).

14. D. Piktialis, "Adaptations to an Aging Workforce: Innovative Responses by the Corporate Sector," *Generations* XXXI, no. 1 (2007): 76–82.
    H. Munson. *Valuing Experience: How to Motivate and Retain Mature Workers.* Research Report 1329 (New York: The Conference Board, 2003).

15. PricewaterhouseCoopers, "Delivering Results: Growth and Value in a Volatile World; 15th Annual Global CEO Survey, 2012," www.pwc.com/gx/en/ceo-survey/pdf/15th-global-pwc-ceo-survey.pdf.

16. Manpower, "2013 Talent Shortage Survey Research Results," www.manpowergroup.com/wps/wcm/connect/587d2b45-c47a-4647-a7c1-e7a74f68fb85/2013_Talent_Shortage_Survey_Results_US_high+res.pdf?MOD=AJPERES.

17. C. H. Loch, F. J. Sting, N. Bauer, H. Mauermann, "How BMW Is Diffusing the Demographic Time Bomb," *Harvard Business Review* 88, no. 3 (2010): 99–102.

18. Dychtwald, Erickson, and Morison, "It's Time to Retire Retirement."

19. Piktialis, "Adaptations to an Aging Workforce"; Dychtwald, Erickson, and Morison, "It's Time to Retire Retirement.

20. Piktialis, "Adaptations to an Aging Workforce."

21. M. May, "Bread before Roses: American Workingmen, Labor Unions, and the Family Wage," in *Families in the U.S.: Kinship and Domestic Politics*, ed. K. V. Hansen and A. Ilta Garey (Philadelphia: Temple University Press, 1998), 143–56.
    E. Jordan, "The Exclusion of Women from Industry in Nineteenth-Century Britain," *Comparative Studies in Society and History* 31, no. 2 (1989): 273–96.
    M. Crain, "Feminizing Unions: Challenging the Gendered Structure of Wage Labor," *Michigan Law Review* 89, no, 5 (1991): 1155–221.

22. J. R. Commons and H. Sumner, *A Documentary History of American Industrial Society*, Vol. VI: Labor Movement 1820–1840, 2 (Cleveland, OH: The Arthur H. Clark Company, 1910), 283.

23. M. Toossi, "A Century of Change: The U.S. Labor Force, 1950–2050," *Monthly Labor Review* (May 2002): 15–28.

24. H. N. Fullerton, "Labor Force Participation: 75 Years of Change, 1950–98 and 1998–2025," *Monthly Labor Review* (December 1999): 3–12.

25. Ibid.

   G. Burtless and R. A. Moffitt, "The Effect of Social Security Benefits on the Labor Supply of the Aged," in *Retirement and Economic Behavior*, ed. H. J. Aaron and G. Burtless (Washington, DC: Brookings Institutio, 1984).

   H. Cremer, J.-M. Lozachmeur, and P. Pestieau, "Social Security, Retirement Age, and Optimal Taxation," *Journal of Public Economics* 88, no. 11 (2004): 2259–2281.

   J. Gruber, "Disability Insurance Benefits and Labor Supply," NBER Working Paper No. 5866, December 1996.

   R. L. Lumsdaine, J. H. Stock, D. A. Wise, "Retirement Incentives: The Interaction between Employer-Provided Pensions, Social Security, and Retiree Health Benefits," in *The Economic Effects of Aging in the United States and Japan* (Chicago: University of Chicago Press, 1997).

   D. O. Parsons, "The Decline in Male Labor Force Participation," *The Journal of Political Economy* (1980): 117–134.

26. A. Mason, R. Lee, A.-C. Tung, M.-S. Lai, and T. Miller, "Population Aging and Intergenerational Transfers: Introducing Age into National Accounts," NBER Working Paper 12770, 2006, www.nber.org/papers/w12770.

   E. Grundy, "Reciprocity in Relationships: Socio-Economic and Health Influences on Intergenerational Exchanges between Third Age Parents and Their Adult Children in Great Britain," *British Journal of Sociology* 56, no. 2 (2005): 233–255.

   J. Fritzell and C. Lennartsson, "Financial Transfers between Generations in Sweden," *Ageing and Society* 25, no. 6 (2005): 397–414.

   M. Albertini, M. Kohli, and C. Vogel, "Intergenerational Transfers of Time and Money in European Families: Common Patterns—Different Regimes?" *Journal of European Social Policy* 17, no. 4 (2007): 319–334.

   E. Duflo, "Grandmothers and Granddaughters: Old-Age Pensions and Intra-household Allocation in South Africa," *World Bank Economic Review* 17, no. 1 (2003): 1–25.

   A. Case and A. Menendez, "Does Money Empower the Elderly? Evidence from the Agincourt Demographic Surveillance Site, South Africa," *Scandinavian Journal of Public Health* 35, no. 69 (2007): 157–164.

   L. Juarez, "The Effect of an Old-Age Demogrant on the Labor Supply and Time Use of Elderly and Non-Elderly in Mexico," *B.E. Journal of Economic Analysis and Policy* 10, no. 1 (2010): 1–25.

   A. Mason and R. Lee, "Population Aging and the Generational Economy: Key Findings," *Population Aging and the Generational Economy: A Global Perspective* (UK: Edward Elgar Publishing Limited, 2011), 3–31 (Chapter 1).

27. Michael A. Smyer and Marcie Pitt-Catsouphes, "The Meanings of Work for Older Workers," *Generations* 31, no. 1 (Spring 2007): 23–30.

   Juan A. Aquino, Daniel W. Russell, Carolyn E. Cutrona, and Elizabeth M. Altmaier, "Employment Status, Social Support, and Life Satisfaction among the Elderly," *Journal of Counseling Psychology* 43, no. 4 (October 1996): 480–489.

Johannes Siegrist and Morten Wahrendorf, "Participation in Socially Productive Activities and Quality of Life in Early Old Age: Findings from SHARE," *Journal of European Social Policy* 19, no. 4 (2009): 317–326.

28. Ming-Ching Luoh and A. Regula Herzog, "Individual Consequences of Volunteer and Paid Work in Old Age: Health and Mortality," *Journal of Health and Social Behavior* 43, no. 4 (2002): 490–509, www.jstor.org/stable/3090239.

29. Andiara Schwingel, Mathew M. Niti, Catherine Tang, and Tze Pin Ng, "Continued Work Employment and Volunteerism and Mental Well-Being of Older Adults: Singapore Longitudinal Ageing Studies," *Age and Ageing* 38, no. 5 (2009): 531–537.

30. William T. Gallo, Elizabeth H. Bradley, Michele Siegel, and Stanislav V. Kasl, "Health Effects of Involuntary Job Loss among Older Workers: Findings from the Health and Retirement Survey," *Journal of Gerontology: Social Sciences* 55B, no. 3 (2000): S131–140.

Chapter 9

Boomer Philanthropists: A Golden Age of Civil Society

Susan Raymond
Executive Vice President, Changing Our World, Inc.

*Our aging population promises a future of ever broader and deeper phil-
anthropic activity, becoming the core of vibrant communities, strengthening societal institutions and the nation itself, and ushering in a new
Golden Age of civil society.*

It was a crystal-clear day on a picturesque road between Kabul and
Jalalabad, a rare day off from a three-week, economic-development trip.
My colleagues and I of course were aware that it was a time of sim-
mering political and social upheaval in Afghanistan. Still, the roadblock
appeared unexpectedly as we drove the isolated macadam road. The next
20 minutes were formative. Having the cold steel of a nervous young
gunman's AK47 pressed against one's head tends to focus the mind.
Luck or providence or both were with me that day, as our local driver

convinced the men to lower their weapons and brought the confrontation under control.

Later, I could not help wondering about the parents and grandparents of those young men. How had a society premised on the wisdom of elders, on the ties between generations literally across millennia, become an unstable cauldron of young gunmen? Raised by the strong hand of my own grandmother, I knew how much older people can imprint the values that bind communities, and how their leadership provides the linkage that keeps societies stable and strong.

Afghanistan's profound history includes an often-deep sense of shared purpose at the village and tribal level that extends across generations. I feel great sadness that this wisdom of elders has been lost to faction, that the dominant forces are those that naturally pull people apart, not the values and cultures that unify them.

After my Afghanistan experience, and others less life threatening in places riven by similar conflict, I have reflected on what holds civil society together, and in particular on the role of older generations. What gives a community its sense of its shared identity, its shared fate, and its shared opportunity? What creates an identity that not only rises above factionalism but is so imbued in the community DNA that factions (which almost never can be eliminated) become simply a peripheral part of life? How can that identity be maintained and strengthened in a world of rapid change, a world where anyone's sense of place can be defined less by physical diameters than by the scope and speed of an app download? Where is the glue that holds civil society together?

Philanthropy as Leadership

Over the years I have observed that philanthropy is a critical part of that glue—and that an aging demographic is a central part of philanthropy. Our aging population today promises a future of ever broader and deeper philanthropic activity, becoming the core of vibrant communities, strengthening societal institutions and the nation itself, and ushering in a new Golden Age of civil society.

To be precise, I do not mean philanthropy as money. For many of us, philanthropy conjures the funds that flow to charity, the hundreds of billions of dollars that the wealthy and the not so wealthy provide to nonprofits of all sizes and types. While money is important, philanthropy, in reality, is not simply about money at all. Philanthropy is individual voluntary leadership that steps onto the community societal commons and commits itself to the betterment of the whole. Philanthropy is the hours spent on a school board listening to complaints and finding middle ground, the nights spent balancing the books of a church women's association, the time committed by retired Elks and Moose and Knights who stock food pantry shelves.

Money is just the way we see and measure that leadership—it is not the leadership itself. This leadership finds private individuals stepping forward to put themselves in service of broader needs, not because of shared faction or shared ideology, but because service is part of a community's identity and culture. Engaged civic leadership pulls attention toward common problems and shared interests.

Older and Kinder

This kind of commitment by older people has a long history. Benjamin Franklin founded the Library Company of Philadelphia, the Pennsylvania Hospital, and the first volunteer fire department. He was president of the Pennsylvania Society for the Abolition of Slavery when he was 79. At age 63, George Washington made what then was the largest gift to higher education, a contribution to Liberty Hall Academy in Lexington, Virginia, what is today Washington and Lee University. Thomas Jefferson was 75 when he donated his entire personal library collection—said to be the finest in the nation—to the Library of Congress, to replace the volumes burned by British troops in the War of 1812.

An aging population is a key asset in philanthropy and in civil society engagement. It is certainly not that people of any age cannot and do not lead, nor that philanthropy is realized only with age. But a mature population can solidify a core commitment to community, which in turn strengthens civil society and advances the common good. With age, people are more likely to volunteer and more likely to contribute resources; a vibrant aging population can become the core engine of a thriving community.

How so? A 2013 study commissioned by Blackbaud and conducted by Sea Change Strategies[1] finds that philanthropy from baby boomers (ages 49 to 67) and "matures" (age 68 or older) accounts for 60 percent of the donors and 69 percent of the dollar value of all charitable giving in the United States. These two groups represent about 40 percent of the population, so their propensity to give is far in excess of their demographic proportionality.

Moreover, their philanthropic engagement tends to be more locally focused than that of other generations. Generation X (born between 1965 and 1980) and Generation Y (born between 1981 and 1995) are much more likely to be philanthropically engaged in global human rights and international causes. There is nothing wrong with that, of course, nor is it particularly surprising given the increasingly global nature of their education and their lives, and their instantaneous, worldwide communication. Older generations, on the other hand, seem to refocus on where they live, on the communities closest to them, and on the issues that are directly within their line of sight—on religious institutions, mentoring, and neighborhood well-being.[2]

This philanthropic relationship between aging and civil society is not simply a matter of money, as I stated previously. It is about engagement. Today, that philanthropic life is becoming a greater part of the core of community as the nation ages, and as more years of good health and active lives characterize this aging trend.

Older Americans today volunteer at rates higher than did the seniors of past generations. When members of the Silent Generation (born between 1931 and 1945) were in their fifties, just 23 percent of them volunteered, compared to nearly 30 percent of baby boomers today.[3]

This engagement also is more nuanced and complex than ever before. A study by the National Conference on Citizenship found that only 15 percent of millennials (aged 18 to 29) were engaged in their communities in multiple ways (giving, volunteering, serving on boards of directors) compared to 38 percent of baby boomers.

Engagement for older generations is not random kindness. It is a fundamental and fulfilling part of their lives. Their year-over-year retention in volunteering is 70–75 percent, indicating that civic engagement is a continuous process for older people who have the time and flexibility to stay involved in their communities.

Some mature philanthropists are household names—for instance, Bono, who in his early 50s has become a tireless humanitarian while still a rock idol. Other examples don't come from the bold-faced names in the news, but from the Main Streets of every town across the country:

- Eighty- and 90-somethings like Pendleton Woods. The MetLife Foundation, and the National Association of Area Agencies on Aging, awarded him a Lifetime Achievement Award for his nearly half-century of commitment to the Epilepsy Foundation of Oklahoma, which he helped found; his work with veterans; and his 75-year involvement with the Boy Scouts.[4]
- Retired business executives like Leonard Kaplan, at 85 a tireless philanthropist in Greenville, North Carolina. When he was 80, he created the Alliance for Global Good and was the anchor donor for its fund providing social enterprise grants and helping relief and development nonprofits diversify their revenue.
- Donors like Isha Salas-Desselle, another MetLife awardee, who, with her husband, sold the family business and home in Trinidad to found the Turning Point Center Homeless Shelter for the elderly in Houston.[5]

A Golden Age of Civil Society

The aging of the population promises more of the same engagement and, with it, the potential for long-term strengthening of the nation—even a new Golden Age of civil society. True opportunity awaits. With more people involved for longer periods of time, the societal commons will reap a community effort for the shared interests of many organizations and individuals.

The obvious indicators of commitment—time and money—are important in creating strong civil societies. But they are only surface manifestations of the strength that aging can build in civil society. These outer signs do not reveal the deeper scope of that Golden Age.

An aging population is a repository of knowledge and history, as well as culture. Therein resides the most important long-term aspect of this Golden Age. A deeply engaged, aging population is a bridge across generations to a continued culture of philanthropy in all of its dimensions.

Take Brian Crimmins, the 30-something chief executive of Changing Our World, Inc., which provides philanthropy consulting to nonprofits and corporations. His parents, who in their mid-70s are still active philanthropists and volunteers, spoke fervently to their children about the importance of community commitment. Brian firmly believes that "values education" was his central motivation for making nonprofit and philanthropic work his career.

My own life is perhaps testimony to this same multigenerational effect, and how it becomes part of a family's DNA. My grandmother—who raised three families during the Depression when parents could not afford to care for their own children—was not a talker. She did not chat. I recall no discussion of giving to community. She did not need to talk about it. It was simply understood and expected.

Now, being part of today's aging demographic ourselves, my husband and I have conveyed the same understanding to our children. My eldest son had his cadet wages garnished at West Point to support a children's charity. My daughter created the Kids Helping Kids Club of Larchmont, New York, at age seven. She was invited to Warsaw, Poland, to present a $100 check to a children's hospital, the beneficiary of her club's summer lemonade stand.

My younger son started a club at his all-boys high school to purchase wigs for breast cancer sufferers who could not afford them during chemotherapy. Cleverly, he convinced the school cafeteria to serve vegetarian casserole and spinach on the days when his club sold the melted-cheese hoagie sandwiches that a local deli provided the club at a discount. The boys flocked to buy his hoagies when faced with the lunch alternative.

Through their commitment to philanthropy and volunteerism, older Americans communicate to younger generations the values of community building. They convey a culture of giving that provides fundamental and precious building blocks for a robust civil society. The Golden Age promises a bridge to sustained community health, as older Americans set precedents for younger generations in this philanthropic commitment.

However, the bridge across generations will not be built of rusted steel. It won't be a tableau of older Americans sitting in porch rockers shouting into the empty wind. Instead, these seniors increasingly convey the culture of engagement by using the very media technology through which Gen X and Gen Y live their lives.

Already, a third of people over 65 use social networking sites, as do more than half of those aged 50 to 64[6]—a 10-fold increase by older age groups in eight years. Social networking among those over age 65 is growing faster than for any age group. When they spread the word about their causes on websites and social media, they set an example for vast audiences of younger people.

The Rising Role of Women

The growth of philanthropy also is enhanced by the increasing role of women, who have long been leaders in philanthropy in its broadest sense. Today, 29.3 percent of women volunteer compared to 23.2 percent of men.[7]

Women's volunteerism dates to the early days of American history. First ladies from Martha Washington on have been leaders equal to their male counterparts in commitment to common cause.

Abigail Adams was a tireless advocate for equal access to education for women. Dolley Madison was the first president's wife to publicly associate herself with a charity, an orphanage for girls. She also helped to gather donations for the Western exploratory expedition of Lewis and Clark. Abigail Fillmore helped to create the first permanent reference library in the White House. The rest of this list encompasses nearly every woman of every age who occupied a position of influence in the nation's early history.

In the coming Golden Age, women's philanthropic roles will likely become more intense for two reasons: trends in education and trends in wealth. Volunteering rises with education and employment, as time, resources, and personal networks enable that commitment. Women in today's aging demographic have increased their capacity in all of those areas, positioning themselves even more conveniently for philanthropic activity.

More than 42 percent of people with a college education or higher volunteer, compared to 17 percent of those without a college education. Further, nearly a third of people who have jobs volunteer, compared to less than a quarter of those who are unemployed.[8]

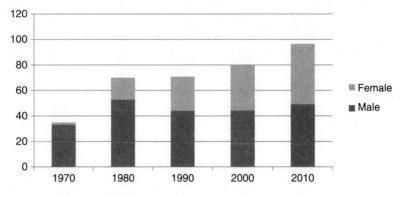

Figure 9.1   First Professional Degrees Awarded, by Gender
Source: National Center for Education Statistics.

The people earning those college degrees increasingly are women. As noted in Figure 9.1, less than a quarter of first professional degrees (MBA, JD, etc.) were awarded to women in 1980; today half are. In 1980, half of all master's level degrees were awarded to women. Today nearly two thirds are, as seen in Figure 9.2.[9]

We can anticipate that as these women join the aging population, their civic engagement will align with the current statistical patterns linking education and employment with volunteerism. Increasingly we will find them in the ranks of Golden Age philanthropists.

Women's philanthropic potential also is bolstered by the diversification of wealth. In 1970, 7 percent of married households had wives

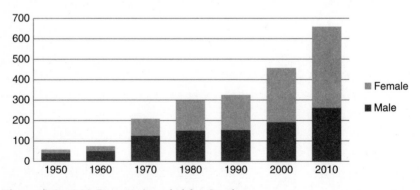

Figure 9.2   MA Degrees Awarded, by Gender
Source: National Center for Education Statistics.

earning more than husbands, a proportion that rose to 38 percent by 2012.[10]

Indeed, women comprise 43 percent of those with gross assets of $1.5 million or more. In terms of overall wealth, 1.2 million women hold $14.6 trillion. Women own 29 percent of all private businesses in the United States.[11] If these women-owned firms were a country, they would rank just behind Germany in economic size.

Hence, women are poised to be tomorrow's monetary philanthropists. On the other hand, we may never know about their giving—or their money. Sixty-three percent of women with wealth would prefer that people did not know they were rich![12]

That doesn't mean they are passive. At least three-quarters of women are actively engaged in managing their family's wealth.[13] Wealthy women also have a deep sense of community responsibility. More than 43 percent of women with at least $1.5 million in assets serve on nonprofit and community boards.[14]

Philanthropy among wealthier women also represents a broader community commitment than it does for rich men, who tend to see their philanthropy more as a way to deepen the intergenerational cohesiveness within a family.[15]

These growing roles for women in wealth and in private institutional leadership bode well for a civil society Golden Age as our population ages. They will strengthen and reinforce the overall tendency for age and engagement to trend together.

Philanthropy and Ethnicity

Finally, we must understand how the ethnic diversity of an aging American population can be harnessed to the philanthropy and volunteerism at the core of civil society. Over the coming two decades, the non-white population aged 60 and older will grow markedly. The total aging population will become more diverse, and each ethnic group within the population will become older.

The giving of time and resources for the common good is present in all cultures and ethnicities. Still, U.S. data indicate that rates of volunteering are lower in some groups than in others, and lower in all ethnic groups than in the white population. This data may be off base; we may not be asking the question the right way or understanding how culture defines philanthropy and engagement. I suspect that this is the explanation. It would not be the first time that survey takers and opinion-polling mavens got the question wrong.

Yet philanthropy in its truest sense is so fundamental to the strength of civil society that it is critically important for nonprofits to understand how to engage the resources and effort of all aspects of our changing demography. If we are not doing it well, we need to figure out how to do a better job. If we are doing it well, we need to know that we are. We will not have a Golden Age of civil society unless it reflects the values and behaviors of all members of our aging society.

Reinforcing the Golden Age

If historical trends prevail, the aging population, in combination with its philanthropic values and commitment to strengthened communities, will produce a stronger nation. Because it will happen naturally, it may, therefore, happen quietly, without appropriate recognition. This is the challenge. We do not need quietude. We especially do not need quietude in an age of political shouting, when the public recognition prize goes to the one with the most-well-developed set of lungs. It is not quietude, but recognition that we need.

The potential for a Golden Age of civil society should not be an obscure topic for academic auditoriums. It should be celebrated and encouraged from rooftops and policy podiums. The role of private philanthropy in civil society and the aging demographic's role in philanthropic leadership should be declared a national treasure. It should be celebrated not as money, not as a substitute for constrained public budgets, not as some guilty "giving back" in recompense for success. Engagement in civil society is not a product of guilt; it is the lifeblood of democracy and our societal commons.

It is time to talk about aging in terms of the ties that bind communities together, to highlight and profile those commitments as a way to help perpetuate them. The challenge clearly is not one of facts; the cases profiled by the likes of the MetLife Foundation show the impact on communities.

The challenge is about impressions. The quiet nature of the giving of older Americans—both in time and treasure—often does not stand out.

Those who study and advocate for philanthropy are often, understandably, impressed by the new philanthropists, those who catch the public eye with billions of dollars in donations at, say, age 40, and who have three or four more decades of giving ahead of them. Their engagement is impressive and of course deserving of celebration itself.

But the harder work often is done in the trenches of civil society. This work is the quiet day-to-day commitment by older Americans to community good and to the (admittedly smaller) monetary contributions that enable problem solving within communities. It is this deeper, more ingrained, more intense work that often goes unrecognized, but it should be honored.

The work of Teach for America, a highly competitive program that selects graduates fresh out of college and trains them to teach in some of the nation's most challenged schools, is deservedly applauded for instilling its young participants with commitment to the community good.

How much equivalent attention has been paid to the AARP's smaller, but highly successful Experience Corps, which puts retirees into classrooms as one-on-one tutors? Although certainly not a perfect measure, a keyword search of the Education Resources Information Center (ERIC) identified 1,169 articles on Teach for America and a total of 7 on the AARP's Experience Corps. More recognition of older Americans' philanthropy and volunteerism can increase awareness and thus participation. And increased participation can expand the bridges between generations across which will flow the continued commitment to community building and strong civil society.

Moreover, efforts by nonprofit and philanthropic organizations to create and even incentivize cross-generational giving, and "twinning" of generations in volunteer commitments, may find a more natural environment for sharing than we perceive. A global survey of high networth individuals indicated that young philanthropists were interested in poverty, peace, and equality, but in middle age those interests shifted to areas such as education and social services. As illustrated in Figure 9.3, their focus returned to fundamental issues of poverty and peace at older ages.[16] There seems to be a natural cycle underneath the yearning of youth and the perspective of age. That "bridge" may be a more natural arc than we might expect.

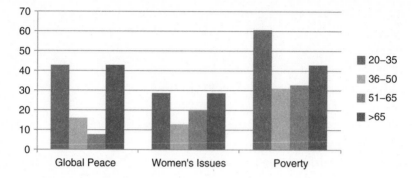

Figure 9.3   Issues Selected as "Very Important" by High-Net-Worth Individuals in Their Philanthropy (by Age Group)
SOURCE: B. Love, S. Raymond, J. Moore, *Giving Through the Generations*, 2009.

Conclusion

The relationship between an aging demographic and philanthropic opportunity naturally is not limited to the United States. The global aging population may have an even greater opportunity to be the bulwark of civil society in nations with young and formative democracies. Many of these newly open nations face a long road to stable governance. Perhaps the best role we can play is to demonstrate how aging and philanthropy work together to provide community stability and strength through individual effort.

For the United States, this is a time of demographic change with important implications. We have before us enormous opportunity: a chance to reinforce our own civil society and to strengthen the traditions of individual commitment to the common good that promise a confident future. This Golden Age civil society, tied to philanthropy and engagement, can enormously benefit the nation's long-term health. It can oxygenate the lifeblood of our commitment to shared values and solutions.

We recognize that no amount of engagement, philanthropy, good will, or commitment to community will prevent or solve all problems. In the first Federalist Paper, Alexander Hamilton, looking back over the new nation's experience, noted that, "It is perhaps more to be wondered at that we have done so well, than that we have not done better." The same could be said of philanthropy and engagement in aging communities.

Perhaps the fact that we have maintained such commitment to fundamental values amid so much social and economic change is more noteworthy than that our results haven't been perfect.

Pendleton Woods, the MetLife awardee, led an effort to solicit 1,500 trees to be donated for 24 Oklahoma counties. Does that solve global warming? Certainly not. Does it improve the community environment? Certainly yes.

The Texas homeless shelter created by Isha Salas-Desselle has served 10,000 individuals, and most have moved on to self-sufficiency. Has this work abolished poverty? Certainly not. Are 10,000 individuals and their communities more stable? Certainly yes.

Furthermore, these are merely quantitative measures; they do not reflect the cascading effect of the commitment of those individuals on the younger generation and generations to come. We have an opportunity to recommit to engagement and strengthen civil society. In accepting that challenge, we can make our communities better, if not perfect, and our nation a stronger, more unified place to live.

That road in Afghanistan led to many questions. What ensures the building of communities of free, prosperous, and committed people who respect each other and work toward mutual concerns? My quest for answers has deepened over the years, more so as I myself have become part of that "aging" population that has so much potential to lead. I do not know the answers fully. But what I have seen is that philanthropy and private leadership committed to community is at least a part of the answer.

Notes

1. Mark M. Rovner, *The Next Generation of American Giving* (Charleston, SC: Blackbaud, August 2013), www.edgeresearch.com/casestudies_files/Edge_Research_Next_Generation_of_American_Giving_white_paper.pdf.
2. Ibid.
3. U.S. Bureau of Labor Statistics, February 2013, "Keeping Baby Boomers Volunteering: A Research Brief on Volunteer Retention and Turnover," Corporation for National & Community Service, March 2007.
4. MetLife Foundation Older Volunteers Enrich America Awards, 2011, www.n4a.org/pdf/OVEAA_2011.pdf.
5. Ibid.

6. M. Duggan and J. Brenner, *The Demographics of Social Media Users—2012* (Washington, DC: Pew Research Center, February 2013).
7. U.S. Department of Labor, Bureau of Labor Statistics, "Volunteering in the United States, 2012," www.bls.gov/news.release/volun.nr0.htm.
8. Ibid.
9. National Center for Education Statistics, U.S. Department of Education.
10. U.S. Bureau of Labor Statistics, "Women in the Labor Force," February 2013, www.bls.gov/cps/wlf-databook-2012.pdf.
11. "The 2013 State of Women-Owned Businesses Report: A Summary of Important Trends, 1997–2013," Commissioned by American Express OPEN, 2013, www.womenable.com/userfiles/downloads/2013_State_of_Women-Owned_Businesses_Report_FINAL.pdf.
12. K. Rosplok, "Gender Matters: Men's and Women's Perceptions of Wealth Are Mostly Aligned," *The Journal of Wealth Management* 12, no. 4 (Spring 2010): 15–30.
13. "The New Wealth Paradigm," (Wilmington Trust/Campden Research, 2010), www.wilmingtontrust.com/repositories/wtc_sitecontent/PDF/new_wealth_paradigm.pdf.
14. *Women and Wealth*, GenSpring Family Offices, 2006.
15. B. Love, S. Raymond, and J. Moore, *Giving Through the Generations* (London: BNP Paribas/Campden Research Report, 2009).
16. Ibid.

Chapter 10

A City for All Ages

Henry Cisneros

Chairman, City View; Former Mayor, San Antonio, Texas;
Former Secretary, U.S. Department of Housing and Urban Development

The vitality of our cities is at stake as we determine how to address our responsibility to residents of all ages. When we enhance the lives of our seniors, our cities are the beneficiaries of the talents and energy that this proud population is eager to share.

The frail woman sadly extended her hands, shaky and blotted with age spots, her skin near translucent as she gripped a doctor's prescription in one palm, a utility bill in the other. "Tell me what I should do," she pleaded. "I can't afford to pay for both." Her anguish was heart-rending. As I tried to set her at ease there in my city hall office, I could think only that no one should face the dilemma she held in her wrinkled hands.

It was an emotional encounter, but I couldn't say that as mayor of San Antonio I was shocked by this particular visitor. Her plight had become all too familiar at my town-hall community meetings. I'd listened to the stories of our seniors, dignified retirees whose years of toil and responsibility had earned them a right to comfort and fulfillment in later life. Instead, they were struggling to find suitable housing, fearful of criminals who snatched their Social Security checks from the mail, and worried about their too-high electricity bills, their isolation, and fear of traffic.

Their problems were stunningly sad. Yet it was clear as well that our senior population was a priceless asset to our city. Many older people remained engaged in the workforce. Others were volunteers and mentors. They were companions, drivers, and helpers to the less hardy. As a group they were a vibrant part of our cultural fabric, a touchstone to what we valued in our past, and a source of wisdom and skills that could enrich our future. Their potential to strengthen our community even more was a challenge they welcomed and embraced.

I came to realize that to fully absorb the vibrancy of this aging population, a city must address a panoply of their interwoven needs. I saw their web of concerns as I began to hear from communities where the residents were aging along with their neighborhoods. These areas were prevalent enough to earn a name from city planners—NORCS, Naturally Occurring Retirement Communities.

As I worked to address their concerns through property tax discounts and other services targeted for seniors, I also saw the evolving needs of my own parents and their neighbors who remained engaged and independent as they aged. As I became more attuned to the realities and possibilities of our aging urban demography, I saw the need for a new vision, for comprehensive strategies to address this group's physical, emotional, and environmental well-being in ways that could only reap benefits for society overall. Meeting these challenges is a crucial, core responsibility of our society.

Nothing less than the vitality of our cities is at stake as we determine how to address our responsibility to residents of all ages. When we enhance the lives of our seniors, our cities are the beneficiaries of the talents and energy that this proud population is eager to share.

Demography and Urban Destiny

The changing face of our cities is tied irrevocably to the demographic shift created by the aging population. The older characteristics of society will have profound effects as cities adapt to the social and economic changes spurred by this changing demography. This shift will be reflected in the ways that people live, work, learn, and gather.

The process is dynamic: At the same time that cultural characteristics define who lives in a city, so those residents reshape their physical and economic surroundings through institutions they build to support their present and future needs. Philadelphia's eighteenth-century Quakers cemented their presence by creating religious, educational, and governing institutions that last to this day. Similarly, the economic engine that we know today as Silicon Valley sprang from a rich twentieth-century mix of migrants—from Asia and Latin America, from top U.S. universities, from global biomedical and technology centers—who together created a vibrant metropolis of technical innovation and investment in the San Francisco Bay Area.

In short, demography is destiny when it comes to metropolitan character and urban institutions. Cities can shape their futures through their capacity to serve the hopes and ambitions of their residents, acting on both the challenges and the opportunities that come with new demographic realities. These opportunities are wide open for the latest and largest demographic trend confronting the cities—the aging of our national population.

Aging in America's Cities

America's urban areas teem with evidence of the aging population. Senior citizens cluster in a nutrition center in the basement of a Polish American church in Cleveland. Japanese American octogenarians assemble for morning tai chi exercises in a Sacramento, California, park. Retired Mexican American veterans undertake community projects in the barrios of San Antonio, Texas. The wave is surging into a tsunami, visible not only in statistics, but also in the costs of elderly health care and in burgeoning markets for products to serve seniors.

Because urban areas house so much of the overall population, the explosion of senior ranks poses challenges for cities. A Brookings Institution report, *State of Metropolitan America, on the Frontlines of Demographic Transformation,*[1] finds the concentration of seniors greatest in both mature industrial areas and retirement destinations. Both have over-65 populations at rates exceeding the national average of 12.8 percent. Seniors are 18 percent of the population in Scranton, Pennsylvania. In Florida, 27 percent of Bradenton, and 16.7 percent of Miami residents are seniors.

"Due largely to 'aging in place,' senior populations in major metropolitan areas such as New York, Philadelphia, Chicago and Los Angeles are projected to grow by at least 18 percent over each five-year period from 2010 to 2030," the Brookings report concludes. Perhaps most surprising is the recent increase in seniors in such new-economy business centers as Raleigh, North Carolina, where between 2000 and 2008, seniors as a percent of residents grew by 38.6 percent. Across the country, from central-city neighborhoods to graying suburbs, metropolitan areas must work to strengthen the lives of these older adults.

Aging and the Living Environment

The twentieth century left a double legacy—an unprecedented increase in life expectancy and improved health for older people—that improved prospects for older Americans to live as self-reliant and contributing community members. To continue this progress we must examine ways that communities can support escalating numbers of older people in attaining healthy, happy, and contributing lives. A key factor, according to research and policymaking experience, is a living environment that is safe, stable, and supportive.

The phrase "living environment" includes both social and physical dimensions, encompassing both dwelling units and the community beyond. To stave off elderly decline, the living environment should sustain health, encourage human interaction, and offer accessibility. Beyond health maintenance and palliative programs, cities can create living environments for improved mobility, social integration, well-being, and independence.

Imagine a city whose leaders say: "We know our population is changing. Our older residents are a greater proportion of our population than ever before. We know their needs evolve as they age and that they can still contribute to society in important ways. Let us therefore think through how we can make the city as user-friendly for them as possible—not with piecemeal programs but with a new vision of how a city can function for its older residents. Let us ask ourselves how we can do things that go beyond merely mitigating the process of aging, to actually enhance the safety, health, and independence of our older residents, which after all should be the goal of a city for its residents of all ages."

Fostering Independent Urban Lives

In practical terms, cities are working on programs and systems to support independent lives for as long as possible. The Milken Institute recently ranked *The Best Cities for Successful Aging*[2] and graded the 100 largest metropolitan regions and 259 smaller areas based on the following criteria:

- The quality of community health care.
- The contribution to general wellness.
- The promotion of financial security.
- Costs of living, especially housing.
- Opportunities for employment and education.
- Accessibility of public transportation.
- Opportunities for community connectedness.

Similarly, author Scott Ball in *Livable Communities for Aging Populations* lists criteria defining lifelong neighborhoods:

- Accessibility across an entire community, from individual homes to neighborhoods, from adjacent retail and services to regional transportation systems.
- Systems to improve and maintain health, available and affordable health care, and a healthy environment.
- A supportive convergence between wellness and community environment, encompassing land uses, public amenities and spaces, and fitness activities.
- A diversity of senior housing options and affordable dwelling types.

Chattanooga Mayor Ron Littlefield, and Bob McNulty, founder of Partners for Livable Communities, recommend in *Independent for Life*[3] that cities:

- Develop a range of housing options to match the needs and expectations of seniors.
- Initiate comprehensive planning for the needs of a maturing population.
- Adapt transportation to enable older adults to remain mobile and engaged in their communities, including improvements to the driving environment and access to public transportation, and modified infrastructure that is more conducive to walking.
- Enable older residents to secure their finances through continued or new jobs, retraining programs, and working with employers.
- Improve overall wellness by offering transportation to health facilities, home-based care, and nutrition and fitness programs.
- Use cultural assets such as libraries, arts organizations, and schools to extend lifelong learning opportunities.
- Strengthen safety by linking law enforcement and social services, and by addressing cases of physical or mental elder abuse.
- Engage older residents in civic work and intergovernmental programs as mentors, tutors, coaches, teachers, and role models, using their skills and experience for meaningful community involvement.

In the ideal city, planners, elected officials, and community leaders overlay such criteria on the full range of city functions and services, starting with a planning framework to adapt urban land mass, public systems, and human services to the new demographics of aging.

Building the City for All Ages

As city leaders think about what the aging population means for neighborhoods and urban services and facilities, they must look beyond disconnected initiatives that characterize traditional city policymaking. We need a framework to integrate all city functions and systems to support aging residents. One planning template has been developed by the New Urbanists, a network of forward-thinking architects and planners whose Smart Growth principles are highly applicable to urban settings that serve older Americans. The guidelines call for extended city building, from the region to the neighborhood to the street or block and to the individual dwelling unit.

Regional Planning

The broadest level of planning—regional planning—is essential because it addresses the "true scale of people's lives," the New Urbanist authors Andres Duany, Jeff Speck, and Mike Lydon write in *The Smart Growth Manual*.[4] "Planning a single town or city is not enough because working, shopping, recreation, education, and other daily activities routinely take people across municipal lines."

Many communities cannot afford programs for the elderly unless they are part of a regionally financed system. Senior nutrition funds, for example, are usually administered through area-wide agencies on aging. A van transportation system for older people should be part of a regional transit agency, tied to other forms of mass transit.

Use of public transit by older people is rapidly increasing, and 80 percent would consider using it more regularly if it were convenient and easily accessible, according to the Milken Institute's *Best Cities for Successful Aging*.[5]

Public facilities with a focus on the elderly should follow extended city-building principles, including, for example, accessible local branch libraries and fully accessorized regional libraries, and small parks as well as large regional parks with swimming pools and walking trails.

The Neighborhood Level

"The smart growth of a region can be measured by the strength of its neighborhood structure," *The Smart Growth Manual* states. "The term 'neighborhood' has the specific technical meaning of being compact, walkable, diverse, and connected," it says. "The neighborhood is not an innovation; it has been the fundamental increment of human settlement throughout history, interrupted only by the 60-year aberration that we now call urban sprawl."

Neighborhood size and organization have direct implications for older people. For them to walk to essential services, a neighborhood must include a mix of homes, retail stores, eating and recreation sites, and public gathering places. A vibrant neighborhood center can serve older people's needs in spaces that are close and safe. Quarter-acre pocket parks, within walking distance of homes and featuring work-out stations for older people, encourage several beneficial trends: fresh air, exercise, peer-group contact and excursions with family members.

Another version of open space is the community garden, where older people can exercise, take pride in their work, gain inspiration from the cycle of life and growth, and enjoy healthy foods nurtured by their own hands. The strength of a city's neighborhoods is inextricably tied to its support for aging residents.

Streets and Blocks

The New Urbanism informs us of ways to influence livability at the street level. For example, in Naturally Occurring Retirement Com-munities (NORCS, the neighborhoods where the majority of people are aging), wide sidewalks enhance safety for older residents, as does relocation of obstacles like utility poles that impede pedestrian and wheelchair movement. Curbs with sloped declines help older people avoid falls, and facilitate wheelchair crossings. Additional street lights attract activity and increase the number of eyes on the street. "The key to neighborhood safety is *natural surveillance*, a term that describes how crime decreases when someone might be watching," *The Smart Growth Manual* notes.

In building new communities, these features should be designed into the streetscape, along with short blocks. Pedestrian social interaction is especially important for older people who cannot drive. Jane Jacobs, in her influential book, *The Death and Life of Great American Cities*,[6] writes that short blocks are indispensable in generating "exuberant diversity" at the street level. Short blocks also discourage speeding by eliminating long straightaways, allowing older people to walk without fear of fast traffic.

Arterial streets within neighborhoods also can be narrowed to respect human scale. Traditional zoning often creates a hodgepodge of structures that negatively impact traffic generation and the walkable character of a block. New Urbanist "form-based codes" permit structures according to their effect, for example, on a safer pedestrian experience. Such thoughtful planning innovations can mean the difference for older residents between shut-in isolation and walkable access, between transportation dependence and self-sufficiency.

The Urban Home

The New Urbanism also guides planning for the individual building or home unit. It stresses retrofitting older homes, as well as constructing new dwellings, for a mix of housing types and price points. The result can be communities with varied housing for older people: cottages, row houses, and apartments and condominiums. Co-housing models include dwelling units built around common space that often has dining facilities and a great room. Ancillary dwellings, often called "granny flats," on the same lot as a primary home are ideal for multigenerational families. Some cities, like Santa Cruz, California, are revising zoning policies to encourage more compact housing where the population is aging.

Another housing innovation, enabling seniors to work in self-employed settings, is the live/work flexhouse, a dwelling that includes a workspace. The mixed uses allow older persons to comfortably pursue careers that offer much to their communities, such as law, financial services, real estate, and counseling, well into their advanced years.

New Urbanism design features applicable to older people include natural light and ventilation, to create sunny spaces and air flow and reduce energy costs. Attention should be paid to energy efficiency in ventilation, heating and air-conditioning, windows and doors, appliances and solar technologies. The Leadership in Energy & Environmental Design (LEED) standards of the U.S. Green Building Council provide important guidelines.

Because older people may be susceptible to sickness and allergies, a healthy indoor environment should consider air purifiers, as well as building materials, paints, and carpeting that do not release hazardous chemicals and mold.

The requirements of the Americans With Disabilities Act and the principles of "universal design" provide a template for home designs that enhance mobility for the disabled and older people. The concept of "visit-ability" is based on the idea that homes should provide basic access to people of all physical capabilities. It calls for at least one zero-step entrance, wider doors, and a half bath on the ground level. Some communities use incentives to encourage accessibility features. Johnson County, Iowa, for example, has created incentives under its Homes for Life Program, which certifies homes at "Level I-Visit-ability" or "Level II-Live-ability," according to accessibility attributes.

Development organizations increasingly are advancing concrete ideas for older residents' dwelling places. Living Communities in New York State builds cottages and patio homes for people over 55, and assisted-living apartments. Other builders are designing homes with elevators, cabinet-free kitchens, pull-cord wall mounts for safety communication, and "check-in" features for caregivers.

A home environment that is emotionally nurturing and physically supportive can help forestall by years, even decades, the loneliness and pain of decline. It can enhance years of health and function during which seniors can participate in and enhance their communities.

A Strategy for Human Service Needs

Also important to quality of life for older people are the many human needs that can be addressed through outreach, personal assistance, social services, and technology support. For example, the isolation that many feel when they can no longer drive and their families live far away does not disappear simply with sidewalk changes or even bus routes for every block. But a well-integrated system of van transport, elderly outreach specialists and communication technologies can work around physical barriers.

A combination of human and virtual connections can be implemented faster than changes in the physical environment. Think of it this way: Efforts to adapt cities for the elderly are in a race with the accelerating aging demographic itself. Social supports to meet urgent needs offer a promising way for cities to keep pace.

Jennie Chin Hansen, former president of AARP, and Andrew Scharlach, director of the Center for the Advanced Study of Aging Services at the University of California–Berkeley, make the case for coordinated community services that are culturally inclusive and locally accessible for older residents.

"These services cannot be designed based on past characteristics of elderly behavior. Instead, the successful programs of tomorrow must help entire neighborhoods and communities become more aging-friendly, supporting well-being and fulfillment throughout our lives," they write.[7] Services must be appropriate across multicultural groups, and should offset language barriers, welcome immigrant groups, address age-related disabilities and safeguard against discrimination.

The highly effective PACE network (Program of All-inclusive Care for the Elderly), operating in 30 states, believes that "it is better for the well-being of seniors with chronic care needs and their families to be served in the community whenever possible."[8] PACE provides a range of medical and support services, among them adult daycare and physical, occupational, and recreational therapies, meals and nutritional counseling, social work, and hospital care.

Responsibility to coordinate aging programs increasingly is devolving to local jurisdictions, partly because federal officials recognize that nationally based elder health care spending is biased toward nursing home care and is more restrictive in home care eligibility. Medicaid spends nearly five times as much for nursing home care as for community care. [9]

New incentives, such as those in the federal Patient Protection and Affordable Care Act of 2010, seek to enable the elderly and disabled to fully participate in their communities. Such incentives aim to save money and also recognize that local physical environments contribute to beneficiaries' well-being.

This devolution requires community-level coordination across types of care. "Community services can help to bridge the gap between existing physical and social structures. Existing supports for aging in place are fragmented, with distinct financing and administrative silos separating essential domains such as housing, health care, and social supports," Chin and Scharlach write. "We need more fully integrated community support services, combining the full spectrum of formal and informal service capacity."

Such urban-level integration of services is the best hope to compensate for failings in our health and aging care systems. "We need to move beyond the focus on meeting individual needs to a broader vision that embraces strategies for enhancing social capital and community capacity," Chin and Scharlach write. This often means working, volunteering, and engaging in civic life, fulfilling the potential and contributions that older people are eager to share.

One way to understand the urban challenges related to aging is to ask older people about their concerns. As part of a project with the Stanford Center on Longevity and AARP, I have conducted town hall meetings to hear from elderly residents directly. Their most prevalent concerns were:

- Frustration at being immobile and dependent on others to run errands and drive them to appointments.
- Deterioration of their homes.
- High utility costs, particularly for heating and cooling.
- Fear of crime, including street assaults and home burglaries.
- Debilitating effects of major impairments and serious frailties.
- Loneliness as a result of isolation from friends and family.
- Fear of falling, getting hurt, becoming ill, and not being able to communicate.
- Pain or feelings of inadequacy in managing the activities of daily living.
- Lack of money for home improvements or maintenance.
- Fear of high volumes of fast traffic on neighborhood streets.
- Danger of misusing appliances such as a stove or oven.

Each of these concerns is real and deeply felt. Cities that value a compassionate setting for their aging residents can address these fears as suggested in Table 10.1.

Table 10.1 Urban Response to Concerns of Older Residents

Concerns of older Residents about Aging at Home	Urban Service Responses		
Frustration at immobility, dependency on others for errands	Use technology to create links to delivery services, such as grocery valet services	Provide public van transport	Create "virtual community" organizations to provide transportation assistance
Deterioration of the home: costs of housing and improvements	Offer a package of certified "life-span" improvements at reasonable costs	Enforce building codes in rental properties	Facilitate access to federal programs offering financial assistance for home repair
High utility costs	Design certified energy efficiency programs targeted to homes of older residents	Provide energy discounts for senior ratepayers	Offer emergency assistance with high utility bills during extreme weather
Fear of crime: home burglary, assaults on streets	Specialize community policing in NORCs focused on older residents and their needs	Use technology to increase in-home security i.e., alarm systems, "life-alert" devices	Upgrade street lighting
Overall effects of impairments and facilities	"Ageify" the home: bathroom and kitchen modifications, proper lighting	Apply communications technologies	Engage "virtual communities" in household assistance or fund home-care health specialists
Loneliness, isolation from friends and family	Offer transportation access to community social settings such as senior fitness and nutrition centers	Encourage creation of virtual community networks in urban neighborhoods	Expand use of home health care specialists

(continued)

Table 10.1 (*Continued*)

Concerns of older Residents about Aging at Home	Urban Service Responses		
Fear of falling or illness without ability to communicate	Build on communications technologies, such as visual Skype, to create links to emergency services	Create a community outreach to check on seniors, especially the most frail	Offer home health care specialists to regularly call on older residents
Pain or inadequacy in managing daily activities in the home	Offer community-based home health care appropriate to the level of debilitation	Match community-based home health care with community health care facilities	Create a clearinghouse to help seniors maximize access to federal health financial assistance
Lack of money for cost of living	Use federal subsidy programs for life-span home packages	Offer financial counseling specific to aging needs	Provide technical advice to explore federal income assistance programs
Fear of high volumes of fast traffic	Provide van transportation linked to communications devices for personalized service	Be attentive to traffic flow issues; mitigate with speed bumps, targeted enforcement, signage, and stop lights	Use senior overlay districts to guide zoning and traffic decisions in NORCs
Danger of misusing appliances such as a stove or oven	When replacing appliances, install with age-appropriate controls and handles	Conduct community briefings to include instruction on safety precautions	Assign home health care specialists to monitor home safety conditions

No major American city has yet implemented an overall strategy to reconfigure land uses and basic services to address the needs of aging residents, although some are making inroads. Washington, D.C., for example is working on an overall strategy to become an age-friendly city. Several progressive leaders in forward-looking cities across the nation are advancing creative ideas, as seen in Table 10.2.

Table 10.2 Targeted Strategies in Cities Addressing Needs of Seniors

Strategy	Examples
Offer affordable housing options suitable for "aging in place"	Cities with low costs of living such as Pittsburgh, Omaha, and Des Moines offer an available stock of quality housing.
	Some high-cost cities—such as New York and Boston—have made large-scale commitments to enlarge their stock of affordable senior housing.
Undertake a comprehensive approach to planning and zoning for the needs of the elderly	New York City has two "senior overlay districts" to guide enactment of measures related to dwelling units, health facilities, recreational sites, and concentrated services.
	The New York City chapter of the American Institute of Architects has formed a working group of housing experts to explore adaptive reuse of apartments for seniors in low-rise walk-ups and high-rise elevator buildings.
Address public safety and personal security by targeting crime initiatives and traffic safety measures	Cincinnati deployed its Madisonville Neighborhood Community Problem-Oriented Policing Team to develop a tactical response for a senior housing complex in partnership with the residents.
	New York City funded the Lincoln Square Neighborhood Center to develop a NORC-supportive Senior Program, including close collaboration with the NYPD to address safety concerns.
Provide access to health care, including quality geriatric services and home health care	Madison, Wisconsin, which ranked first in the Milken study for health care accessibility, manages its own quality health care system.
	Other small metros, such as Jackson, Mississippi, and Little Rock, Arkansas, have extensive medical capabilities at inexpensive prices.
	San Francisco's On Lok Senior Health Services established a national model for the Program of All-inclusive Care for the Elderly (PACE) system of community-based care.

(continued)

Table 10.2   *(Continued)*

Strategy	Examples
Support overall wellness, including nutrition, recreation programs, and public facilities for fitness activities	Bridgeport/Stamford/Norfolk, Connecticut, is ranked second in the Milken study for its many recreational centers and high levels of physical activity among seniors.
	San Antonio Sports for Life program offers dozens of competitive sports programs for seniors into their eighties.
	New York has designed differentiated space in public parks such as Washington Square Park, to assure safe use by people of all ages, including seniors.
Promote financial security through work opportunities, retraining, and income supports	Provo and Salt Lake City (Utah), stand out for opportunities offered to seniors in small business and entrepreneurship, and have strong community college and university programs to assist seniors.
	Other mid-sized metros such as Omaha, Nebraska, and Des Moines, Iowa, encourage their strong service sectors to create employment opportunities for seniors.
	Sioux Falls and Rapid City (South Dakota), have high employment rates for seniors in a state with one of the highest per capita levels of funding for senior services.
Enable connectedness and engagement in community life through outreach programs, lifelong learning, intergovernmental involvement, and cultural initiatives	Pittsburgh, with a high concentration of over-65 residents, involves its community colleges in senior connectedness though education and retraining.
	Boston's Beacon Hill Village uses social networks to connect seniors to transportation, health care, home repairs, and other assistance for aging in place.
	Portland Community College in Oregon supports Life by Design NW to connect seniors to volunteer leadership and community service.
	Burlington, Vermont, funds programs to keep seniors engaged in community life at high levels.
Improve accessibility to public transit and modify street environment to be conducive to safety	New York City, Boston, San Francisco, and Washington, D.C., are ranked high in the Milken study for accessible public transit and accessibility to neighborhood grocery and convenience stores. All have extensive subway systems integrated into other public transit.
	Among cities without subway systems, Salt Lake City has kept fares affordable and Baton Rouge has invested in transportation for seniors.
	San Francisco offers Silver Ride, to provide rides, trip planning, and accompaniment to medical services.

Conclusion

This chapter has offered a window on several aspects of the American urban future. We know that our population is aging, that elderly persons will be a higher percentage of urban residents, and that they can continue to offer vital economic and cultural contributions to our communities. We also know that city governments and nonprofit institutions can work together to make urban life better for people as they age. In the process, we can gain the engagement of a senior population that will enrich life for all of our residents.

What is less clear is whether cities will meet the demographic trend with comprehensive action to benefit their aging residents, and whether they will go beyond palliating the aging experience to reap the benefits that seniors offer their communities, by helping them grow stronger and healthier as they age. The cities face two starkly alternative scenarios.

One is business as usual: Urban residents grow older in greater concentrations but physical systems and social services stay basically the same. Transportation systems remain automobile-based, and more elderly residents are isolated, financially stressed, and vulnerable to crime. Dwellings in aging neighborhoods become less habitable as older residents lose the ability to climb stairs, use bathroom facilities, or open kitchen cabinets without difficulty. They suffer falls that force them to hospitals and nursing homes earlier than necessary, and than their finances allow. Their finances are strained by high utility bills, partly due to nonweatherized homes. They lack guidance on accessing government financial assistance for medical needs.

This scenario of reduced options leaves seniors overwhelmed, alone, and broke, with hopelessness that can affect neighborhoods and cities themselves. These are not civic attributes that brighten the prospects for urban life.

Fortunately another, brighter, scenario is within reach, with some cities already laying groundwork. City leaders create senior overlay districts where the concentrations of older people justify modifications to homes, infrastructure, and human services. Van systems and public transit are linked with home-care specialists who offer accompaniment to medical appointments and grocery shopping. Weatherization and affordable improvements enhance entrances, restrooms, kitchens, and security systems. Police and safety personnel check up on the vulnerable elderly. Local community centers offer health care, exercise regimens, and dietary guidance. Neighborhood recreation programs bring people together to improve strength and stamina, flexibility and balance. City libraries and schools become venues for senior education courses about finances, health, and cultural themes.

The civic attributes inspired by this scenario spark urban life at its best—engagement, reconnection, accessibility, safety, and respect for the values of community. These are civic values rooted in our secular faith, our belief that proactive community care can humanize the realities of time and mortality. These are values that make all of us more humane and make our cities places where people of all ages can work, learn, gather, and live in ways that truly uplift our lives. That should be the measure of a good city.

Notes

1. Brookings Institution Metropolitan Policy Program, *State of Metropolitan America, on the Frontlines of Demographic Transformation* (Washington, DC: The Brookings Institution, 2010).
2. Anusuya Chatterjee and Ross Devol, *The Best Cities for Successful Aging* (Santa Monica, CA: The Milken Institute, 2012).
3. Henry Cisneros, Margaret Dyer-Chamberlain, and Jane Hickie, eds., *Independent for Life* (Austin: University of Texas Press, 2012).
4. Andres Duany, Jeff Speck, and Mike Lydon, *The Smart Growth Manual* (New York: McGraw-Hill, 2010).
5. Chatterjee and Devol, *Best Cities*.
6. Jane Jacobs, *The Death and Life of Great American Cities* (New York: Vintage Books Edition, 1992).
7. Jennie Chin Hansen and Andrew Scharlach, "Community Services," in *Independent for Life* (Austin: University of Texas Press, 2012), 81.
8. Ibid.
9. Ibid.

Chapter 11

Aging and Learning: The Future University

Steven Knapp

President, The George Washington University;
Co-Chair, Age-Friendly DC Task Force

The new reality of an older, relatively healthy population can be expected to shape universities in three major ways: as an object of study, a source of students, and a source of participants in teaching and research.

"That is no country for old men . . ."

These days I run a university, but I was trained many years ago as a scholar of literature. I had been gripped, while young, by the power of poetry. Today, as I consider how the dramatic extension of the human life span is likely to transform universities as we know them, I am struck by the recollection that the first poem that really moved me, oddly enough, was a poem about aging.

Its intriguing title was "Sailing to Byzantium," and it recounted the imaginary voyage of an aging poet to an ancient city (the long-ago precursor of modern-day Istanbul) where, according to this poet, works of art were more important than physical embodiment. Here, in the opening stanza, the poet casts his feeling of alienation from physicality and sexuality as a state of exile from what he calls the "country" of the young:

> That is no country for old men. The young
> In one another's arms, birds in the trees—
> Those dying generations—at their song,
> The salmon-falls, the mackerel-crowded seas,
> Fish, flesh, or fowl, commend all summer long
> Whatever is begotten, born, and dies.
> Caught in that sensual music all neglect
> Monuments of unageing intellect.[1]

It's hard to think of a more stirring evocation of natural fecundity than those "salmon-falls" and "mackerel-crowded seas," or of noble but not quite living perfection than monuments of "unageing intellect." But why contrast the body and the mind in such drastically opposing terms? The next stanza opens with the answer, which is the poet's unhappiness with, even disgust at, his own aging body:

> An aged man is but a paltry thing,
> A tattered coat upon a stick, unless
> Soul clap its hands and sing, and louder sing,
> For every tatter in its mortal dress,
> Nor is there singing school but studying
> Monuments of its own magnificence;
> And therefore have I sailed the seas and come
> To the holy city of Byzantium.

The man behind the imagined poet whose soul sings this poem was the great Irish Nobel laureate William Butler Yeats, who wrote a number of poems about the transition, as one ages, from physical to spiritual and intellectual pursuits. But one learns with some astonishment that Yeats was only 60 or at most 61 years old when he wrote this poem in 1926. How many 60-year-olds in our era would embrace a description of themselves as paltry scarecrows?

I'm not suggesting that Yeats himself fit that description when he imagined that voyage to Byzantium, or even two years later when the poem was published. In fact, we can't be sure that the poet in the poem is literally meant to be Yeats himself. But it remains a striking difference between his era and ours that it would not have seemed surprising to Yeats or his contemporaries to regard the age of 60 as the turning point from physical (and sexual) to intellectual (and spiritual) existence.

Equally striking is the apparent absence in Yeats's era of the anxiety that goes with turning 60 in our day: not so much about the loss of physical vitality—we have numerous drugs and regimens to delay that transition for years and even decades—as the loss of cognitive ability, including those temporary lapses in memory retrieval that are annoyingly called "senior moments."[2] We no longer conceive the decline of physical capacity as the liberation of intellect; instead, we worry that our bodies will remain healthy even as our minds begin to decline. At the same time, we have seen a waning appreciation of the intellectual, practical, and even spiritual benefits of aging—attributes that used to be praised under the rubrics of wisdom and experience but that have receded into the background of a culture that would prefer to view aging as a more or less seamless extension of youth.

Universities in the New World of Aging

How should institutions of higher learning engage this new reality? One has to acknowledge, at the outset, how hard it is for colleges and universities to adjust to large-scale changes of the kind this book addresses. Universities are notoriously conservative institutions, harking back to literally medieval prototypes and still in many ways organized around disciplinary structures and pedagogical assumptions that have retained their basic features not just for generations but for centuries. Still, the new reality of an older, relatively healthy population presents universities with at least as large an opportunity as a challenge.

This phenomenon can be expected to shape universities in three major ways: as an object of study, as a source of students, and as a source of participants in teaching and research. Global aging provides a rich field for new investigations across a range of academic disciplines, as scholars and scientists probe everything from the biological status of the older population to the cultural, social, and economic implications of so massive a demographic shift. While older adults have yet to return to college in numbers proportionate to their growth as a percentage of the population, the university of the future will of necessity find ways of welcoming them to its real or virtual campuses. And higher education will benefit in surprising ways, we can be sure, if it can capture the wisdom, experience, and creativity of older adults and harness those attributes in the service of its core missions.

The Study of Aging

The sheer scale of global aging—that is, the extraordinary rate at which the global population of older adults is projected to grow in the coming decades[3]—points to a major transformation of human existence and experience, with implications for all of our conceptions of human needs and capacities, as well as of the structures of social organization. This phenomenon, unparalleled in human history, portends changes across all aspects of human experience that will demand the engagement of scholars and scientists—and, of course, their students.

Organized research on aging occurs at every university, and mine is no exception. Not surprisingly, much of that research occurs in the fields of medicine, nursing, and public health. In the United States, by far the largest source of public funding for research, after all, is the National Institutes of Health. What *is* surprising is the variety of projects engaging this subject and the number of scholars involved in them—a scope one can only expect to grow as the aging of human populations becomes ever more apparent and as private and public funders of research respond to increasing demands for solutions to the challenges this phenomenon presents.

At the George Washington University (GW), we have research and service initiatives underway in our schools of medicine, nursing, public health, law, business, and arts and sciences. We are fortunate insofar as our location in the heart of the U.S. capital gives those efforts a platform from which they can inform the policies that are bound to affect the lives of older adults. I will cite three examples from my institution—and these could be matched by important work that is going on at many other universities.

First, Loretta DiPietro, who chairs GW's Department of Exercise Science, does advanced work on the role of physical activity in helping people "age in place." She and her colleagues recently discovered that 15 minutes of walking after every meal does a better job of protecting older adults at risk of insulin intolerance (and therefore of developing type 2 diabetes) than 45 minutes of sustained walking.[4]

My second example is the Center on Aging, Health & Humanities. Founded in 1994 by the late Gene D. Cohen, the center comprises an interdisciplinary group of scientists and scholars who study the role of creativity in improving the quality of life for older adults and their families. The scholars then use the results to effect positive changes in public policy.

One approach the center explored during Dr. Cohen's tenure was the treatment of Alzheimer's disease through an intergenerational version of what is broadly known as "biographical intervention." Working with a patient's family, the center's staff would assemble old photographs and spoken narratives into video biographies designed to stimulate the patient's memories and emotions. A striking variation on this model was the creation for each patient—again, with the help of family and friends—of a board game employing biographical flash cards.[5]

Both these examples of university-based research—DiPietro's work on exercise and Cohen's on ways of delaying or mitigating the effects of dementia—might be seen as addressing one of the most obvious downsides of aging, the progressive malfunctioning of biological and neurological systems. What about the upside?

Here is a third example that returns us, in some ways, to the Yeatsian themes with which I opened this chapter. Like Yeats's poem, it involves what can be called the *spiritual* gains that accompany physical losses. The George Washington Institute for Spirituality and Health was founded in 2001 by Christina Puchalski. As the name suggests, it explores the effects of a patient's spiritual orientation (which may or may not involve a formal religious affiliation or set of beliefs) on such matters as the patient's health status or responsiveness to medical treatment. It also considers how medical care itself might be enhanced by taking into account a patient's spiritual attitudes and needs.

According to Dr. Puchalski, spiritual concerns and dispositions play an especially significant role in the lives—and therefore the health—of older adults. She writes in a personal communication (and in what is almost a twenty-first-century paraphrase of Yeats's poem) that:

> A significant body of literature . . . highlights the role of spirituality in aging. As we age, spirituality—broadly defined as a search for ultimate meaning and purpose and the experience of connection to the transcendent, to others, to nature and to the significant or sacred—plays a more dominant role in our lives than when we were younger. As the finitude of life on earth becomes more obvious as we age, the questions about meaning, purpose, and connection become more critical for us.[6]

In the same personal communication, Dr. Puchalski goes on to invoke the intriguing notion of what is known as "gerotranscendence." This is "a relatively new term" describing the stage of life in which "people begin to detach from those parts of life such as titles, money, the acquisition of things and even illness or debility, in favor of a more focused attention on things that matter most"—such things as "legacy building" and mentorship. "In healthy aging," she writes, "attention to the spiritual dimension can help the older person reframe what may seem like a limited phase of life to one that is expansive and full of opportunity for inner growth and for contributing to the next generations."

If we ask, then, how academic research is likely to be affected by the growing visibility and the particular needs of our aging population, part of the answer may be that what Dr. Puchalski and others call gerotranscendence—the underappreciated conjunction of physical decline and the rise of spiritual and aesthetic concerns—will increasingly compel us to think across traditional boundaries, including those between medical science, philosophy, and art and imagination. And that promises to transform the study not just of older adults but of human experience writ large.

Back to School

Whatever form it may take, there is no doubt that academic interest will increasingly focus on the subject of aging during the coming decades as the phenomenon swings into full national and global gear. But growth in the population of older adults is not only a rich and potentially inex-haustible subject of university study; it is also a *potential* source of pro-spective students—at least for those universities that figure out how to engage this newly growing audience.

My emphasis on "potential" is deliberate. So far there is no indication that the percentage of older students enrolled in for-credit higher edu-cation programs is growing. Figures published by the National Center for Education Statistics show that older adults, as a percentage of overall students enrolled in colleges and universities, actually declined between 1998 and 2007 from 18.1 percent to 16.5 percent; since then, the enroll-ment percentage has remained essentially flat.[7] Why, then, should we suppose that the interest of older adults in higher education will grow, or that universities will be ready for them if it does?

Recent debates on the question of whether college is "worth it" have focused, at times in stunningly myopic fashion, on the earning capacity of a college degree–holder during the first few years after graduation.[8] That is one of many reasons why it is refreshing to think about the value of higher education for older adults who are well past the point of embarking on their first careers.

Some will be economically secure enough to seek intellectual enrich-ment rather than professional advancement; indeed, there has always been a small percentage of retirees who do go back to college out of curiosity or a regret at having missed certain intellectual experiences—say, courses in the arts or history—the first time around. The phenomenon of "gerotranscendence" mentioned in the previous section—the shifting of focus from material to intellectual and spiritual pursuits as one ages—may be expected to increase that trend.

Thanks to their many years of work experience, older adults who *do* begin or return to college for the sake of professional training or credentialing may be better prepared than younger students to select and complete the programs they need—and less patient with requirements and teaching styles they regard as unnecessary or distracting. Such students may compel institutions to reconceive their pedagogy in ways that will benefit younger students as well.

One key to serving older adults may be the computerized instruc-tion that some university leaders embrace and others fear as a "disruptive technology"—disruptive in the sense that it promises (or threatens!) to alter the economics of instruction in something like the way robotics has altered the economics of automobile manufacturing, or the Internet has changed the economics of print journalism. These hopes and fears both rest on the assumption that students who can get what they need from online instruction will no longer be willing to bear the labor- and capital-intensive costs of on-campus, face-to-face instruction.

Business models for online higher education are still in their infancy, so it is too soon to guess whether its effects on traditional modes of learning will or will not amount to what the most ardent supporters and critics of these developments currently predict. But we can still ask what these innovations may portend for older adults.

On that score, I can't resist the optimistic conclusion that few populations have as much to gain from online instruction. In my experience—and here I can do no better than cite the example of my own 91-year-old father—there is no reason to suppose that older adults are necessarily less capable than younger ones of finding and processing information that comes to them from Internet sources. At the same time, physical constraints on mobility, as well as their (in many cases) deeply established ties with their places of residence, make it far less likely that older adults will pick up and move to sites of face-to-face instruction than will younger students.

Furthermore, older students generally bring the work habits they developed over decades of employment to their studies. They have a clearer sense of why they are enrolling, and they often have educational or professional backgrounds that have already prepared them for modes of critical thinking that younger students are trying out for the first time.

For all these reasons, older adults may well be the perfect audience for the new generation of online courses and programs that the media assume—prematurely, in my view—will mainly appeal to far younger students. Indeed, there is some statistical evidence to suggest that older adults are currently the most likely consumers of what is often portrayed as the most innovative version of online instruction, the so-called massive open online courses (MOOCs).[9]

No one knows what mix of online and face-to-face instruction will become the dominant model in higher education over the coming years, but older adults are already demonstrating the drive and resourcefulness to avail themselves of whatever opportunities the new instructional modes may present. They also have the maturity and confidence to point out what does or doesn't work in various educational formats.

An excellent case in point is Helen White, who earned a GW master's degree in Sports Management in 2013, one month before turning 60, and recently recounted her experience in an e-mail interview.[10] In 2007, she had been employed as a manager by a large nonprofit organization; when her department was reorganized, she decided that, rather than reapply for her job, she would seek what is now being called an "encore career."

Helen had recently taken up basketball and had rediscovered a love for sports; this now led her to create a senior women's basketball program in the Washington, D.C., metropolitan area. In the process, she discovered what she calls her "passion," which was to find better ways of encouraging older adults to become more active by returning to the sports they had abandoned in their thirties when "the playing field [was] no longer level."

Earlier in her career, Helen had studied and worked in physical education but now perceived a need to update her skills, reestablish her credentials, and develop a network of contacts that would support her mission of becoming "a change agent in the world of senior sports." The GW program in which she enrolled had a hybrid curriculum, involving a mixture of online and classroom instruction—academic instruction that she supplemented by volunteering to work on "a variety of sport management events and activities."

Helen reported finding it "challenging to sit at an uncomfortable desk for a three-hour weekly class" in which all the other students were considerably younger than she. She also found it hard to socialize with her fellow students outside of class, and one has to think that a worry about social isolation is a deterrent to some older adults who might otherwise return to college. Still, she found the younger students "more tech savvy" than she and was grateful for their willingness to guide and encourage her forays into the use of new technologies.

Most of Helen's courses, in any case, were online and "included students with a broader range of work experiences and ages" who benefited, she believes, from the opportunity to share their "real-world experiences." But she missed the opportunity she had in face-to-face classes of getting to know her professors; she also found that content in classroom courses tended to be more current than material packaged for the online offerings.

Overall, Helen reports that she had "a good academic experience" but also came away from it with some important observations about how universities might do more to recruit and support older adult students. "Before targeting older adults," she writes, "universities need to understand that market": the needs, goals, and experiences that differentiate them from younger adults; the fact that entering a graduate program can be intimidating for those who have long been out of school; and the related challenges faced by older applicants when it comes to performing on standardized admissions tests.

Universities, Helen thinks, should give more weight to life and work experiences in the admissions process, and indeed should make the further development of such experiences an integral part of the curriculum, rather than leaving it up to the students themselves to look for jobs, volunteer work, or internships outside their courses of study. "Perhaps," she concludes, "every course should include an experiential component."

Some of this kind of innovation is underway, here and there, at most universities. But scattered innovation won't be good enough if universities are serious about opening their physical and virtual doors to older adults. And serious they will become as demographic realities continue to settle in, and as all of us in higher education increasingly understand that our missions, our economic viability, and our social and cultural relevance will depend on our success in engaging this rapidly burgeoning proportion of humankind.

Learning from Older Teachers and Scholars

The pressure of new demands from new customers is a source of innovation in any industry. But what if we think of older adults not only as customers who demand innovation but also as agents who help produce it? It is now time to ask what older adults might contribute to the scholarly and instructional activity that lies at the core of every institution of higher education.

We can all point to scholars who remained fully active, engaged, and inventive well beyond what used to be the official age of retirement.

(My dissertation director, the great and still active literary scholar M. H. Abrams, turned 100 last year.) I will mention just two illustrations from my current institution: Thomas Buergenthal, the distinguished jurist (and Holocaust survivor) who, at the age of 76, returned from a decade of service on the International Court of Justice to resume his career of teaching and scholarship in the field of human rights; and Seyyed Hossein Nasr, the world-renowned scholar of philosophy and religion, author of several dozen books, the first Muslim to deliver the Gifford Lectures at the University of Edinburgh, and a scholar still active at age 80.

Such examples of scholarly longevity are impressive and inspiring in their own right and certainly illustrate the upside of aging. These are scholars whose contributions late in life are firmly based on efforts and achievements accumulated over decades. But what about older adults who have not built a lifetime of scholarly achievement but may be turning their attention to higher education after careers outside the scholarly world, careers perhaps in the practical application of what scholars have discovered? Is there a role for them as teachers and scholars in the university of the future?

This is the most speculative moment in this chapter, because currently I am not aware of a well-developed model—or *any* model—for older adults who seek an "encore career" in higher education. For instance, we do not have significant numbers of older adults applying to doctoral programs or seeking the degrees that would qualify them to climb the notorious "tenure ladder" from assistant to full professor. Indeed, there might be a significant social and intellectual cost to encouraging older adults to ascend that ladder: the number of new college and university jobs available to young scholars has declined to the point where we are in danger of losing whole generations of scholars and scientists—in part because of how long senior professors are delaying retirement. Anything that made it even harder for young scholars to get a start in their professional lives would be problematic.

But there are many ways in which older individuals who have finished successful careers, whether inside or outside the academy, might contribute significantly to the work of higher education without having to mount the tenure track. One example of how they are already doing so is a program in GW's Department of Medicine in which a cadre of retired internists foster and evaluate the skills of third-year medical students in conducting physical examinations and taking patients' histories—the elements of literally hands-on care that, in an age of increasing reliance on technology, are still important components of effective diagnosis and treatment.[11]

There is no reason why such intergenerational training and mentoring might not be applied to numerous other fields, from the arts to public policy to civil engineering. And while these "encore" instructors are conveying their wisdom and practical know-how to their students, the universities fortunate enough to employ them in that capacity might experiment with ways of collecting, archiving, and/or publishing their professional memories. Such documentation might extend the utility of what these instructors know far beyond the circle of students with whom they directly interact. One way to accomplish that might be to engage the encore instructors themselves in developing modules in online courses aimed at broad audiences.

Indeed, encore instructors might help extend higher education by participating in the delivery of the MOOCs or "massive open online courses" mentioned earlier. For more than a year now, the pages of education journals and the popular media have been filled with both enthusiastic and skeptical articles about the courses, which distribute lectures by star faculty from elite universities to global audiences comprising many thousands of students.

Whatever position one takes on the intrinsic quality of MOOCs, there is no doubt that variations in cultural background and language proficiency pose a challenge for any form of online instruction that crosses international boundaries, especially for students who have not been exposed to the assumptions of Western pedagogy.[12] One way to begin addressing that problem might be to supplement the online lectures emanating from universities in the developed world with face-to-face sessions led by preceptors strategically placed in developing countries. Retirees with an interest in travel might be ideal candidates for such a role—somewhat along the lines of older adults who, after retirement, sign up for a stint in the Peace Corps.[13] That's one more of no doubt countless ways in which older adults might become active and valued "extenders" of higher education.

Conclusion

The point of these examples has not been to identify the best, let alone the only, ways universities can or should respond to the world-changing phenomenon this book explores. We have only sampled the many ways in which the phenomenon of aging is adding to the intellectual repertoire of higher education, while at the same time providing them (potentially!) with a vast new audience and a rich new supply of scholars and teachers.

As communities, universities are extraordinarily dynamic and diverse, with myriads of talented people constantly coming and going and seeking new ways of pursuing intellectual and creative projects; the potential points of intersection between those communities and the talents and interests of older adults are literally countless.

Universities as *institutions,* on the other hand, have not often been as innovative as they might be. As it happens, however, we are living in an era in which changing demographics and mounting economic pressures are forcing universities to explore new models in every sphere of their activities. The conjunction of that demand for innovation with an unparalleled increase in healthy human longevity inevitably will mean that experiments of the kind I have described or imagined will continue to multiply—one of the many ways in which the aging of humankind will inevitably shape the future of universities.

Notes

1. William Butler Yeats, "Sailing to Byzantium," in *The Poems of W.B. Yeats*, ed. Richard J. Finneran (New York: Macmillan Publishing Company, 1983), 193.
2. Current neuroscience provides ample reason to doubt that such lapses point to fundamental deficits; see Barbara Strauch, "Aging: The Secret Life of the Middle-Aged Brain," *Huffpost Healthy Living*, April 19, 2010, www.huffingtonpost.com/barbara-strauch/aging-the-secret-life-of_b_543298.html; and Maia Szalavitz, "Today's 90 Year Olds Are Mentally Sharper than Their Predecessors," *TIME*, July 11, 2013, http://healthland.time.com/2013/07/11/todays-90-year-olds-are-mentally-sharper-than-their-predecessors/#ixzz2Yq60dJah.
3. See Introduction, Figure I.4, Aging of the World Population.
4. Loretta DiPetro, Andrei Gribok, Michelle S. Stevens, Larry F. Hamm, and William Rumpler, "Three 15-Min Bouts of Moderate Postmeal Walking

Significantly Improves 24-h Glycemic Control in Older People at Risk for Impaired Glucose Tolerance," *Diabetes Care* 36, no.10 (June 2013): 3262–8. doi: 10.2337/dc13-0084.

5. Gene D. Cohen, "Two New Intergenerational Interventions for Alzheimer's Disease Patients and Families," *American Journal of Alzheimer's Disease* 15, no. 3 (2000): 137–42.

6. E-mail communication to the author from Christina Puchalski, August 15, 2013.

7. National Center for Education Statistics, "Projections 2018," Table 13, http://nces.ed.gov/programs/projections/projections2018/tables/table_13 .asp?referrer=list. The absolute numbers have increased slightly since 1998, when adults older than 35 constituted approximately 2.6 million out of a total of 14.5 million; the corresponding numbers in 2007 were approximately 3.0 million out of 18.2 million. In short, there were more older adults going to college in 2007 than in 1998, but the growth in their attendance did not keep pace with the overall growth in the number of people going to college.

8. See Michael Lindgren, "In Four Books, Four Different Visions for Fixing Higher Education," review of *Is College Worth It?*, by William J. Bennett; *Hacking Your Education*, by Dale J. Stephens Perigee; *Paying for the Party*, by Elizabeth A. Armstrong and Laura T. Hamilton; and *College Unbound*, by Jeffrey J. Selingo, *Washington Post*, August 9, 2013, WP Opinions, www .washingtonpost.com/opinions/in-four-books-four-different-visions -for-fixing-higher-education/2013/08/09/e0049db4-c7c2-11e2-9f1a -1a7cdee20287_story.html.

9. Yuliya Chernova, "New Study Sheds Light on Free Online Course," *Wall Street Journal*, July 31, 2013, http://blogs.wsj.com/venturecapital/2013/07/31/new -study-sheds-light-on-free-online-courses/; "MOOCs for Seniors," Open Ideo, http://www.openideo.com/open/mayo-clinic/ideas/moocs-for-seniors.

10. Helen White, e-mail communication with the author's staff, August 12, 2013.

11. Thomas Kohut, "The Art of Healing," *GW Medicine and Health*, Spring 2012, www.gwmedicinehealth.com/spring-2012/the-art-of-healing.

12. For an especially pointed commentary on this challenge, see Ghanashyam Sharma, "A MOOC Delusion: Why Visions to Educate the World Are Absurd," *Chronicle of Higher Education*, July 15, 2013, http://chronicle.com/ blogs/worldwise/a-mooc-delusion-why-visions-to-educate-the-world-are -absurd/32599.

13. I am grateful to Paul Berman for this intriguing suggestion, as well as more generally for his thoughts about the potential relationship between older adults and online education.

Part Three

PERSPECTIVES AND POSSIBILITIES

Old age is not a disease—it is strength and survivorship, triumph over all kinds of vicissitudes and disappointments, trials and illnesses.
— Maggie Kuhn

Chapter 12

Aging in a Majority–
Minority Nation

Fernando M. Torres-Gil
*Director, UCLA Center for Policy Research on Aging;
Professor of Social Welfare and Public Policy,
UCLA Luskin School of Public Affairs*

*New immigrant groups offer opportunities to revitalize our economic,
social, cultural, and national security. As the population grows older, we
have a self-interest in recognizing and responding to these opportunities.*

It was like being in a foreign country. Having never lived anywhere
but California I arrived at Brandeis University in the 1970s, to study
gerontology and geriatrics, as a young graduate student, polio survivor,
grandson of migrant farmworkers, and one of the first Latino students
from the Southwest to attend a Boston-area college.

This chapter was co-written with Courtney Demko, doctoral candidate at UCLA Luskin School of
Public Affairs. Ms. Demko contributed intellectual ideas and demographic analysis as well as editing.

I found myself assigned to interview white retirees in New Hampshire as part of a survey of long-term care facilities in New England. The subjects were God-fearing, patriotic men who found it rather strange for a young, disabled Latino to inquire about their personal lives. I later learned that Brandeis faculty members had qualms about sending me into this uncharted territory, concerned that my ethnicity might not be well received. To the contrary, I not only completed the surveys but I made new friends among these research subjects.

How? By drawing on my personal background, understanding their concerns and appealing to their good sense and compassion. Acceptance and understanding from both sides were key to these interactions. Looking back on the experience, I can see it as a microcosm of the challenge that faces our society these many years later when the U.S. demography is dramatically shifting, when older people and ethnic minorities are the two fastest growing population segments in the nation.

While the United States since its earliest days has been a nation of demographic change, with immigration and a Manifest Destiny serving us well for more than 200 years, we are about to embark on a demographic challenge unlike those of previous eras: the aging of the United States as it also becomes a majority-minority country.

The United States anticipates a near-doubling of its older population by 2030, when Hispanics already will be the largest minority group. Thanks to unprecedented growth, all minorities and racial groups will account for over half of the U.S. population by 2050.

What does this mean for the future of the United States? Will fear and insecurity create racial discrimination and ageism or trepidation like that felt by my Brandeis professors? Or will we have the foresight to prepare for, and invest in, this new America?

Fortunately, public debate about these changes appears to be shifting from fear and reticence to the recognition that this diversity can be good for the country. A growing group of policy elites and strange bedfellows—conservative, libertarian, liberal—is acknowledging the economic benefits of aging and diversity.

What is apparent is that the new immigrant groups offer intrinsic opportunities to revitalize our economic, social, cultural, and national security. As the population grows older, we have a self-interest in recognizing and responding to these opportunities. If we follow that self-interest, we will find that minorities and immigrants are a crucial component for the country's future and an important backbone of the workforce.

But how can the public—Mr. and Mrs. Main Street—and in particular, older white retirees, who are the most uncomfortable with these dramatic changes, come to recognize the benefits and necessity of fully embracing the New America?

The Great Challenge

For too long we have viewed diversity, immigrants, and minority groups as a set of problems and conflicts. Revising this narrative would change the public discourse to one of how to invest in the well-being and productivity of these populations and at the same time benefit society at large.

From that perspective, we can view the transition to a majority-minority society as a grand opportunity for ensuring a youthful and productive workforce and avoiding the demographic issues faced by Japan, Italy, and other nations with declining fertility rates and an aversion to foreign workers and immigrants.

The United States has been through it before, the recurring cycle of a nation whose history is replete with new groups of immigrants. Whether arriving legally or through extrajudicial means, these groups have over time moved from downtrodden and exploited people to become Americans who are a vital part of mainstream society.[1] Each group—Dutch, Anglo Saxons, Eastern Europeans, Irish, Germans, Chinese, Japanese, Filipinos, Mexicans, Armenians, and Persians—has gone through this social and political transition and emerged successfully as a robust citizenry of the United States.

However, there is no guarantee that this impressive tradition of acculturation will continue. Each epoch is replete with conflicts and traumas and requires a renewed commitment to the values of this great American experiment.

What makes the current epoch different is that the United States also faces a demographic transformation based on age and longevity: We are simultaneously becoming an older population and a majority-minority nation, a profound demographic shift never before experienced in this country.

Our challenge is to understand the complexities of these changes and to address the growing insecurities and fears, especially among older people who fear that somehow they will lose as immigrants flood in, and that the American dream and character that they cherish will be lost amid this sea of new arrivals. The question today is: Can we recognize the self-interest we all share in ensuring that the newcomers succeed in becoming full members of U.S. society, and once again meet this challenge despite the inevitable discomfort and dislocation of new arrivals?

The nation faces two key milestone years: 2030 with the maturation of the aging baby boom generation,[2] and 2042, when we will see what it means to be a majority-minority nation. These two dates can be benchmarks by which to measure how we respond to the changing demographics.

The Hispanic population will more than double between 2012 and 2050, becoming 30 percent of the population and the largest minority group, as seen in Figure 12.1. By that time the number of adults over 65 will have more than doubled, creating the largest "senior citizen" group in our history.[3]

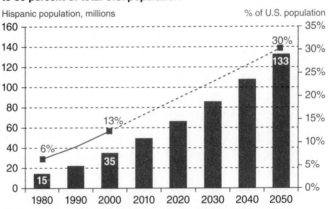

By 2050, the Hispanic population will increase to 30 percent of total U.S. population

Figure 12.1   Increase in Hispanic Population, 1980–2050
SOURCE: U.S. Census Bureau, 2002b and 2008c; Hayutin, A., Dietz, M., & Mitchell, L. (2010). *New Realities of an Older America: Challenges, Changes and Questions*, Stanford Center on Longevity. Retrieved from: longevity3.stanford.edu/wp.../New-Realities-of-an-Older-America.pdf.

Other racial and ethnic groups also are increasing, and the United States in 2042 will become a majority-minority nation for the first time.[4] But while the non-Hispanic older white population steadily declines, as seen in Figure 12.2, this group will continue to exercise inordinate electoral influence. Given that older persons are more likely to vote than younger groups, elderly whites may control the political agenda in the midst of a growing young Hispanic and immigrant population.

Rather than viewing this demographic transformation as a problem, we can realize the upside by accepting it as a positive change and developing a roadmap for public policy actions to once again integrate the newcomers into American civic and social life. By doing so, we can retain this country's soft power as a democratic and open society and in turn enhance our global leadership.

Although increasingly diverse, the older population will remain majority white non-Hispanic.

Population 65+ by race and ethnicity, %

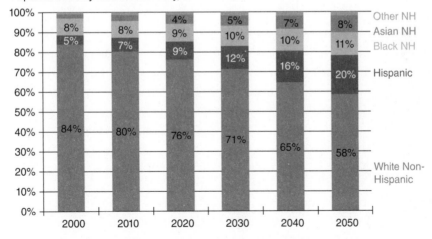

Figure 12.2   Older Population by Race and Ethnicity

NOTE: NH = non-Hispanic; Other NH = non-Hispanic and two or more races, American Indian and Alaskan Native, or Native Hawaiian and Pacific Islander.

SOURCE: U.S. Census Bureau, 2008c; Hayutin, A., Dietz, M., & Mitchell, L. (2010). *New Realities of an Older America: Challenges, Changes and Questions*, Stanford Center on Longevity. Retrieved from: longevity3.stanford.edu/wp . . . /New-Realities-of-an-Older-America.pdf.

The Political Tempest

We are in the midst of a transition to a new America and, as with previous demographic transitions, it can be hard to see the virtues and opportunities that lie ahead. The political arena is replete with debates about the advantages and disadvantages of a nation becoming more diverse and older. Public policy debates center on the solvency of entitlement programs, in particular Social Security and Medicare. Can this country afford these programs, when some 80 million baby boomers draw on those benefits? Record budget deficits and a $17 trillion national debt raise alarmist visions of Greece's financial crisis and national insolvency.[5] Debates around immigration reform and whether an estimated 11 million undocumented persons should have a pathway to citizenship create a new sense of nativism: America for Americans.[6]

The rise of a Tea Party dedicated to minimalist government, as well as a continuing public aversion to increased taxation, and the irony that the nation's first black president lost a key electorate—those over 65—create confusion about the future direction of the United States and even fears about retaining the "American character."

Perhaps the most alarmist view of these ongoing debates was covered in a prescient *National Journal* article by Ronald Brownstein. He capsulated the concerns of many, suggesting that the growth of the elderly population in the midst of increased diversity will create a "generational mismatch" between the competing needs of older whites (e.g., low taxes) and younger Hispanics (e.g., increased public expenditures).[7] This, in turn, will aggravate tensions over diminishing public resources and balkanize an already divided electorate.

But does this have to be the case? Are we destined to face conflicts among the elderly, minorities, and immigrant groups? Can we find common cause and chart a roadmap for a more benign and hopeful rationale for viewing the political debates around demographic changes as an opportunity? A detailed overview of those demographic changes can reveal the opportunities and benefits awaiting the United States with a narrative that allows for political consensus to take advantage of these changes. My personal journey informs that future narrative.

A Journey of Ethnicity and Aging

Born and raised in the twentieth century and growing older in the twenty-first century, I view the nexus of aging and diversity from an intriguing platform. My mother's parents were immigrants from Mexico, having fled the revolution there for a safer place to raise their children. Both grandparents followed the proverbial immigrant saga: serving as farmworkers in the agricultural fields of California, struggling to raise 10 children and eventually saving enough to buy some properties in Northern California. Their children—my mother, aunts, and uncles— were first-generation Americans, seeking acceptance in a world where Mexicans were viewed as second-class citizens, obligated to do low-wage and undesirable work.

Yet World War II and the postwar economic prosperity enabled my uncles to serve their new country as proud patriots and my aunts and uncles to move into the middle class with jobs that paid decent wages and, for some, provided union benefits. My cousins began the journey into college, with the option to acculturate. Mexicans in particular and Latinos in general were a distinct minority in numbers, influence, and civic contributions. Yet by the end of the twentieth century, they began to exhibit political, cultural, and civic influence.

Through this time, my family—my mother and siblings—followed their own destiny. My mother married a bracero—a Mexican national who came to the United States during the war years to replace a work-force that was fighting abroad. He met my mom while working in the fields with her family. They married and had nine children; I was the second born. But, like some others, my father returned to Mexico, leaving my mom and their children to fend for themselves, forced to rely on public housing and the generosity of the robust social welfare safety net of the 1950s through 1970s, as well as charity from community groups.

We were most fortunate—growing up in a time of high-quality public education, public benefits that gave us a decent life, and civic organizations that supported the poor and vulnerable. And of course, we had a mother who believed in the values of discipline, church, patriotism, and education. The upshot of this story: All nine of her children are college graduates and, benefiting from the "Chicano movement" of that time and its affirmative action policies, have professional careers and good lives.

This saga became more complex when I, as a child, acquired polio during the epidemic of the 1950s. Through the good graces of Shriners Hospital and a grandmother who dedicated her traditional healing practices to my rehabilitation, I, too, acquired an education and a professional career. A footnote to this immigrant saga: The public housing that gave us shelter and safety is being replaced by a new residential village, and it will be anchored with a community center that will bear my mother's name: the Maria J. Torres-Gil Community Center, in honor of her community organizing and success as a single mother.

So what does this story say about the demographic changes facing the United States and the need to revise the narrative from one of fear to one of opportunity? Today the state in which I grew up is majority-minority, and Latinos are the largest minority group. We are no longer a side note to the economic, social and cultural fabric of California. The young Chicanos of the 1960s are now the political leaders and entrepreneurs of this great state. The immigrant families, whether having arrived as braceros, as illegals, or through family reunification, are the workforce and the consumers of goods and housing. And the values of our immigrant grandparents and family members—a work ethic, family, education, discipline, church, and patriotism—have given California and the nation a vitality and energy that is a replica of what previous immigrant groups have given this nation.

One has only to look at other nations where birth rates have declined and immigration and foreign workers are not welcomed or integrated into the host societies—for example, France, Germany, Italy, Japan, and South Korea—to see what could have occurred in California and the United States had we not accepted a steady infusion of immigrants, like my relatives. But this story also is about the good public education, health care, shelter, and public benefits my brothers and sisters received—the very safety net that has eroded in this century. If there is a message in our personal journey, it is to recognize and accept demographic change and to adapt and invest in order that the future outcomes bode well for the nation. Together, Latinos and baby boomers will define the new demographic portfolio of the nation.

Boomers and Latinos—Demographic Destiny

The future of the United States is based on a few key demographic trends: longevity, the growth of minority/ethnic/immigrant groups, and fertility rates. As discussed elsewhere in this book, the population is aging in large part simply because people are living longer—average life expectancy will move into the eighties after 2030[8]—and the simultaneous rapid aging of the baby boom generation.[9] Perhaps more profound is that U.S. fertility rates at the same time are declining, to 1.9 births per woman in 2010, below the replacement level of 2.1.[10]

Added to these changes are two lesser-known but pertinent developments: Latinos are also aging and they too have a baby boomer cohort. As Figure 12.3 shows, Latinos and baby boomers have a demographic destiny. In 2000, 10 percent of baby boomers were Latino and therefore make up a significant portion of the demographic change that is occurring.[11] Thus, understanding the characteristics of this largely unknown segment of the population will help policymakers prepare for the future.

This demographic overview points to a transition evolving by 2050—aging baby boomers, Latinos as the largest minority group, and the decline of white, non–Hispanics as the majority population. This change is not to be feared. Rather we should understand and adapt to it.

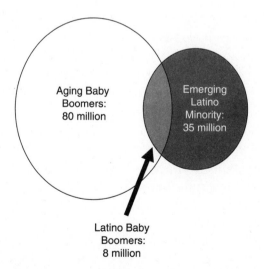

Figure 12.3   A Confluence of Two Populations: The "Hidden Boomers"
DATA SOURCE: UCLA Center for Policy Research on Aging.

A Symbiotic Convergence

The United States is fortunate to be faced with a growing population of new ethnic groups that, as before, can invigorate the nation. At the same time we see a growing group of elders that can be a resource. Taking advantage of these new dynamics may not be easy, with some politicians and groups attempting to portray these changes as the demise of the nation. How we respond will determine whether we continue the 300-year success of integration and acculturation of emerging groups.

Examples abound at the personal, community, and global level to demonstrate the demographic good fortune awaiting our country. On a personal level, we can pose an intimate question: Who will take care of us when we are old and unable to care for ourselves? Caregiving and the need for long-term care is a pending crisis for aging baby boomers as they face the inevitable chronic conditions and vicissitudes of living longer. We assume the caregivers will be our family members—spouses and children—but that isn't guaranteed.

Already, one-third of baby boomers are living alone,[12] while the available pool of potential caregivers is projected to decline. Who will fill the gap? Answer: minorities and immigrants. One has only to enter a nursing home or long-term care facility to likely find the following "age/race stratification:" The patients, especially those in more expensive facilities, will be female and white. The owners and investors of the for-profit facilities tend to be white males. The administrators tend to be white males and females. The visiting MD is likely to be a white male. The nurses are likely to be white, immigrant, and minority females. The hands-on staff—the LVNs and aides who feed, bathe, and clean the patients—are almost exclusively minority and immigrant.

Equally as important, the janitorial and service staff is minority and immigrant. The upshot is an English-speaking, white, frail elder receiving her care from a non–English-speaking minority or immigrant. Granted, this is an illustration, but it is close to the reality in many long-term care facilities, including what I myself found in the nursing home/rehabilitation facility where I recovered from a surgical procedure a few years back. Because I spoke Spanish and was comfortable with the Filipino, Caribbean black, and Latino janitors and aides, I was accorded special treatment including a private room, the best wheelchair, and a higher level of attention from an overworked and underpaid staff.

Issues of caregiving and long-term care are but one example of why we need to examine the benefits of diversity as our nation gets older. On an economic and community level, we can ask the question: Who will buy our homes? Dowell Myers, a noted urban planner from the University of Southern California, gained notoriety by documenting that in a society where whites are aging and having fewer children, they will face a conundrum when they seek to sell their homes to move elsewhere.[13] The potential buyers of their homes will have to be the growing young population of immigrants and minorities. But will they have the education, jobs, and financial resources to afford buying the homes of older whites ready to retire elsewhere? This scenario points out the self-interest that all older persons can have in investing in the social, educational, and economic needs of emerging minority and immigrant groups.

The third example is more global. Examining the situation facing other nations with fertility levels below population replacement levels demonstrates what would await us if we did not embrace diversity. Japan is a well-recognized example of a nation with a declining population and fertility level that is well below the replacement level.[14]

Japanese leaders realize that the economic stagnation of the last 20 years is due, in part, to an aging population whose members are more likely to be savers than consumers of goods and services. This would not be problematic, except that Japan values racial homogeneity and remains uncomfortable with diversity. Japan is forced to recruit foreign workers for its long-term care industry, but it restricts their ability to be part of Japanese society. To remain in the country, these workers must become fluent in Japanese and, during economic downturns, are likely to be sent back to their home countries. This situation does not bode well for an aging nation that is losing population.

South Korea presents an even more extreme case, with a replacement level of 1.1, discrimination against foreign workers and people in mixed-marriages, and an unwillingness to integrate foreign workers who are recruited to do the "3D"—dirty, dangerous, demeaning—work.

These examples are among many that show the benefits and opportunities in the United States as we become an older, more diverse society: the immigrant and minority pool of potential caregivers; an expanding workforce that can be the country's future consumer base; and a proud history of integration and acculturation of all groups. But how might we make a compelling case to a conservative, white, English-speaking, retiree that he or she should welcome immigrants and minorities?

The Common Ground

I speak to a variety of audiences—professional, minority, political—about the complex policy implications of aging, especially in light of public concern about entitlements, federal budgets, and the future of Medicare and Social Security. Increasingly, I also am speaking about diversity; and with immigration reform on the national agenda, issues of public policy, aging, diversity, and immigration.

My litmus test of my effectiveness in presenting my case is in how I reach audiences of older, white, and conservative retirees in places like Orange County, California, and the Midwest. I have gone to these "lion's dens" and argued that white retirees need young Hispanics and other immigrants. How do I present a compelling case to these audiences, given that they have been the least likely group to vote for our first black president, or support the Affordable Care Act and a pathway to citizenship for those who have broken our nation's laws by entering the United States illegally?

As mentioned earlier, in meeting New Hampshire retirees during my graduate school years I was able to connect with them by understanding their concerns and trying to reach their sense and compassion. From my initial public speaking experiences, I similarly have built approaches to present complex issues to conservative audiences in a manner that appeals to their good sense and values. To that end, I present the following case for understanding and accepting that the United States will be a majority-minority nation:

1. I acknowledge that their values matter and are valid, and that this nation is about fairness, equality, merit, and playing by the rules.
2. I agree that not everyone plays by the rules and that those who came to this country illegally in fact have broken our laws. I concur that immigrants who overstay their visas and/or bring their elderly parents and enroll them in our public welfare system (e.g., in-home supportive

services, SSI) are "gaming the system," and this must stop. And I empha-
size that anyone desiring U.S. citizenship must learn English, register to
vote, and commit to this nation's democracy and constitution.

3. Having supported their sincere reasons for frustration with those
   who take advantage of our nation's openness and generosity, I then
   speak to their priorities as older persons by reinforcing the absolute importance of preserving Social Security, Medicare, and old-age
   benefits. Polling indicates that all elders, regardless of ideology or
   partisanship, depend on these crucial programs.

4. I then ask the rhetorical question: How will we ensure the sustain-
   ability of entitlement programs and ensure that we have sufficient
   funds (e.g., taxes) to maintain these benefits, especially in light of
   federal debts and deficits?

5. The answer: by ensuring that we have sufficient numbers of young
   people and an expanding workforce able and willing to pay the taxes
   that fund these public benefits.

6. But who will be that future workforce? We face a decline in birthrates among non-Hispanic whites to the extent that this group will
   decline in number and be unable to infuse the workforce and tax-
   payer base.

7. Yet, there are other groups that can replace a declining white population and can, with adequate support and investments, be the future
   workforce and taxpaying population that supports social programs.
   They also can volunteer for our armed forces and defend our nation.

8. And who might those groups be? Answer: Hispanics, Asians, and
   future immigrants, all of whom have replacement rates above 2.1.

Thus, regardless of how we feel about new arrivals, we have a self-
interest in enabling them to integrate and acculturate, like previous
immigrant groups. And, as the United States population ages, we are
fortunate that we are still growing in numbers and that today's minorities
and immigrants can be the future of this country.

I have found that, in almost every case, this new narrative has my
audiences paying attention. While they may disagree with specific issues
like bilingual education or driver's licenses for undocumented residents,[15] they may begin to realize their self-interest in proposals like the
Dream Act and a pathway to citizenship.

Shifting Political Winds and Alliances

There is evidence that this revised narrative is gaining currency. In 2013, *Health Affairs*, an influential policy journal, used 2009 data to show that immigrants in the United States accounted for a net surplus of $13.8 billion paid into the Medicare hospital trust fund while native-born Americans depleted that same fund by $30.9 billion.[16]

Leading Republicans, like Senator John McCain of Arizona, argue that older Americans should recognize that immigration reform would stimulate the economy, create jobs, reduce the deficit, and improve the solvency of Social Security and Medicare.[17] Even the ideologically conservative House Budget Committee chairman Paul Ryan speaks favorably about the importance of immigrants (and 11 million undocumented persons) to the nation's economy.[18]

These strange bedfellows are natural allies to more liberal and pro-immigration reform groups. What is needed is a narrative like mine that highlights our self-interest, regardless of age, income, race, or ideology, in accepting the demographic reality and taking advantage of a growing group of minorities and immigrants who believe in the "American Dream." This won't be easy. As in the past, there will be tensions.

But if we can make a compelling case to older white conservatives, then we have reached a crucial segment of the electorate. As an aging baby boomer, I know that my children and grandchildren will grow and age in a nation that is much different than it was in the last century. And unlike my grandparents, my mom, and my aunts and uncles, my children and grandchildren will not be a minority. With proper investments in their future, we can be confident once again that they will make invaluable economic and societal contributions to our country, and that our nation will continue to prosper and be a beacon for the world.

Notes

1. M. Barone, "The Saturday Essay: A Nation Built for Immigrants," *Wall Street Journal*, September 21–22, 2013, C1–C2.
2. See Introduction, Figure I.6, U.S. Over-65 Population, 1950–2030.
3. G. Vincent and V. Velkoff, "The Next Four Decades: The Older Population in the United States: 2010 to 2050 Population Estimates and Projections,"

U.S. Department of Commerce Economics and Statistics Administration, U.S. Census Bureau, 2010.

4. Ibid.

5. J. Calmes, "Budget Office Warns That Deficits Will Rise again Because Cuts Are Misdirected," *New York Times*, September 18, 2013, A13.

6. J. Angel, L. Yarnell, F. Torres-Gil, K. Whitfield, K. Markides, "Hispanics and Mexican Americans Health and Aging in the 21st Century," Lyndon B. Johnson School of Public Affairs, University of Texas, Austin, 2009.

7. Ronald Brownstein, "The Gray and the Brown: The Generational Mismatch," *National Journal*, April 16, 2012, 14–22.

8. See Introduction, Figure I.2 U.S. Life Expectancy at Birth.

9. See Introduction, Figure I.6 U.S. Over-65 Population, 1950–2030.

10. M. Mather, "Fact Sheet: The Decline in U.S. Fertility," Population Reference Bureau, 2012, www.prb.org/Publications/Datasheets/2012/world-population -data-sheet/fact-sheet-us-population.aspx.

11. U.S. Census Bureau, "U.S. Census Bureau Projections Show a Slower Growing, Older, More Diverse Nation a Half Century from Now," www.census .gov/newsroom/releases/archives/population/cb12-243.html.

12. S. Reinhard, D. Redfoot, and B. Cleary, "Health and Long-Term Care: Are Immigrant Workers Indispensable?," *GENERATIONS: Immigration in an Aging Society* (Winter, 2008–2009): 24–30.

13. D. Myers, "Aging Baby Boomers and the Effect of Immigration: Rediscovering the Intergenerational Social Contract," *GENERATIONS: Immigration in an Aging Society* (Winter, 2008–2009): 18–23.

14. B. J. Kim and F. Torres-Gil, "Aging and Immigration: the Case of South Korea with a Look at Italy and Japan," *GENERATIONS, Immigration in an Aging Society* (Winter 2008–2009): 80–87.

15. Barone, "A Nation Built for Immigrants."

16. L. Zallman, S. Woolhandler, D. Himmelstein, D. Bor, and D. McCormick, "Immigrants Contributed an Estimated $115.2 Billion More to the Medicare Trust Fund Than They Took out in 2002–09," *Health Affairs*, http://content .healthaffairs.org/content/early/2013/05/20/hlthaff.2012.1223.

17. American Association of Retired Persons, "Opinion," *AARP Bulletin*, September 2013.

18. N. Cook, "Cash Chase," *National Journal*, July 27, 2013, 6.

Chapter 13

Healthy Ageing and Well-Being in Britain and the World

Baroness Sally Greengross
Member, UK House of Lords;
Chief Executive, UK International Longevity Center

Our twentieth-century institutions can survive and flourish in the twenty-first century, but they need to respond to new demographic demands by setting new goals. Ending Alzheimer's, creating age-friendly environments, and eliminating ageism are universal challenges that all countries must face in an era of population ageing.

Elevation to the UK House of Lords in 2000, as Baroness Greengross of Notting Hill, was a great honor for me. I already had spent much of my adult life working on issues affecting older people in the United Kingdom. Ageing, after all, is an issue that is not only nationally important but also crucial to each and every person. Recognizing the need for equality among age groups led me to Age Concern England, which I headed from 1987 to 2000.

Unfortunately there remains much to be done to get away from the antiquated age-rigid approaches that still dominate much of the land-scape when it comes to our ageing population around the world. At the same time, across the globe, societies are afflicted with the social, moral, health, and fiscal nightmares stemming from the explosion of age-related dementia, including Alzheimer's disease. This is the major driver of my work, and as vice chair of the All-Party Parliamentary Group on Dementia and Ageing and Older People, I am passionately committed to helping solve this challenge.

Like the rest of the world, the United Kingdom is ageing. Unlike the rest of the world, Britain maintains a comprehensive, publicly funded health care system that is a source of great pride to modern-day Britons. The overlap of these two phenomena is at least part of the reason that British newspapers regularly proclaim that the National Health Service (NHS) is on the brink of collapse. Such sensationalism has brought the question to the front of everyone's mind in the United Kingdom: Can the NHS survive in the twenty-first century as the British population ages? And, more generally, can last century's health institutions meet this century's demands?

To both questions, the answer is yes and no. Yes, the NHS and other health systems can survive and even flourish if they make significant structural changes—and also benefit from equal changes in the rest of society. However, the NHS, in particular, will be destined for certain demise if British societal institutions do not change to meet the challenges of an ageing population. Moreover, last century's mode of ageing—with its poor health and pensions—will equally encumber British economic growth. Indeed, just as the future of the NHS relies upon healthy and productive ageing, so does the rest of British society. All societal institutions must meet the challenges brought by ageing populations.

What the world needs is a new path of ageing that stresses good health and ongoing productivity. If such a model can emerge, Britain's prospects remain bright, and the NHS may become the United Kingdom's most vibrant symbol of success in an ageing world. To achieve this goal, the NHS and other institutions in Britain and throughout the world must focus on promoting health and well-being. It is only through concentration on these issues that the ageing can continue to participate at the highest levels of society.

This goal must build upon three pillars that are particular but not unique to the United Kingdom: preventing and treating Alzheimer's disease; creating age-friendly environments; and eliminating ageism from the workplace and all other aspects of society.

Certainly, the challenge of creating a new path of ageing is not Britain's alone. Nor are these three pillars unique to the United Kingdom. The challenges brought by an ageing population and the solutions to promoting health and well-being throughout society apply to all countries throughout the world, whether they are emerging or developed, whether they have public or private health care systems.

In looking at the particulars of ageing in Britain, we can see how ageing can become a catalyst for much-needed institutional reform. Our twentieth-century institutions can survive and flourish in the twenty-first century, but they need to respond to new demographic demands by setting new goals. Ending Alzheimer's, creating age-friendly environments, and eliminating ageism are universal challenges that all countries must face in an era of population ageing.

Ageing in Britain

The greying of Britain, as in the United States and the world, is well under way. In 2000, the over-60 demographic segment made up nearly 21 percent of the population. This percentage will swell to 30.7 percent by 2050, making nearly one in three Britons over 60.[1] Numerically, the over-60 population will nearly double in size from 2000 to 2050, and during this time the over-80 segment will grow by nearly 150 percent, according to estimates by the United Nations Population Division.[2]

Increased life spans and consistently low fertility rates are the proximate forces of ageing in Britain as in the world. In 1950, the average person in Britain would not live to see his or her seventieth birthday, but the average baby born today can expect to live past 80.[3] Since the end of the baby boom of the 1960s, Britain's fertility rate has remained below "replacement level," as it has for numerous European nations. For nearly half a century, just over 1.5 British babies have been born per woman during her lifetime.[4] Ultimately, this adds up to the emergence of a "top heavy" population structure, one in which "pensioners" make up an ever-growing segment of the population.

While the global picture is similar, one could argue that Britain's demography is "younger" and more able to exploit its "demographic dividend" than that of many of its economic peers, like Italy, Japan, and South Korea. Nonetheless, the United Kingdom must develop strategies to enable its ageing population to remain healthy and productive. If the NHS is to survive and thrive—and if the United Kingdom is going to prosper economically—then this "neediest" section of its population must become one of its most socially and economically valuable.

Increased Pressure on a Fragile NHS

The ageing of the British population is increasing pressure on an already distressed NHS. Nations that are seeking to revise their own health care systems to accommodate their ageing populations would do well to observe how the dynamic is playing out in the United Kingdom.

Even as the full force of the ageing demographic has yet to hit the country, the British health care system is overburdened and struggling. In 2011, 9.4 percent of the United Kingdom's gross domestic product went to health care, on par with the 9.3 percent average of other nations of the Organisation for Economic Co-operation and Development (OECD). However, for this expenditure, the United Kingdom had only 2.8 practicing physicians and three hospital beds per 1,000 residents, compared to OECD averages of 3.2 physicians and 4.8 beds.[5]

Citizens and politicians alike have seen the stress on the hospital system—and the unfortunate results. Mortality rates are high, and inefficient emergency systems and staff cannot manage current demand, much less near-term projections that arise with ageing. Prime Minister David Cameron has noted that Britain does the NHS no favors by continuing to ignore its shortcomings: "I love our NHS and I never want to do it any harm, but we don't serve our NHS by covering up problems and difficulties."[6]

The current struggles forebode further difficulty as the population ages. In July 2013 the British press reported that England's largest hospital trust, Barts Health NHS Trust in London, was losing £2 million a week; and 11 NHS trusts have collectively forecast a deficit of £200 million for 2013. Further down the road, the NHS anticipates a funding gap of £30 billion between now and 2020.[7]

Why is the NHS under such distress? The simplest answer is an increased demand on resources. According to the NHS, the problem is "a combination of factors, such as an ageing population, outdated management of long-term conditions, and poorly joined-up care between adult social care, community services, and hospitals.[8]"

Of those factors, the ageing of the population is the most critical. In its report, "The NHS Belongs to the People: A Call to Action," the NHS notes that ageing creates a number of challenges for the organization:

- Nearly two-thirds of people admitted to hospital are over 65.
- More than 2 million unplanned admissions per year are for people over 65, accounting for nearly 70 percent of hospital emergency bed days.
- When older people are admitted to a hospital, they stay longer and are more likely to be readmitted.
- Older patients account for the majority of health expenditures; one analysis found that health and care spending on people over 75 was 13 times greater than on the rest of the adult population.[9]

To a system that has not developed an informed response to the changes brought by an ageing population, such challenges will be not merely encumbering, but crippling. I suggest three ways to promote healthy, productive ageing, ease the burden of the NHS, and open new possibilities for ageing adults. These suggestions also will be instructive to other nations as they look ahead to the health care challenges of their own ageing populations.

Conquering Alzheimer's Disease

Throughout history, communicable diseases have been the greatest public health threat. In the last century especially, diseases such as HIV/AIDS, malaria, and tuberculosis presented the greatest peril to human health. Today, however, as the World Health Organization has noted, an incredible two-thirds of deaths worldwide are caused by noncommunicable diseases (NCDs) such as stroke, diabetes, and heart disease.[10] On one hand, this is a testimony to the success of global vaccination programs and other public health outreach that has quelled the threat of communicable disease. On the other hand, it is a warning sign that, as the global population ages, a new health challenge emerges.

While the World Health Organization and the United Nations both have highlighted the rise of NCDs, too little attention is given to what might be the most menacing NCD of them all—Alzheimer's disease. The International Longevity Centre UK (ILC-UK), and the Alzheimer's Disease International and HelpAge International, however, have been pressing to include Alzheimer's disease as a noncommunicable disease. Progress has been promising, but success is far from certain.[11]

Alzheimer's and other dementias, while slow to end in fatality, are disabling to their victims, demanding to their families, and destructive to the function of national health care systems. Moreover, dementia is fiscally devastating. Worldwide, costs associated with dementia amount to 1 percent of GDP.[12]

In the UK, the NHS projects that by 2021 the number of cases will exceed one million and cost upwards of £23 billion a year.[13] Because the risk of Alzheimer's increases with age, the ageing of the population will usher in ever-greater incidences of the disease. Ultimately, research into preventing, treating, and curing Alzheimer's is not only a compassionate endeavor, but also a necessary investment. In 2010, the UK government put £26.6 million toward Alzheimer's research.[14] By comparison, in the same year, the member organizations of the National Cancer Research Institute spent an incredible £504 million on research[15]—for diseases that cost the nation significantly less than does dementia. This investment does not match the level of need.

In a hopeful sign, Prime Minister David Cameron has led an effort to turn this trend around, both in Britain and across the globe. In March 2012, Cameron announced that research funding for dementia would increase to £66 million by 2015,[16] and he set the goal of raising dementia diagnosis. This goal does not, of course, get us where we need to be, but it does signal progress.

In addition, in May 2013, the prime minister pledged to make Alzheimer's a top priority for the G8 during the UK's presidency of the organization. "As more people live longer, [Alzheimer's] is fast becoming one of the biggest social and health care challenges we face," Mr. Cameron said.[17]

This pledge was highly encouraging given the G8's past success in taking the lead on global health concerns—most notably its role in creating the Global Fund to Fight AIDS, Tuberculosis, and Malaria. Yet, as USAgainstAlzheimer's chairman George Vradenburg has noted, "Other stakeholders must join the G8 governments to turn lofty ambition into goal-oriented action."[18]

Indeed, if we fail to improve our methods of diagnosing, treating, and preventing Alzheimer's, the burden on the NHS and other health care systems around the globe will be overwhelming. Alzheimer's disease lacks the visibility of the pink-ribboned breast cancer movement, and it has no spokespersons like HIV/AIDS or Parkinson's. But leadership like Mr. Cameron's may prove decisive. It indicates that Alzheimer's is gaining a higher global profile, and it will attract more R&D funding and attention. Others must follow through to ensure that Alzheimer's doesn't become the disease that ruins lives, families, medical systems, and national economies.

Advancing Age-Friendly Environments

Improved public health requires more than treating illness and disease. Improved health for individuals—and thus for society as a whole—begins not in the hospital, but in the home and in the community. The very environments in which we live play a crucial and underappreciated role in promoting health and well-being.

To the ageing person, the environment is especially important. The young are more mobile and can travel as they wish. They have a relatively easy time navigating various inconveniences that can limit the possibilities available to older people. As they are often confined to a narrow community, the quality of life for older adults can depend upon the restrictions and affordances of their communities. In the United Kingdom, a number of efforts have been created by the ILC-UK to work towards better, sustainable communities for older people, such as Lifetime Neighbourhoods and Localism and Neighbourhoods for all ages.

In Britain and around the world, cities have a special role to play in promoting healthy, productive ageing. The city is the most appropriate environment for older people, according to Elizabeth Burton, professor of sustainable building design and well-being at the University of Warwick.

"Most of us have grown up believing in the rural idyll—that people move from city centres to suburbs, from suburbs to small towns, and small towns to villages," she writes. "But there is a recognition now that as people age and their mobility reduces, they may no longer be able to drive, and their world shrinks—it is therefore much better to live closer to amenities in a higher density of people."[19]

Professor Burton's insight is critical, and an increasingly popular one around the world. The World Health Organization (WHO),[20] for example, has launched a Global Network of Age-Friendly Cities and Communities. This network, at the forefront of age-friendly development, is leading the promotion and development of cities that are "inclusive and accessible" and "promote active ageing." With 138 member-communities across 21 countries, the network is leading the effort to renovate outdoor spaces, transportation, communication, civic participation, and more. An Age-Friendly City is a great place to live not just for the elderly, but also for everyone, as addressed at length elsewhere in this book.

In Britain, the cities of Manchester and Brighton & Hove have joined the WHO's Global Network, committing themselves to its age-friendly principals and goals.[21] Another independent UK Age-Friendly Cities Network mirrors the WHO program, with membership from Belfast, Brighton & Hove, Cardiff, Camden, Edinburgh, Glasgow, Leeds, Manchester, Newcastle, Nottingham, Sheffield, and Stoke-on-Trent.[22]

Furthermore, Newcastle University's Institute for Ageing and Health[23] is working on a Campus for Ageing & Vitality, which will enable older adults access to education, health care, business, retail, and social engagement. The entire campus is built upon age-friendly principles: accessible, easy-to-use transportation; clean, safe environments; public spaces allowing for rest; and so forth.

Because these developments are still in their infant stages, there is no hard evidence that age-friendly cities demonstrably improve health of the ageing. Yet, there is a significant body of research showing the opposite—that isolation and exclusion lead to negative mental and physical health outcomes. Looking ahead, it should be a top priority of advocates to assemble a body of literature that examines the health outcomes of age-friendly cities and communities. Such evidence would further support the development of such environments and, ultimately, pave new paths of healthy, productive ageing.

For the NHS and others, the take-away of age-friendly development is simple. Active ageing leads to healthy ageing, and environments either enable or inhibit activity. Want to encourage older adults to walk? Give them safe streets. To eat healthy foods? Give them easy access to fresh produce. To make it to their medical appointments? Give them good transportation. Indeed, age-friendly development is far more than "do good" policy. It is an investment in the cost-reduction of the health system; and it is a path to economic inclusion.

It also is an opportunity for business growth. In the United Kingdom, those aged 65 to 74 have the second-highest household wealth, preceded only by those aged 55 to 64.[24] For the organizations that make it their business to be age-friendly, commercial rewards may follow. It's truly a win-win-win scenario.

Eliminating Ageism

The inclusion of older adults into social and economic life demands that ageism be eliminated. Ageism—the act of discriminating against certain persons because of their age—is an overlooked, but common practice in Britain and the rest of the world. Ageism exists throughout all of society: in health care, at work, in schools, and beyond. While ageism can never been morally justifiable, it is especially pernicious in the twenty-first century.

A wealth of literature attests to the social and economic benefits that older adults bring to society. As workers, consumers, managers, mentors, and more, older adults are contributing at the top-levels of public- and private-sector work. Indeed, we are learning more and more that an ageing society can only realize its full potential if older adults are fully and indiscriminately integrated into the economy.

Thus, while it is morally imperative to eliminate ageism throughout all of society, it is especially prudent to eliminate ageism in the workplace. Until 2011, the British government sanctioned a default retirement age, by which employers could force employees to retire at 65 solely because of their age.[25] Thankfully, that mechanism has been removed. Yet, while the *letter* of the law may be erased, the *spirit* of it remains.

Today, Britain retains one of the worst records in Europe on age discrimination. One recent survey by a private law firm found that 72 percent of respondents would still impose a mandatory retirement age if the law had not been changed.[26] The European Social Survey found that nearly two out of five British respondents had been shown a lack of respect due to their age; and another half of respondents said that they did not have a single friend over 70.[27]

It also is evident that without a mandatory retirement age, firms simply shift to making a productivity-based case for dismissing older workers. In many ways, this reinforces the stereotypes and ageist attitudes against older workers as less-productive members of the workforce, in complete opposition to what the legislation intended.[28]

Ageism is the most commonly experienced form of prejudice in the United Kingdom, more prevalent than both racism and sexism.[29] Such attitudes, of course, make for unwelcoming workplaces, a costly problem especially as Britain struggles to regroup its economic fortunes, because ageing workers have vital roles to play.

One recent study from the Center for Retirement Research at Boston College, for example, shows that ageing workforces are highly productive.[30] Other research shows that some companies are even using an ageing workforce as a catalyst for improvement. The German carmaker BMW's 2017 Pilot Project, for example, created a team of older workers that was faster than average-aged assembly lines and had a lower rate of error and absenteeism.[31]

Other companies around the world have piloted similar programs, and results have led to one clear conclusion: Age discrimination in the workplace isn't just bad ethics, it's bad business.

Moreover, prolonged working lives lead to increased health. The Institute of Economic Affairs and the Age Endeavour Fellowship, reported in *Work Longer, Live Healthier: The relationship between economic activity, health and government policy* that:

- Retirement decreases the likelihood of being in "very good" or "excellent" self-assessed health by about 40 percent.
- Retirement increases the probability of suffering from clinical depression by about 40 percent.

- Retirement increases the probability of having at least one diagnosed physical condition by about 60 percent.
- Retirement increases the probability of taking a drug for such a condition by about 60 percent.[32]

The relevance to health care and the NHS budget is obvious. Health outcomes are improved by environments that welcome older workers and encourage their participation. Conversely, ageist environments push older adults into retirement and turn producers into patients, thus exacerbating the drain of resources on the health system.

Conclusion

Britain's ageing challenge is unique: The NHS is a distinctly British institution, and its place in the British heart and economy is unparalleled. Yet, the challenge to the NHS is similar to that of health systems the world over: Institutions must be updated and upgraded not only to account for but also to embrace the dynamics of an ageing population.

The three priorities that I have suggested—addressing Alzheimer's, advancing Age-Friendly Environments, and eliminating ageism—will help all nations achieve the "upside of ageing." For Britain and the NHS, the time for reform is now. For the rest of the world, it isn't far off. I hope that Britain and the NHS can serve as a model of success.

Notes

1. Population Division of the Department of Economic and Social Affairs of the United Nations Secretariat, *World Population Prospects: The 2012 Revision*, online database, http://esa.un.org/unpd/wpp/index.htm.
2. Ibid.
3. Ibid.
4. Ibid.
5. OECD Health Data 2013, "How Does the United Kingdom Compare," www.oecd.org/unitedkingdom/Briefing-Note-UNITED-KINGDOM-2013.pdf.
6. Daniel Martin and Sophie Borland, "The Devastating Dossier of Needless Hospital Deaths," *Daily Mail* (London), July 17, 2013, www.questia.com/library/1G1-337095361/the-devastating-dossier-of-needless-hospital-deaths.

7. Chris Ham, "Why the NHS Is about to Be Hit by an Even Bigger Crisis," *The Telegraph*, July 19, 2013, www.telegraph.co.uk/health/10190727/Why-the -NHS-is-about-to-be-hit-by-an-even-bigger-crisis.html.

8. NHS England, "The NHS Belongs to the People: A Call to Action," www.nhs .uk/NHSEngland/thenhs/about/Documents/nhs-belongs-to-the-people -call-to-action.pdf.

9. Ibid.

10. World Health Organization, *The Top Ten Causes of Death*, Media Centre Web Page, http://who.int/mediacentre/factsheets/fs310/en/index2.html.

11. International Longevity Centre, "Non-Communicable Diseases in an Ageing World," July 7, 2011, www.ilcuk.org.uk/index.php/publications/publication_ details/non_communicable_diseases_in_an_ageing_world.

12. "World Alzheimer Report 2010, The Global Economic Impact of Dementia," www.alz.co.uk/research/files/WorldAlzheimerReport2010Executive Summary.pdf.

13. NHS England, "The NHS Belongs to the People."

14. Sarah Boseley, "Dementia Research Funding to More than Double to £66m by 2015," *The Guardian*, March 26, 2012, www.theguardian.com/society/2012/ mar/26/dementia-research-funding-to-double.

15. Oliver Childs, "Near-Doubling of UK Cancer Research Funding in Less than 10 Years," Cancer Research UK, June 29, 2011, http://scienceblog .cancerresearchuk.org/2011/06/29/near-doubling-of-uk-cancer-research -funding-in-less-than-10-years.

16. Sarah Boseley, "Dementia Research."

17. Nigel Morris, "Britain Will Use G8 to Aid Dementia Research," *The Independent*, May 15, 2013, www.independent.co.uk/life-style/health-and-families/ health-news/britain-will-use-g8-to-aid-dementia-research-8616366.html.

18. George Vradenburg, "The Global Moment for Alzheimer's: The G8 Leads," *Huffington Post*, June 17, 2013, www.huffingtonpost.com/george-vradenburg/ the-global-moment-for-alz_b_3442362.html.

19. Tim Smedley, "Are Urban Environments Best for an Ageing Population?" *The Guardian*, November 19, 2012, www.theguardian.com/sustainable-business/ blog/urban-environments-ageing-population-design.

20. World Health Organization, "WHO Global Network of Age-Friendly Cities," www.who.int/ageing/Brochure-EnglishAFC9.pdf.

21. Age-Friendly World, www.agefriendlyworld.org/afcc/united-kingdom.

22. UK Age-Friendly Cities Network, www.bjf.org.uk/age-friendly/news/uk -age-friendly-cities-network.

23. Newcastle Initiative on Changing Age, www.ncl.ac.uk/changingage/campus.

24. "Over 55 to 64 Years Olds Have Much of the Country's Wealth Says Audley Retirement," *Mindful Money*, April 18, 2013, www.mindfulmoney.co.uk/ retirement-planning/over-55-to-64-year-olds-have-most-of-the-countrys -wealth-says-audley-retirement.

25. Brian Groom, "Business Pleas on Retirement Age Ignored," *Financial Times*, January 13, 2011, www.ft.com/intl/cms/s/0/85fed034-1f4d-11e0-8c1c -00144feab49a.html?siteedition=uk#axzz2e3LjwiJI.

26. Brian Groom, "Ageism More Widespread than Sexism," *Financial Times*, March 31, 2013, www.ft.com/intl/cms/s/0/8a17e304-97d7-11e2-97e0 -00144feabdc0.html?siteedition=intl#axzz2e3LjwiJI.

27. Ibid.

28. International Longevity Centre, "Ageism and Age Discrimination: Some Analytical Issues," August 19, 2010, www.ilcuk.org.uk/index.php/publications/ publication_details/ageism_and_age_discrimination_some_analytical_issues.

29. European Social Survey, "Experience and Expressions of Ageism," www .europeansocialsurvey.org/images/downloads/Dec2012/Experiences%20 and%20Expressions%20of%20Ageism%20-%20Topline%20Results%20(UK) %20from%20Round%204%20of%20the%20ESS_FOR%20WEBSITE.pdf.

30. Center for Retirement Research at Boston College, "The Impact of Population Ageing and Delayed Retirement on Workforce Productivity," May 2013, http://crr.bc.edu/wp-content/uploads/2013/05/wp_2013-111.pdf.

31. Michael W. Hodin and Mark Hoffman, "Snowbirds and Water Coolers: How Ageing Populations Can Drive Economic Growth," *SAIS Review of International Affairs*, Summer-Fall 2011, http://muse.jhu.edu/login?auth=0&type=summary&url=/ journals/sais_review/v031/31.2.hodin.html.

32. Institute of Economic Affairs, "Retirement Causes a Major Decline in Physical and Mental Health, New Research Finds," May 16, 2013, www.iea.org.uk/in -the-media/press-release/retirement-causes-a-major-decline-in-physical -and-mental-health-new-resea.

Chapter 14

Financial Security: Longevity Changes Everything

Dan Houston
President—Retirement, Insurance and Financial Services, the Principal Financial Group

Today's worker, armed with the right savings vehicles, sound guidance, and self-discipline, can ensure that aging is a time of fulfillment, as opposed to a time fraught with financial stress.

The two most defining moments for me both occurred before my twenty-second birthday. I had already convinced Joanie, the love of my life, to marry me, a union that happily stands more than 30 years later.

In graduating with four job offers, I was doubly fortunate, and my career decision ultimately came from the heart as well. I joined a company with a mission I could embrace—to help growing businesses and their employees achieve financial security and success.

The author thanks Jeff Rader for his writing and research.

The job, with the Principal Financial Group, quickly became a cause for me—my life's work. I soon learned that today's worker, armed with the right savings vehicles, sound guidance, and self-discipline, can ensure that aging is a time of fulfillment, as opposed to a time fraught with financial stress. Today's aging generation has more choices than ever before about how to spend the years traditionally categorized as "retirement." Ensuring the financial well-being of this older population will not only benefit its individuals, but the economy and the country as a whole.

Over the years, I've spoken with literally thousands of plan sponsors and financial advisors about financial security, and I have advocated before the U.S. Senate on retirement savings and the importance of workforce education.

I've concluded that much remains to be done to ensure the nation's aging population is financially independent. We can do more to help workers prepare for postemployment life, and working with policymakers and the industry, we can take their financial security to a new level.

This process will not just benefit retirees—there is tremendous, proven upside for all stakeholders in stepping forward to drive financial readiness for the years after age 50.

The reward for aging adults is most obvious—they gain financial independence. For employers who assist employees by providing savings plans, it goes beyond attracting and retaining employees. They achieve meaningful improvements in employee productivity and reduced costs.

For financial advisors, retirement plan service providers, and asset managers, major opportunities exist to increase assets under management and revenue: Today's pre-retirees have financial assets of almost $7 trillion, the LIMRA Retirement Study estimates. The number of workers in their peak savings years is projected to increase by as much as 36 percent by 2023.[1]

Further, beyond the aging baby boom generation, 80 million millennials will need to save at higher rates than previous generations, making retirement savings a strong growth market for the foreseeable future.

Finally, for policymakers, improving the financial security for older people helps ensure that the United States remains a model for the world in creating and operating effective retirement systems.

The New Retirement

The mind-set around retirement is evolving—I'd contend for the better—with longer life spans playing a key role. Couples age 65 now have a 45 percent chance that at least one will live to age 90, according to the Society of Actuaries.[2]

Far from slowing down, many are using this longevity to pursue activities that enrich their own lives and inspire the rest of us—from the man who marked his eightieth birthday by participating in the Race Across America, to the woman who at age 71 convened a small knitting group that has donated thousands of winter scarves to needy children.

The "retirement" years have become a new phase—an age of exploration and discovery. A time for new studies and passions. A time to find new ways to be active and engaged, and make positive, meaningful contributions to society.

In 2012, 20 million seniors volunteered nearly 3 billion hours of time, which the Corporation for National and Community Service valued at $67 billion.[3] And many are pursuing new careers. MIT Technology Review reported in 2012 that twice as many founders of successful U.S. technology businesses were over 50 as were under 25.[4]

In hundreds of conversations every day with individuals in or nearing this next phase, our employees at The Principal hear many uplifting stories about how people use the time that was so scarce when they were working and raising a family.

Due to increases in life expectancy, this may be the first time in history where someone spends more years in retirement than in a traditional working career. Still, living 20, 30, even 40 years in this new phase of life comes with a substantial cost—one that has to be funded. It's an increasingly challenging prospect given inflation, the high cost of health care, and the risk of outliving savings.

Off Track

For all the people who have built the financial means to pursue their dreams in their older age, a strong body of research and experience points to a harsh reality—too many are not living within their means, thinking about their financial futures, or embracing the notion of self-sufficiency. Too few are making savings a priority.

In the United States, just a quarter of pre-retirees rate themselves as very prepared for retirement, according to the LIMRA Retirement Study (2012), *The Pre-Retiree Market: Surveying the Landscape*.[5]

Fewer than 4 in 10 pre-retiree households (age 55 to 70 and not yet retired) have financial assets of at least $100,000, an amount that would generate guaranteed lifetime income of just $400 or so per month. Among problems revealed by LIMRA's findings are that pre-retirees and workers:

- **Think they need less income in later life than recommended**—under-estimating, on average, by 16 percent. For most workers, saving 15 percent a year (including any employer contribution), along with Social Security benefits, will replace 85 percent or more of preretirement income, enabling people to maintain their lifestyles in retirement.

- **Anticipate needing to withdraw assets to cover basic living expenses at unsustainable rates**—at 9 percent on average, that rate will deplete assets in less than 13 years (4 percent is the recommended rate).

- **Underestimate unreimbursed health care costs in retirement**—it will cost around $250,000 for a moderately healthy retired couple to cover unreimbursed health care expenses and premiums throughout an average retirement.[6]

- **Overestimate their ability to work for income in retirement**—more than two-thirds of workers expect to be able to supplement income by working in retirement. By contrast, just one in five retirees actually works, a statistic that reflects availability of work, as well as ability to work.

- **Do not focus on planning, and their older years are not a top priority**—just 2 percent of workers identify saving or planning for retirement as their most pressing issue.

- **Are in debt**—55 percent of workers (and 39 percent of retirees) report having a problem with their level of debt.

- **Are not saving for their later years or are not saving enough**—43 percent of workers report neither they nor their spouse currently is saving for the future, and 57 percent report less than $25,000 as the total value of their household's savings and investments.

Thus, it was unsurprising that EBRI found just one in eight workers very confident about having enough money to live comfortably in later years, and only a minority very confident about having enough money to cover key expenses. These studies clearly demonstrate that to benefit from the upside of aging, workers need help with planning and implementing financial strategies.

A Foundation for Success

The challenge is significant, but not insurmountable. A lot of good work already is in progress, and each of the stakeholders—workers, employers, financial advisors, retirement plan service providers, asset managers, and policymakers—can act to fix this very fixable problem.

I believe that over the next 20 years, we can get 90 percent of workers on track to replace 85 percent of preretirement income. Without qualification, the defined contribution (DC) system gives us the foundation necessary for this success. DC provides a vehicle for employees to save, as well as for the employer to set aside a certain amount (or percent) of money for the employee.

This DC system already is the key driver of nearly $3 trillion in retirement accounts for pre-retirees, LIMRA finds. Today's aging Americans have amassed retirement assets in record amounts, with the average per household up nearly six-fold since 1975.[7] Meanwhile poverty among older people has fallen from nearly 30 percent in 1966, to 9 percent in 2011.[8] While that's still too many poor people, and those living in near-poverty add to the travesty, the numbers indicate we are moving in the right direction.

If DC has been so successful, why are so many workers so under-saved? I'd offer several complicating factors: First, only half of private-sector employees have access to an employer-sponsored retirement benefit, according to the National Institute on Retirement Security.[9]

Additionally, while we have moved into the era of personal responsibility, too many workers lack needed discipline and have failed to prioritize financial security.

Businesses complicate the issue because too many of them view the retirement benefit as a cost, not an investment. So they don't encourage employee participation or urge them to save at higher rates. A vocal minority mourns the shift to defined contribution from the old defined-benefit (DB) pension system. They've ignored DC's successes, and overstated the historical breadth of DB coverage and level of income replacement.

The Way Forward

In general, the industry can deliver retirement solutions through incremental innovation, particularly in plan design, enrollment, delivery of guidance/advice, and investment portfolio construction.

Importantly, we have a vast body of research and data—from EBRI's work on retirement confidence and LIMRA's focus on pre-retirees, to insights from the Plan Sponsor Council of America and the Investment Company Institute, not to mention our own professional experience. The Retirement Ecosystem graph, Figure 14.1, depicts each of the stakeholders in retirement readiness.

Figure 14.1   The Retirement Ecosystem

Worker Call to Action

The responsibility for funding and decision making around financial security continues to shift to individuals. As they consider options for their lives after age 50, workers first must get up to speed on the basics: the importance of starting early and the power of compounded growth. For example:

Mary at age 25 puts $2,500 a year in an IRA for 10 years, then makes no additional contributions. John at age 35 starts an IRA, saving $2,500 a year for the next 20 years. When both are 65, Mary has more than $270,000, 30 percent higher than John, assuming a 7 percent annual rate of return per year, despite making just half of John's total contribution.

Workers also must embrace the retirement savings opportunities offered by their employers. Although these options remain unavailable to many, our experience showed that nearly 40 percent of 3.7 million people eligible to participate were not taking advantage of their retirement benefit.[10]

Workers fall short as well when it comes to planning. People plan for vacations and careers, even for death—half of U.S. adults with children have a will.[11] But planning for transitions, retirement, or other activities in their later years is clearly another story. Among those 55 or older, LIMRA found only one in seven had a formal written financial plan, and that the majority had failed to accomplish even the most basic postemployment planning activities.

Unfortunately, even when retirement plans offer advice to employees—6 in 10 plans do so—only 19 percent of eligible participants take advantage of that resource, according to the Plan Sponsor Council of America.[12]

Financial security isn't just about saving for retirement, but involves comprehensive financial planning for competing demands on household finances at different stages of life—paying off student loans and credit card debt, building a rainy day fund, buying a house, building a college fund, saving for retirement or new ventures in later years, and constructing an investment portfolio that an older person won't outlive.

Some basic, uncomplicated approaches will help people increase their savings and ensure more comfortable years later in life. People first need to curb their passion to spend and develop a passion to save. Americasaves.org was one of 94 million hits when I searched the Internet for "easy ways to save." Under "saving tips," 54 suggestions pop up, most of them relatively painless ways to save up to several hundred dollars a year.

Attention to personal health also is an area that provides tangible benefits, something people often fail to understand. Wellness unquestionably helps lower health care spending out of pocket. For example: A diabetic spends $2.30 for every dollar a healthy individual spends;[13] and obesity results in 40-percent higher medical costs and 80-percent higher prescription drug costs.[14]

Smoking is just plain costly: A pack-a-day smoker who quits could save more than $71,000 over 20 years.[15]

People should think and act as long-term investors, which means having the discipline to stay the course despite market volatility. There is far too much unnecessary "leakage" from retirement plans. For instance, nearly a third of participants dipped into savings to pay for basic expenses.[16]

Employer Call to Action

In an environment where businesses face both local and global competition, it makes sense for employers to cut costs. One result has been the decline of defined benefit plans, another the rise of voluntary benefits.

However, some employers focus only on costs without considering the associated financial upside of providing employee benefits. Some realize that wellness improves worker productivity. But what they may not recognize is the negative impact of financial stress on the productivity of their employees and thus the company's balance sheets. A couple of relevant statistics:

- For every dollar an employer spends on a wellness program, the company saves $3.27 in medical costs, plus $2.73 through lower absenteeism costs.[17]
- A 2010 Federal Reserve study found that employee financial stress costs employers an average of $5,000 per employee per year in lost productivity.[18]

Encouragingly, employers increasingly measure plan success by their workers' "retirement readiness," instead of traditional yardsticks like participation rates. The new endgame needs to be helping workers achieve a sufficient retirement income-replacement ratio. Employers should provide access to retirement planning tools, offer one-on-one assistance at the worksite, and encourage employees to maximize savings by providing a meaningful matching contribution.

Advisor Call to Action

In financial planning, we need more holistic approaches that help people sort out competing demands on limited resources: Do I pay off credit card debt or contribute to my 401(k) account? If I pay off $1,000 of credit card debt (15 percent interest), I eliminate the liability and the interest charge, increasing my cash flow by $150 over the next year. At a 20 percent tax rate, I could instead put $1,250 into my 401(k) account, reducing my take home pay by that same $1,000.

Assuming a 50-percent employer matching contribution, or $625, my $401(k) account reaches $1,875, excluding any asset appreciation. I'd still have the credit card debt and the additional interest expense. But my net worth is $725 higher, primarily because the employer matching contribution exceeded the interest on my debt.

Holistic planning also contemplates risks that can derail financial security. Perhaps the most shocking result coming out of EBRI's 2013 Retirement Confidence Survey was that only half of workers and retirees said they could come up with $2,000 if an unexpected need arose in the next month.

Sixty-nine percent of the private sector work force has no long-term disability insurance,[19] and in terms of life insurance, more than three-quarters of adults are either uninsured or underinsured.[20] So I'd challenge advisors to push workers toward building an emergency fund, as well as acquiring life and disability income insurance.

Advisors also should incorporate business-owner succession strategies. For the many Americans who own businesses, this ownership often represents their largest asset, totaling more than $4 trillion in value for pre-retirees overall, according to LIMRA.

Employee stock ownership plans, or ESOPs, are a way for business owners to sell some or all of their companies. The owner sells the business to an ESOP trust, which is a qualified retirement plan primarily invested in company stock. Over time, the business makes retirement plan contributions to the ESOP, and as the ESOP repays the loan it used to acquire the company, shares are allocated to employees. Looking at our own data,[21] participants in ESOPs have an average 6.7 percent in 401(k) contributions, and an additional 11.9 percent in ESOP contributions for a total of 18.6 percent—2.7 times what the average 401(k)-only participant (6.8 percent) is setting aside.

While a consensus is elusive, most industry studies recommend replacing 80 to 90 percent of preretirement income. Employees generally need to save between 11 and 15 percent per year to accomplish this.

Although ESOPs don't tend to work for companies with fewer than 30 employees or without strong cash flows, it is an ideal option for some business owner clients.

Lastly, advisors need to be experts in retirement income planning and implementation—with a focus on helping seniors create a sustainable stream of retirement income through product allocation, investment portfolio construction, and advice on maximizing sources of guaranteed income such as Social Security.

Retirement Plan Service Provider Call to Action

Between the financial crisis and the aging of the baby boomers, the industry has done a lot of soul searching, coming to an important conclusion: We need to move from delivering good retirement plans to delivering best-in-class retirement programs—programs that influence better savings behaviors, and drive better outcomes for workers not only in the accumulation phase, but also in the decumulation phase. My challenge to the industry is four-fold:

Streamline Enrollment—Companies and their employees don't want long meetings or content-heavy brochures and forms. They want simple, understandable, and streamlined, with emphasis on key points like recommended savings rates for retirement and the impact of savings on take-home pay.

Improve Plan Design—Thanks to the Pension Protection Act of 2006 (PPA), and its automatic-enrollment provision, defined contribution (DC) is better positioned than ever to get the nation's aging demographic on track for savings. But while nearly half of plans have auto enrollment, just one in nine of those has a default rate of 6 percent or higher, just 1 in 12 applies to all nonparticipants, not just new hires, and just 4 in 10 have adopted automatic escalation.

Clearly, both plan providers and advisors need to push plan design that utilizes "auto" features in a more optimal way. EBRI defined success as a large enough 401(k) balance that, when combined with Social Security, provides a total real replacement rate of 80 percent.[22] Success rates for both the lowest and highest income quartiles improved 30 percentage points when:

- The maximum level of employee contributions allowed by the plan sponsor increased from 6 to 15 percent.
- Automatic annual increases occurred at 2 percent per year up to the maximum.
- The employee did not opt out of automatic escalation.

There will continue to be room for the industry to refine and improve plan design going forward. For instance, employers should structure matching contributions so workers must save at a higher rate to receive the full employer contribution (matching 25 cents on the dollar on the first 8 percent saved instead of matching dollar for dollar on the first 2 percent saved). We found that workers participating in plans that had restructured in this way could achieve 30 percent higher monthly income in retirement.

Expand use of tools and guidance—Deloitte[23] found the demand is there: that employers are seeking intuitive websites, more robust tools, and innovations like webcasts where participants can receive financial education on demand. As we study our own customer base, we continue to find that access to planning tools, including interactive online tools, and education can influence worker behavior and drive meaningfully better outcomes. Employees who used one such tool saved 39 percent more on average than those who had not used it.[24]

Deliver comprehensive, integrated retirement solutions— Retirement plan service providers can play a key role, along with advisors, in helping participants determine if they are on track to achieve their goals, and to initiate corrective actions. The providers should consider offering workers tools and resources to capture all their savings and investment accounts, so planning and guidance are based on a complete picture as opposed to a single account.

Investment Manager Call to Action

Having suffered two major market downturns since 2000, and a sustained low interest–rate environment, today's investor is right to question traditional portfolio strategies. Using the 2008 tail event (40-percent market drop) as an example, an investor earning subsequent returns of 6 percent a year would take more than eight years to fully recover. For an investor already in retirement, any significant drop is even harder to recover from.

To help retirees build resilient investment portfolios, we must rethink portfolio construction, developing new outcome-oriented products that address four key risks—inflation, market volatility, income, and longevity, as seen in Figure 14.2.

Solving for Inflation Given longer life spans, and the fact that even low inflation can erode purchasing power over time, inflation is the greatest risk facing older investors today. A dollar invested in the S&P 500 in 1971 appreciated to $2.27 at the end of 1982. Yet on an inflation-adjusted basis,

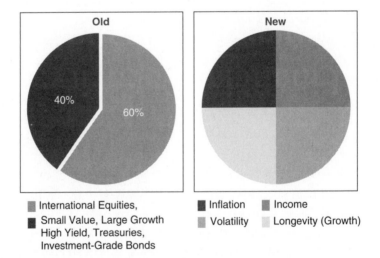

Figure 14.2 Rethinking Portfolio Construction

that dollar depreciated to 96 cents. At just 3 percent inflation, a retiree's purchasing power is halved over the course of a 25-year retirement.

Inflation risk cannot be diversified away using only traditional asset classes. Advisors and investors need to move toward real asset and real return strategies—such as Treasury Inflation-Protected Securities, commodities, Global REITs, natural resource stocks, and Master Limited Partnerships—to address the risk, and provide true diversification.

Solving for Volatility   The chances of a retiree outliving his or her assets depends not just on average annual total returns but on the pattern of returns:

Beginning portfolio value	Year 1 return	Year 2 return	Year 3 return	Average annual return	Ending portfolio value
Portfolio A—500,000	+6 percent	+11 percent	+7 percent	+8 percent	$629, 481
Portfolio B—500,000	+18 percent	-30 percent	+36 percent	+8 percent	$561,680

Alternative Strategies   Using tools such as leverage, short selling, and alternative assets can complement traditional long-only investment portfolios to achieve greater diversity of investments and minimize the impact of market volatility.

Solving for Income and Growth   With investors' potential to live 20, 30, and even 40 years in retirement, asset managers have a lot of opportunity to help seniors manage the risk of outliving their savings. Building on the industry's track record in asset allocation, for instance, we developed a fund that brings together multiple asset types and multiple asset managers to provide consistent income and address the need for capital appreciation.

Policymaker Call to Action

As mentioned, the Pension Protection Act went a long way to establish defined contribution as the vehicle for building retirement security in the United States. That said, several key challenges remain in the policy arena. I would challenge policymakers to take action to encourage businesses, especially small and medium-sized organizations, to create plans—too many still don't have plans in place for their employees.

We also need ways to help those nearing retirement save more—as an example, having the catch-up provision kick in at age 45 instead of 50. And policymakers should listen to industry concerns about changes to investment advice rules—it is critical that changes don't have the unintended consequence of making it harder for the masses to access guidance.

With much of today's inaction stemming from workers' lack of basic financial understanding, we also need to seek ways to champion financial literacy.

Finally, the policy world must fix the Social Security system—people are relying on Social Security to cover at least some portion of their income in retirement. The "insolvency" date keeps moving closer, to 2033 based on the government's May 2013 estimate, while the over-65 population is projected to more than double between 2010 and 2050.[25]

The Final Challenge

None of this is going to be easy, but if we want to change the game, we must first change some mind sets. There's too much focus on what isn't working, and not enough focus on the strong foundation and the meaningful successes. As there should be, there's a lot of focus on risk. But there's not enough focus on the reward, on the upside—the types of outcomes we can help workers achieve, if we work together, and the benefits to society of having financially secure seniors who can continue to contribute through active community involvement, entrepreneurship, and mentoring.

Notes

1. The LIMRA Retirement Study, "The Pre-Retiree Market: Surveying the Landscape," 2012.

2. Society of Actuaries, "Key Findings and Issues: Longevity," June, 2012.

3. Corporation for National and Community Service, "Senior Volunteering at a 10-Year High," press release, May 6, 2013.

4. Vivek Wadwha, "Innovation without Age Limits," *MIT Technology Review*, February 1, 2012, www.technologyreview.com/news/426760/innovation-without-age-limits.

5. The LIMRA Retirement Study, "The Pre-Retiree Market."

6. EBRI, "Funding Savings Needed for Health Expenses for Persons Eligible for Medicare," EBRI Issue Brief, December 2010.

7. Investment Company Institute, "The Success of the U.S. Retirement System," 2012,.

8. US Census Bureau, "Income, Poverty and Health Insurance Coverage in the US: 2011," issued September 2012.

9. National Institute on Retirement Security, "The Retirement Savings Crisis: Is it Worse than We Think?" June 2013.

10. The Principal Financial Group, "Total View 2011," www.nxtbook.com/nxtbooks/principal/totalview2011/#/1.

11. Daniel Bortz, "Important Things to Consider when Preparing Your Will," *US News and World Report*, http://money.usnews.com/money/personal-finance/articles/2012/09/26/important-things-to-consider-when-preparing-your-will.

12. Plan Sponsor Council of America, "55th Annual Survey of Profit Sharing and 401(k) Plans," October 2012, www.psca.org/55th_survey.

13. American Diabetes Association, "The Cost of Diabetes," www.diabetes.org/advocate/resources/cost-of-diabetes.html.

14. *Health Day News*, November 28, 2011.

15. Generated at www.women.smokefree.gov, assuming a pack of cigarettes costs $5.31, the national average according to the site as of July 30, 2013.

16. EBRI, "The 2013 Retirement Confidence Survey," Employee Benefits Research Institute, March 2013, www.ebri.org/publications/ib/index.cfm?fa=ibDisp&content_id=5175.

17. The Principal Financial Group, "Wellness = Retirement Savings," April 2012.

18. Ruisha Cian, "The Toll of Financial Stress in the Workplace," www.kiplinger.com/article/business/T020-C000-S001-the-toll-of-financial-stress-in-the-workplace.html.

19. Social Security Administration Fact Sheet, 2013, www.ssa.gov/pressoffice/factsheets/colafacts2013.htm.

20. Many Americans Misinformed About Cost of Life Insurance, *LifeHealthPro*, September 10, 2012.

21. The Principal Financial Group, "The Total View 2011," www.nxtbook.com/nxtbooks/principal/totalview2011/#/1.

22. EBRI, "Issue Brief No. 349," November 2010, www.ebri.org/pdf/briefspdf/EBRI_IB_011-2010_No349_EBRI-DCIIA.pdf.

23. Deloitte, "Annual 401(k) Benchmarking Survey, 2012 Edition," www.deloitte
.com/view/en_US/us/Services/consulting/human-capital/
c9bd901987c5e310VgnVCM1000003256f70aRCRD.htm.

24. The Principal Financial Group, "The Principal: 401k Participants Using
Online Tool Defer 39 Percent More." Press Release, February 28, 2011.

25. U.S. Census Bureau, Population Division, 2008 National Projections: Summary Tables, "Projections of the Population by Selected Age Groups and Sex
for the United States: 2010 to 2050, www.census.gov/population/projections/
data/national/2008/summarytables.html.

Chapter 15

New Transitions: A Changing Journey of Life and Health

Philip A. Pizzo

Former Dean, Stanford University School of Medicine; David and Susan Heckerman Professor of Pediatrics and of Microbiology and Immunology, Stanford University School of Medicine; Founding Director, The Stanford Distinguished Careers College

The whole issue of retirement increasingly is irrelevant, or at least less important, when we understand our lives as a continuum of interwoven threads that blend and intersect unpredictably—rather than a series of discreet stages.

The question to me was startling, and perplexing. "How do you like being retired?" It was so far from my reality that I hardly knew how to answer my friends and colleagues. True, I had just stepped down, at the end of 2012, from a 12-year tenure as dean of the Stanford University School of Medicine—a transition I had long planned and had announced publicly nearly two years earlier. In fact, when I first disclosed my transition plan, most of my colleagues anticipated that I would be leaving Stanford for another "big job." Few believed that I wasn't on my way to another position in government or in the private sector despite my proclamations that I was planning a different journey.

While I admit that I felt honored to have served as dean of a major medical school, I also felt it was important to have a planned transition—one that would foster personal and institutional rejuvenation—while my career was still "on the rise." However, I never intended to convey that I was "retiring." In fact, I have long believed that it is unwise to step away from physical and mental challenges, social networks, and the intergenerational interactions that a workplace supports and fosters. Accordingly, I had decided not only to take a full-time Stanford teaching position in pediatrics and microbiology and immunology, but I also was about to embark on an exciting new project that in itself involves career transitions.

But I was 68 years old at the time of my transition, and although I felt vibrant, fit, and engaged, it was clear from the questions I was receiving that, in the eyes of my own professional and personal community, this was when I should be thinking about "retirement." Yet retirement, at least what they seemed to envision, was never part of my plan, and as a physician, I do not think it should be part of anyone's life plan per se—at least in its traditional definition.

For today's aging demographic, the upside of aging is rooted in two important points: First, the whole issue of retirement increasingly is irrelevant, or at least less important, when we understand our lives as a continuum of interwoven threads that blend and intersect unpredictably—rather than a series of discreet stages—childhood to adolescence to adulthood; education to employment; early, mid, and later careers; full-time to part-time to retirement, cradle to grave.

Second, we have an opportunity to positively influence our own life continuums by taking action to preserve health and an overall sense of well-being. While there are many things in life that we cannot control, we can take advantage of the many opportunities to maintain a healthy and robust lifestyle, and approach each day with a sense of excitement that we will do something meaningful.

With these two ideas prominently at work in my own life, I am embarking after a 45-year career in medicine (since beginning medical school), not on a "retirement" journey but into a completely new chapter—designing a Stanford-based program that fosters a new paradigm for adult education and career transformation. It will be one dimension of a broad range of opportunities that could become available through universities and colleges in the years ahead, an effort to establish an upside and new paradigm for aging, successfully and meaningfully.

The Life Continuum

I see the life journey as less about starts and stops, or beginnings and endings, than about transitions, discoveries, and redirections. Our later years need not be a static time, but a continued life journey that is undulating and intersecting, where peaks and valleys are not pinnacles or chasms, but transition points and opportunities for creating additional knowledge and purpose.

However, we have been acculturated to believe that our career paths are linear and that beginning a new journey later in life is counter to normalcy, at least as defined to date. In a number of professions, the dominant corpus of learning and acquisition of knowledge takes place during higher education, with subsequent growth and development accrued by employment and life experiences. In others (such as medicine, law, accounting) there are requirements for "continuing education," but these programs rarely open new pathways of education or new career opportunities. This "continuing education" is primarily designed to renew and keep current one's foundational competence and to meet regulatory or license/credential requirements.

People often tend to stay closely aligned to their areas of initial preparation, although they may change jobs or focus within the confines of their professional disciplines. In many jobs, knowledge, experience, and even wisdom reach a peak after two or three decades. Burnout can occur or a person's thinking can lose its flexible and creative edge. One antidote is for people to change their knowledge specialties and focus every several years as a way of staying fresh—even if it means existing at the edge of their comfort zones.

Traditionally, however, people have tended not to take up new career directions later in life—or have a realistic opportunity to do so. Instead, they are conditioned to see one career that leads to "retirement," followed by various avocations or hobbies. I am not casting negative aspersions about hobbies but rather advocating that we make whatever we do as meaningful and socially valuable as possible for as long as possible.

In today's aging population, many people are diverging from the conventional linear model while looking for new meaning in their "senior" years. Some, like me, choose to do things that are different than the career they've so far experienced, taking up activities that allow them to continue to grow and contribute to society.

Such later-in-life transitions can be part of the unpredictable life continuum: the journey that has not followed a prescribed and consistent path, or even the trajectory for which our educational focus prepared us. For example, concentrating in philosophy in college never led to the PhD I initially contemplated, but it did enhance the analytic and ethical thinking that would later help me face challenges in human relations and in academic leadership positions. Training in both the specialties of pediatric infectious disease and hematology-oncology could have led to very different career paths individually, but combining them empowered me to become an early leader in pediatric AIDS research, something I didn't anticipate early in my training.

As well, communication skills that I developed as a pediatric oncologist, in difficult conversations about life and death with children and their parents, helped me to deal with complicated personnel issues when I later became an administrator in research institutes and universities. I have been a teacher of young physicians and scientists as well as medical students, experiences that stand me in good stead as I now plan a curriculum for college students and those interested in continued education, building it on intersections of science and medicine with history, literature, philosophy, and the arts.

These unexpected and unplanned threads of learning, knowledge, and wisdom provide connections that can link our past to the present and future.

Knowing When to Change

Ironically, my choice of pediatrics as my clinical focus was predicated on the belief that I didn't want to care for aging adults, something that flies in the face of my current focus on transitional careers and life journeys.

In fact, my early pediatrics experiences influenced my thinking about life transitions in ways I would not have anticipated.

Specifically, during my pediatrics internship at the Boston Children's Hospital in the early 1970s, I encountered two individuals whose attitudes influenced my own preparation for older adulthood. Both had been major innovators and leaders in the care of children. One had virtually created the field of pediatric surgery and the second had laid the foundation for cancer chemotherapy. Both of these luminaries were in their seventies (an age that was "older" in the early 1970s than it is today). Sadly, both lost the respect of their peers and their positions of leadership—in the case of the surgeon because he refused to stop performing surgery in children although his technical skills were waning, and in the renowned cancer leader's case because he had become rigid and constrained while his peers were creating new paths and insights.

The inability of these two trailblazers to recognize when and how they should "transition"—and how that eclipsed their admirable contributions in the minds of others—had a major impact on my life plans and journey. I resolved I would not allow that to happen to me.

By contrast, I later encountered an exceptional leader at Stanford who followed a different path as he aged. This scientist proactively closed down his lab in his early seventies, when he felt he was no longer attracting the best trainees. Instead he transitioned to the role of a senior statesman, advisor, and colleague and has remained stimulated and excited by the work he continues to do—even though it is different from that which led to his primary fame and success.

Timing a Transition

In a life continuum, transition does not have to occur in a set chronological timeframe, although to be successful it should be anticipated and planned—at least by envisioning options. It is always better for the individual to have control over her or his transition than to risk it being imposed by employers or others.

The standard of age 65 as a retirement benchmark was guided in earlier generations by expectations of longevity and eligibility for retirement programs. In reality, neither age 65 nor even the concept of "retirement" has much relevance to life and successful aging in the twenty-first century. No specific age for a career transition is readily defined, since timing depends on one's prior career pathway, satisfaction, personal finance, and many other important factors. In many career pathways, individuals in their fifties and sixties are the most likely to consider life and career transitions.

These considerations can also occur at earlier and later stages of life and work, a pattern likely to become more common in the future as life spans lengthen and the opportunities for continued personal growth and development become more available. Today, some career transitions and terminations occur because they are built into a profession, and others because they are sought or expected. Investment bankers tend to transition in their mid-fifties, for example, while other professions cap the working age due to concerns about age-related judgment, like the age 65 maximum for airline pilots.

Physicians and health care providers may encounter physical, cognitive, or other challenges that impact the ability to carry out procedures and interactions that were standard at earlier stages of the life journey—but no clear age for transition has yet been established.

Retirement requirements and norms, which differ worldwide, force many people into retirement despite their potential for additional years, or even decades, of future productivity and socially valuable activities.

At the same time, U.S. life expectancy continues to increase—as it has for the past 150 years—with the average reaching into the eighties by 2030.[1] It is not possible to put a figure on the age when human biology has run its course, but it seems plausible that children born today can expect 100 or more years of life. The U.S. population of seniors will escalate over the next decade as the baby-boom generation crosses the 65-year threshold at some 10,000 each day.

While it is true that age-related cognitive declines are inevitable, the timing at which they occur is highly variable—and can be influenced by exercising both body and mind. Even after the baby-boom generation has eclipsed, people's longer lives will necessitate fundamental changes in how we assess and address our personal and work lives after 50. We need to anticipate the upside of aging more effectively.

Longevity and health mean added years of work, relevance, and productivity. But that does not mean we should cling to old patterns that may no longer fit us. After witnessing the sad denouements of the two luminaries I had encountered at Boston Children's Hospital, I determined that when it came time for my own career transition, I would basically start over in a new field—history. Through 40 years steeped in science and medicine, I have been reading history as a preparation for enrolling in graduate school one day. Although now it appears I will take yet another path entirely, I was long comforted in the fact that I had a plan for continued rejuvenation—not an ending or "retirement" but transformation from my prior life journey. My journey has included experiences that were not discrete, age-focused opportunities, but new experiences building on one another at different trajectories.

Flexibility and adaptation are important to a life journey, as is being willing to develop new pathways and to celebrate the future instead of hanging on to the past. People often are uncomfortable with transitions and the personal and professional instability they generate. We become comfortable with who we are or have been, but uncertain of who we might be. We can become stuck in place and then lose ground. The result may be precipitous decisions, which ultimately truncate opportunities for growth and evolution. That in turn can isolate and negatively impact the prospects for healthy and meaningful transitions. When these experiences and concerns prompted me to put together a "Senior Transitions Task Force" for Stanford's School of Medicine faculty in 2006, a large number of over-50 faculty members completed a survey about their plans and expectations for career transition. Nearly a third indicated that they had done little-to-no planning about career transition, especially financial planning. While the absence of planning is not necessarily catastrophic, it does risk limiting options and opportunities.

Unfortunately, a well-delineated resource to guide senior career transitions is not available to most people. With that in mind, we set up a website with resources for medical school faculty as a nascent step.[2] We all need resources to help with life and career transitions. And along with financial security, we need to sustain social networks and health and well-being to optimize our chances for continued success.

Health Opens Options

As a physician I have long believed that a lifestyle fostering health and well-being is essential for sustaining a demanding career and a happy life. Simple things like diet and exercise can make a tremendous difference. Certainly it is both possible and desirable to continue physical exercise with aging. While performance ultimately declines with age, sustaining aerobic exercise improves cardiovascular health and is one of the most notable deterrents to dementia. And one can be happy, even thrilled, with age-corrected performance metrics that compare continued success to younger individuals.

Personally I have derived the greatest pleasure and fitness from long-distance running, which I began in my late twenties to help overcome the physical limitations of childhood asthma. Amazingly, after I broke through a fitness barrier, running seemed to make my asthma better, and I soon graduated to running marathons, which I have continued over the years. Running and fitness not only improve endurance and help reduce stress, but also can promote a general feeling of being able to meet difficult challenges in other areas of life. Put another way, physical well-being promotes emotional health and overall endurance.

Each of us needs to find our own comfort zone with exercise and wellness, but their connections are inextricable. Moreover, as our life spans lengthen, preservation of health through simple things like exercise and diet become ever more important. We are fortunate today in that information and guides to help us maintain wellness have never been more readily available. Among many resources online are:

- A 2013 report from the Centers for Disease Control entitled "The Stage of Aging and Health in America."[3]
- A set of recommendations from AARP, the American Medical Association and the CDC on "Team Up to Stay Healthy." [4]
- A report from the Merck Institute and the Gerontological Society of America on "The State of Aging and Health in America."[5]
- Resources on health aging from the National Institutes of Health.[6]
- Tips from the Mayo Clinic on healthy aging.[7]

Inevitably we all will lose aspects of our physical and even cognitive abilities. This is part of aging and something we seek to offset or delay by combining our passion and commitment to work or new projects with social networking, intergenerational interactions, financial security, physical and cognitive health recalibration, and holistic thinking.

My own rigorous running schedule of 40 to 70 miles per week for several decades became part of my life and identity. A sudden injury that I experienced underscored how a life journey can be impacted and altered in ways that are hard to control. Nearly a year of severe chronic neuropathic pain—during which I was unable to do any vigorous exercise—presented enormous challenge, resulting in deep reflection extending to clinical depression. Thankfully, with persistence and medical care I regained much of what I lost—but I no longer take that for granted.

Vulnerability to loss of physical competence and capability is also part of the aging process—and requires adaptation and resolve to overcome. The goal is to avoid the declines in physical and cognitive well-being for as long as possible. However, some of these declines inevitably will challenge some of our prior areas of life success. In medicine, for example, there comes a time when technical prowess becomes more limited or cognition impeded, making functioning as a doctor ill advised. While wisdom can supplant knowledge, many doctors have reason to limit their duration of clinical practice or to alter its scope and activities.

Of course, these losses can be devastating, especially if they haven't been replaced by alternate vocations or avocations. While I am particularly attuned to these issues in professions like medicine, they also apply to virtually every walk of life.

Contemplating Transformation

As I contemplated my own career transition, the threads and connections of my personal journey began to shape a new vision for the future where academic institutions might play a new, pivotal role quite different from that of the past. Without question, education has its longstanding foundation in preparing individuals for lifetime careers. Such preparation invariably begins in the first two to three decades of life and rarely anticipates, or even permits, second, let alone third or more, careers later in life. Many colleges and universities provide "continuing education" for the public, including opportunities for advanced degrees. However, these tend to be knowledge explorations for the joy of learning, not intended to redirect or promote new paths or vistas for people exploring different career paths, whether in a familiar or new field. Similarly, evolving online learning technologies can open new vistas for learners of all ages, but are unlikely to lead to new directions for those who are more advanced in their careers.

This combination of factors has given rise to a unique opportunity to reconsider the role of higher education for individuals who already have been successful in career pathways and who are seeking a new direction. Such directions might lead to volunteer-based opportunities or to new employment paths around the world.

To date, very few such programs exist. The relatively new Advanced Leadership Initiative at Harvard University is a notable exception. This led me to think that my own institution, Stanford University, could also play an important role in creating a new direction, an opportunity for adult education to be transformational for individuals, institutions, communities, and the world. With that in mind I designed the Stanford Distinguished Careers College in hopes of creating a model for other universities by fostering a new paradigm for adult education and career transformation. This program is best viewed as one dimension of a broad range of opportunities that could become available through universities and colleges (including community colleges) in the years ahead.

A New Kind of Sabbatical

The concept of a sabbatical leave is deeply rooted in academia, used by faculty to refresh, renew, or begin new academic journeys—in research, education, and beyond. The term comes from the Latin *sabbaticus* and can be found in the Bible (Leviticus 25) as a time to rest from work or have a hiatus that can last from months to a year.

Some businesses similarly offer a "sabbatical" to allow employees to refresh and redirect their research or work. A sabbatical can be a time of transition from one field or discipline to another, a way of opening doors and vistas to a new period of productivity and creativity.

The program at Stanford will build on that tradition in a way that highlights the ability and responsibility of accomplished leaders in the global community. The Stanford Distinguished Careers College focuses on the renewal of individuals who have already demonstrated success in one life journey, and wish to explore another career or goal—an investment well worth making given this cadre's potential to positively impact not only their own lives but also communities and society more broadly.

The program is a pilot through which participants can explore questions that I believe have profound individual and societal impacts. In helping midlife individuals transition to new life journeys, the experiment aims to foster healthy and successful aging—to increase years of well-being while compressing periods of decline and deterioration that not only impact individuals but represent an incredible economic and societal toll on our nation.

The participants will explore, develop, and prepare for new careers and life transitions—a pathway to new ventures and journeys, the very purpose of a "sabbatical." Key objectives and components include:

- A new education and training model to develop a cohort of experienced leaders who will have a transformative impact on the workplace and community, locally and globally.
- Creating ideas that could make communities and the world more livable, safer, and more environmentally sound, utilizing technology and innovation in new and simpler ways to improve life.
- Fostering a national dialogue about life transitions, healthy aging, and personal transformation.
- Deepening the knowledge of program participants, whether in their own expertise or new areas of learning, and in doing so creating something special that can advance the world.
- Intergenerational learning communities both within and outside the sabbatical program which add new perspectives and wisdom to Stanford's academic settings.
- Assessing participants' personal health and well-being and defining ways to improve health habits for a longer and more productive life.
- Assessing ways to improve and sustain cognitive skills and learning opportunities over time.
- Providing a new definition to the value and importance of higher education.

The kind of possibilities that might arise include a teacher's transition from the graduate level to the elementary level, or the policymaking arena; a physician's design of new health care delivery systems or redirection of a clinical career; or a business leader's pursuit of entrepreneurship focused on engineering and the environment, or on global health.

Developing ways to alter the life trajectory, keeping it at a higher functioning plane until biological capacity is exhausted, is a better formula for all of us. That will mean finding ways to democratize programs like those at Harvard and Stanford and extend their benefits to individuals in diverse and different communities, locally, nationally, and globally. This, too, is an opportunity.

Reaching for the Upside

By celebrating new ventures and opportunities, looking forward rather than backward, we can reach for the upside—in aging and in life. There are many forces and vehicles of discrimination that can damage our morale and sense of self. But we can choose to rise above them by staying positive, embracing opportunities for transition and change at all points of our life journeys, and pursuing the physical well-being that allows us to make the most of our opportunities. We can't reclaim the past but we can continue to reach upward to the future.

Notes

1. See Introduction, the graphic for U.S. Life Expectancy at Birth.
2. Stanford School of Medicine, "Senior Faculty Transitions," http://med.stanford.edu/academicaffairs/senior-faculty.
3. Centers for Disease Control, "The Stage of Aging and Health in America," 2013. www.cdc.gov/aging/pdf/state-aging-health-in-america-2013.pdf.
4. www.ama-assn.org/resources/doc/public-health/ama-aarp-brochure.pdf.
5. Merck Institute of Aging and Health the Gerontological Society of America, "The State of Aging and Health in Society," www.agingsociety.org/agingsociety/pdf/state_of_aging_report.pdf.
6. National Institutes of Health, "Healthy Aging," http://nihseniorhealth.gov/category/healthyaging.html.
7. Mayo Clinic, "Healthy Lifestyle, Healthy Aging," www.mayoclinic.com/health/healthy-aging/MY00374/TAB=indepth.

Chapter 16

Life Reimagined: The Second Aging Revolution

A. Barry Rand
Chief Executive Officer, AARP

We are transforming our ideas, attitudes, and practices around aging. We are seeing the emergence of a different set of expectations, and of practices, skills, and purposes, that will massively alter the landscape of life after 50 in America.

What's next? Increasingly, today's 50-and-older population is asking this question. It's a question that foretells the full range of possibilities that life has to offer as we grow older—possibilities that did not exist for earlier generations. It's also a question that reflects the spirit of optimism, hope, and indeed expectation that aging brings with it real possibilities for new and enriching opportunities. And it is a question that encourages us to reimagine our lives, to discover and fulfill our purpose. The answer to the question, "What's next?" defines a life reimagined and the upside of aging.

The story of one retired business executive tells the tale of an emerging "what's next" generation that is leading the second aging revolution and defining how our world and our lives are changing. This story dates back almost four years—but in many ways it stretches back more than 50 years, to an earlier generation.

This executive had wrapped up a rewarding 30-year career at a major corporation, followed by an intense turnaround stint as CEO at a second high-profile business, and then another demanding run as CEO of an international enterprise. Now, with financial security, it was time to live the retirement promise that evolved from the first aging revolution more than 50 years earlier: surrounded by family, free to sit on boards of directors, and unburdened by the heavy responsibilities of corporate life, he could now focus instead on lowering his golf score. It was the retirement life to which he thought he aspired.

Fulfillment, however, was elusive. Missing was a sense of engagement, the challenge of using his lifetime of leadership and experience for a larger purpose, the satisfaction of doing something that mattered in people's lives. Retirement, the goal of a generation, turned out to be an unsatisfying destination.

So, when the phone rang one day with an offer to become CEO of one of the country's most prominent social change organizations—a chance to lead a new national conversation about a whole new phase of life—he jumped at the challenge. He "un-retired" and embraced the upside of aging—a chance for life reimagined.

By now you've probably gathered that "he" is "me." The social change organization is AARP, and we are deeply immersed in the national conversation to reimagine what aging in America is all about.

Something important and deep and permanent is changing in American life—and while it has much to do with aging, it has even more to do with living. For a number of deep-seated reasons, we are transforming our ideas, attitudes, and practices around aging. We are seeing the emergence of a different set of expectations, and of practices, skills, and purposes, that will massively alter the landscape of life after 50 in America.

My own story is the story of an entire cohort of people for whom the old notion of "the golden years" no longer offers an easy fit. It envisions a whole new phase of life, a period that comes after middle age and before old age. And it is about the desire of more and more women and men to use this new phase of life as an opportunity for continued growth, development, exploration, and self-discovery.

This quest envelopes a burgeoning movement of people with the talent and the time to make a difference through all the years of their lives. Their journey is at once personal—each of us has his or her own version—and universal. Together we are all embarked on a profound, shared journey.

As important as the questions that arise from reimagining life after 50 are the answers we develop—these will ripple through all of the generations that follow. As we reimagine aging, we are reimagining the future—and we are reimagining life.

The Changes behind the Change

No one knows for certain how, why, or when our society will experience a fundamental shift, an alteration of the social seismic plates that lie beneath the surface of everyday life. This happens rarely in our society. It occurred in the 1950s and early 1960s when we created the retirement life stage. It also happened at the turn of the twentieth century with the advent of adolescence as a concept. And before that, we have to go back to the late eighteenth century with the invention of childhood as a distinct stage of life, not just a miniaturization of adulthood. These are monumental shifts in how we live our lives, and they have lasting impact. That's what we're facing now with the aging of the boomers.

A number of factors are propelling the transformation of aging in America. First, there are more of us—78 million members of the baby boom generation. Every single day, 10,000 boomers turn 65, and that will continue for the next 17 years. This is a generation that has transformed everything it has touched at every step of its life journey, from the day it arrived in public school, triggering the need for more kindergartens, to the decade-long turmoil its coming of age caused in the 1960s. Its arrival at the doors of parenthood launched a furious marketplace of new maternity, baby, and child products. And now, arriving at a new phase of life, this generation is reimagining how aging looks, feels, acts, and sounds.

Second, we are living longer and healthier. We've added more than 30 years to the average American's life since 1900 when life expectancy was 47 years. The new phase of life is not just about more years, but about more engagement with life itself. The importance of increased longevity is in the way it alters the essential experience of life. In other words, it's not only about living longer; it's about living more fully.

Third, we are working longer and more productively. For many people, of course, this decision is a necessity, not an option. But for many others, work is a conscious choice. This represents a remarkable shift from previous generations. AARP's own research shows that more than two out of every three older Americans say they plan to work past the traditional age of retirement—and of those, more than one out of three say they will keep working for enjoyment, not only for money. One in 10 says he or she wants to take the entrepreneurial path and start a business.[1] Work, for members of this generation, is about money—and engagement, connection, and the continued use of their talents and experiences.

Finally, we are living with meaning. This is a generation that has long been concerned as much with making a difference as with making a living. Finding and expressing purpose in life has been a hallmark of this generation. Now, as we get older, this search for purpose and meaning takes on more urgency and intensity. In a life journey, this generation knows, the ultimate discovery is self-discovery, and the age-old mantra, know thyself, is the first step in a life of meaning and purpose.

As we at AARP conducted our research for a new approach to aging that we call Life Reimagined, we found that more and more people are reaching traditional retirement age while realizing that they're not ready to retire. They want to do more, to contribute to society. They're not done yet. As one AARP member told us, "I haven't retired, I've just changed directions."[2] They want to explore the possibilities ahead. People are reimagining their lives, their careers, and their relationships. The one core theme that consistently emerged from our research was the idea of "finding one's purpose," or "finding one's calling" and "living a life of meaning."[3]

Any one of these new developments on its own would have been enough to signal a change in direction for aging. Taken together they amount to a huge shift in the country's attitudes and practices. The aging of the boomers is creating the second aging revolution.

The First Aging Revolution

The first aging revolution came in the 1950s and early 1960s with the emergence of a new life stage that became known as "retirement." In the years after World War II, older Americans were not a national asset—nor was retirement a desirable destination. In fact, the prolific author Lewis Mumford wrote that at no point in the history of American society had any group been so rejected as older people were then.[4]

Old age was regarded as a life in purgatory, and old people were considered a massive social problem. That plight, that nightmare, was what Dr. Ethel Percy Andrus set out to change with the support of her AARP band of "useful citizens." It all began when Dr. Andrus, a 72-year-old retired high school principal from California, found a retired schoolteacher living in a chicken coop on a measly pension. She didn't have health insurance because no one offered it to people her age. Dr. Andrus began a quest to find a company that would provide health insurance to this teacher and other older Americans. Forty-three companies turned her down before she found one that would work with her to defy conventional wisdom and create a group health insurance plan for older people. This was the birth of AARP, an organization that would become a leading advocate for policies and programs to make life better for people as they aged.

For the older Americans coming out of the Great Depression and World War II, the challenge was elemental. With lives shaped by economic hardship and physically demanding work, they were searching for security.

Events on a global scale had systematically stripped them of their confidence that life could be anything but uncertain; everything they had experienced had taught them that they could expect only struggle and hardship. Now, as they reached the end of their working lives, and, with it, the end of their income, they were staring into an already difficult future, burdened further by financial strain.

In less than half a century, aging in America underwent a fundamental transformation to make life better for people as they aged. From a life in purgatory, old age became a life secured. From a life of uncertainty, old age became "the golden years." New policies, programs, and practices produced an entirely new life experience for millions of older Americans.

Social Security began to provide people with a secure foundation for income in retirement. More employers offered workers defined pension benefit plans. In 1965, we added Medicare to ensure that older Americans would have basic health care, and Medicaid to protect and lift up the poor. The Age Discrimination in Employment Act was passed in 1967 to protect workers 40 and over from employment discrimination based on age. In this new story line, older Americans had earned, through lives of hard work, the right to a comfortable and secure retirement.

Not surprisingly, an infrastructure grew up to support and sustain these new realities. The country witnessed the birth of thriving new industries that catered to the needs of this first-ever generation of genuine retirees: Everything from housing to health and entertainment to education changed to accommodate their needs, interests, and wallets.

While it is important to recognize the fundamental transformation of individual lives and social expectations in the shift of aging from a dreaded period of life to one of dignity, we should never forget how important that struggle was—nor should we assume that for millions of Americans the struggle is over. Too many older Americans still must contend with inadequate health care, poor nutrition, inadequate housing, uncertain finances, and crushing loneliness.

For too many of our older citizens, there still is no upside of aging. For them, the answer to the question, "What is next?" is our ongoing commitment at AARP—to win for them a life secured with Social Security and Medicare, affordable health care, and livable communities—so that they can live their best lives and pursue their passions. At the same time, we recognize the fundamental shifts occurring in the social and economic structure of this country, changes that are enabling a new generation to ask the question, "What's next?" and come forward with a new answer.

Redefining the "Golden Years"

That old story line of a traditional retirement still holds true for millions of Americans. It describes what they aspire to, what they work for, and what they genuinely want for their lives after 50. But at the same time, the children of that first-ever retirement generation—the baby boomers—are writing their own story. And just as they rebelled against societal conventions in the 1960s, they are rejecting some of the assumptions the old story made about their parents' lives.

For example, more of them plan to continue working. They also see the traditional retirement years as a time of freedom to pursue interests and hobbies, and to spend time with family, and less as a time of leisure.[5] One AARP member in Denver, Colorado, summed it up well, "When I was 20, I never thought I would be able to do this much when I was 60."[6]

Told in graphic terms, that old story described the trajectory of life as a parabola, an arc that started at the bottom-left corner of a graph, advanced steadily to a midpoint, and then declined to the bottom-right of the graph.

That line implicitly conveyed only the first half of life as full of promise, when people were learning, growing, and developing. For the first 50 years or so, our lives were full of opportunities and responsibilities—from growing a family to advancing a career.

But after 50, according to that old chart, life began a gradual and inexorable decline. The line went down. People's lives went down. And for this new 50-plus generation, that declining line poses both a threat and a challenge. It suggests that there is nothing to be done other than to accept decline. While that may not be the only way to interpret that old trajectory, it is an interpretation that this generation does not accept. Nor does it match their real life experiences.

Through the eyes of the baby boomer generation, that decline, those "golden years," is not the desired destination. The goal is not as passive as a well-earned retirement. Instead, given the gift of longer life, better health, greater engagement, and more possibilities, the 50-plus generation of today holds new and very different ideals—a story of life reimagined, as well as life secured.

A new chart accompanies their aspirations, this time with an arc that begins in the lower-left corner and rises to the center point. But instead of heading back down, it dips briefly—an acknowledgment that age does bring changes, both physical and mental—before heading back up. Then, this new trajectory of life levels off and extends forward for those extra years that we have come to expect. This trajectory represents the transformation of aging.

If the dramatic revolution that delivered a secure life to that previous generation was the first great transformation of aging, this current revolution that is bringing us life reimagined is the second great transformation.

Just as that first revolution brought with it an entire system of policies, programs, and practices—as well as an economic and social infrastructure to make it possible—so will this second revolution engender its own framework to respond to a generation that is demanding the promise of life reimagined. And just as the first aging revolution brought society a new life stage called retirement, this second aging revolution brings with it a new life stage we at AARP call the Age of Possibilities.

Reimagining Life

When Matt Thornhill and John Martin, founders of the Boomer Project and authors of *Boomer Consumer*, asked boomers what period of their lives was their personal best, they were surprised that many said they had not reached their peak. Many boomers are still looking forward at things they want to do and accomplish. They believe the best years of their lives are still ahead.[7]

In a way, that defines the Age of Possibilities. Because of increased longevity and relatively good health, many people 50 and older have opportunities their parents never had—to find and fulfill their purpose in life, make the world a better place, and live lives their parents could only dream of.

And, if our research at AARP is any indication, they are doing it. More and more people are choosing to remain in the workforce longer, or to return to work in some capacity after having retired. For some this is a choice—for others a necessity. A report in 2010 by *Bloomberg News* found that U.S. employees old enough to retire now outnumber teenagers in the workforce for the first time since 1948.[8] According to our own research, almost half of all employees ages 45 to 50 envision working into their seventies and beyond.[9] Moreover, since 1995, the 50-plus age group has been the fastest-growing segment of the population with home-based businesses.

People 50 and over are the new consumer-spending majority. They account for at least half the sales of women's apparel, appliances, housing, groceries, take-out food, entertainment, health insurance, and new cars and trucks. They buy three-fourths of all prescription drugs and about half of over-the-counter medications. They also purchase one-quarter of all toys and account for the dramatic increase in the rate at which people join health clubs.[10]

As people aged 50-plus explore new possibilities, they want to experience life to the fullest, so it's not surprising that travel is high on the list. People in their fifties took nearly twice as many leisure trips in 2009 as they did in 2001. Those in their seventies, while increasing their number of trips less dramatically, traveled more miles when they left home.[11]

These statistics only begin to scratch the surface of how boomers are changing the culture of aging. But one thing is clear from our ongoing research: For the past two decades we have seen the emergence of a positive, optimistic, and forward-looking generation that doesn't see itself as old, and it is looking for ways to define and experience the upside of aging.

Boomers created this new "age of possibilities" because they reject the notion that their possibilities are shrinking as they get older. They want to use their years of experience not to "wind down," but to reach even higher.

People are reimagining their lives. They are applying their life experiences to carve out new paths, taking action to overcome fears and achieve their aspirations, and building a greater sense of community. They're looking for new purpose—a cause or passion. They're developing new skills, learning and discovering, and finding new interests and pastimes. Many are seeking new jobs, often in disciplines new to them. There's the truck driver who fell in love with Zumba aerobics while working on his own fitness and became a full-time Zumba class instructor; the 30-year postal worker who had a passion for photography and is now a world-class photojournalist; the successful tax attorney who wanted to give back and became a full-time volunteer firefighter.

This generation is blazing a new trail. As the first aging population to grapple with the meaning of this new phase of life, they must find a set of practices to help discover the way forward, recognizing that each individual's life is an experiment of one. Each person gets to explore his or her own life-reimagined journey; and at the same time, none of us should have to go it alone as we embark on this transformational adventure. But until now, no courses have offered the essential life skills for this twenty-first-century transformation: how to live longer and healthier, with more purpose, choice, curiosity, and courage.

AARP created its Life Reimagined strategy to help people turn their goals and dreams into real possibilities. Growing older is no longer just about "retirement," but about reimagining possibilities and pursuing rewarding experiences for a richer and more fulfilling life.

Even more fundamental and profound is a shift from the old story about aging to the new story about living, a focus on growing whole instead of growing old. Instead of accepting decline, Life Reimagined celebrates discovery. The goal of retiring is supplanted by an explicit goal of reimagining an engaged and personally fulfilling life. In this shift, people can replace what I think of as the "D-words" of aging—decline, dementia, dependency, disease, and disability—with the "C-words"—choice, connectedness, curiosity, courage, caring, compassion, creativity, and contribution. That transition to a new mindset embodies the upside of aging.

It matches the spirit of a generation of men and women who are determined to live their lives on their own terms, to the fullest. But while the aspiration is clear, the challenge of finding the way forward—of actually diverging from long-held assumptions—still stymies many people.

To reimagine life at any age requires a contemplative series of actions that can help answer the defining question: "What's next?" Today, we are at a "what's next" moment, both as individuals and as a society. Whether it's about work or money, relationships or health, people across the country are asking, "What's next?"

What's next for our society when America for 50 years has considered retirement the destination, and now that isn't the only option, or, for many, even the best option?

What's next for parents who have raised their families and now find themselves empty nesters, for those leaving long-held jobs after reaching retirement age, for long-married people who are newly single, for parents who are in the midst of rearing their children and find they must now also care for their aging parents?

The Life Reimagined strategy was developed to help people answer these life-changing questions. Designed for the millions of people who are seeking inspiration, information, and guidance, it offers a philosophy and a map to help guide them through this powerful transition, from an approach to aging that emphasized security to one that emphasizes possibilities. It involves a series of self-directed steps for people, beginning with reflection on what they want out of the next phase of life. Once they have focused on goals and priorities, the Life Reimagined philosophy encourages them to seek counsel from trusted friends, explore and evaluate different options, and, importantly before taking action, to consider what they need to discard emotionally and physically to enable them to move forward.

This structure's value is in its concreteness and its reality-tested approach to personal growth, development, and fulfillment. It is also a methodology for connecting to others and building a broad community of committed people.

Life Reimagined is the cornerstone of the second aging revolution, especially for today's generation of aging Americans who seek something other than the retirement experience that grew from the first aging revolution, and for those seeking to answer to the "what's next" question. There is no one-size-fits-all solution. We are mapping this new territory as we explore it, writing the new story for a new generation, a story that is comprised of millions of individual stories—like my own. As we create the upside of aging, what we are doing today will gradually but inevitably transform not only how we age in America, but more broadly and more importantly, how we live in America, today and in the future.

What Is Next?

Looking back at the last 50 years of aging in America, it is important to recognize the basic transformation of individual lives and social expectations that resulted in the first aging revolution. At the same time, we need to recognize the fundamental shifts that are emerging in the social and economic structure of this country, and that are driving the second aging revolution and enabling a new generation to find promising, rewarding answers when they ask, "What's next?"

For the new generation of aging Americans, the promise of life reimagined is fresh and powerful. It refutes the idea that life after 50 is about decline. It contends, instead, that this period, like life before 50, is what each of us makes of it. It argues that, equipped with essential life skills, and acting with choice, curiosity, and courage, each of us can explore new possibilities and chart new adventures.

And finally, we can build a movement that takes aging in America in a new and better direction—from simply growing older to growing more whole and ultimately, to growing more wise, more fulfilled, and more connected to each other, creating a society where all people can age with independence, dignity, and purpose. The goal, after all, is not just to add years to our lives, but more importantly, to add life to our years.

Notes

1. AARP, "Staying Ahead of the Curve 2013: Snapshot of the Wants and Needs of Older Workers," May 2013, www.aarp.org/content/dam/aarp/research/surveys_statistics/econ/2013/Staying-Ahead-of-the-Curve-2013-Snapshot-of-the-Wants-and-Needs-of-Older-Workers-AARP-rsa-econ.pdf.
2. AARP, "Relevance and the New Reality: Insights, Strategy, and Language for AARP and Life Reimagined," July 2012.
3. Ibid.
4. Lewis Mumford, *The City in History: Its Origins, Its Transformations, and Its Prospects* (New York: Harcourt Brace Jovanovich, 1961).
5. AARP and GFK Custom Research North America, "Baby Boomers Envision What's Next," June 2011, assets.aarp.org/rgcenter/general/boomers-envision -retirement-2011.pdf.
6. AARP, "Relevance and the New Reality."
7. Matt Thornhill and John Martin, *Boomer Consumer* (Jacksonville, FL: Linx Books, 2007).
8. Andrew Cinko, Michael McDonough, and Courtney Schlisserman, "Workers over 65 Vie with Teens in Labor Market for the First Time Since Truman," *Bloomberg News,* July 13, 2010.
9. AARP, "Staying Ahead of the Curve 2013."
10. Bill Novelli, *50+ Igniting a Revolution to Reinvent America* (New York: St. Martin's Press, 2006), 145.
11. Nancy McGuckin and Jana Lynott, *Impact of Baby Boomers on U.S. Travel, 1969 to 2009,* AARP Public Policy Institute, Insight on the Issues 70, October, 2012, www.aarp.org/content/dam/aarp/research/public_policy_institute/liv_com/2012/impact-baby-boomers-travel-1969-2009-AARP-ppi-liv-com.pdf.

I have taken a moment here to rest, to steal a view of the glorious vista that surrounds me, to look back on the distance I have come. But I can rest only for a moment for with freedom comes responsibilities, and I dare not linger, for my long walk is not yet ended.

—Nelson Mandela

About the Editor

Paul H. Irving is president and a member of the board of the Milken Institute. In addition to executive management, Irving leads initiatives to improve aging lives across America and the world, expand global capital access, and enhance philanthropic impact. Under his leadership, the institute produced the widely acknowledged *Best Cities for Successful Aging* index. He speaks frequently on aging, philanthropy, and leadership, and his work has been featured by news outlets including *PBS NewsHour*, *Forbes*, CNN, the *Wall Street Journal* and *USA Today*. Irving sits on the boards of East West Bancorp, Encore.org, and Operation Hope; the dean's council of The George Washington University School of Public Health; the board of counselors of the USC Davis School of Gerontology; and the national advisory board on aging of Partners for Livable Communities. Previously, he was an advanced leadership fellow at Harvard University and chairman, CEO, managing partner, and head of the financial services group of Manatt, Phelps & Phillips, LLP. Irving was recognized by *The Best Lawyers in America* for more than 10 years and named a California Super Lawyer by *Los Angeles* magazine. He attended New York University, Harvard University, and Loyola Law School, Los Angeles, where he served as an adjunct professor and received the Board of Governors Award for outstanding contributions to society and the law.

About the Authors

Laura L. Carstensen is the founding director of the Stanford Center on Longevity, which explores innovative ways to solve the problems of people over 50 and improve the well-being of people of all ages. She is a professor of psychology and the Fairleigh S. Dickinson Jr. professor in public policy at Stanford University. Best known in academia for socioemotional selectivity theory, a life-span theory of motivation, Carstensen has published more than 100 articles on life-span development with her students and colleagues. She is the author of *A Long Bright Future: Happiness, Health, and Financial Security in an Age of Increased Longevity* (2011). She has chaired two studies for the National Academy of Sciences, resulting in the noted reports "The Aging Mind" and "When I'm 64." A fellow in the Association for Psychological Science, the American Psychological Association, and the Gerontological Society of America, Carstensen is also a member of the MacArthur Foundation's Research Network on an Aging Society and the National Advisory Council on Aging. She is the recipient of numerous awards, including a Guggenheim Fellowship and the Distinguished Career Award from the Gerontological Society of America. Carstensen received a BS from the University of Rochester and PhD in clinical psychology from West Virginia University.

Henry Cisneros, the former U.S. Secretary of Housing and Urban Development and former mayor of San Antonio, Texas, is executive chairman of CityView, which works with urban homebuilders to create affordable dwellings. As President Clinton's HUD secretary, Cisneros initiated the revitalization of public housing developments and formulated policies that contributed to record U.S. homeownership rates. During three terms as a San Antonio councilman and four as mayor, he helped rebuild the city's economic base through massive infrastructure and downtown improvements. In the private sector, Cisneros formed Cisneros Asset Management and was president and chief operating officer of Univision Communications, where he is a board member. He is an officer of Habitat for Humanity International, chairman of the San Antonio Economic Development Foundation, and a member of the advisory boards of the Bill & Melinda Gates Foundation and the Broad Foundation. Cisneros is an author or editor of several books, including *Independent for Life: Homes and Neighborhoods for an Aging America*; *Interwoven Destinies: Cities and the Nation*; and *Opportunity and Progress: A Bipartisan Platform for National Housing Policy* with former HUD Secretary Jack Kemp. He holds a BA and a master's degree in urban and regional planning from Texas A&M University, an MPA from Harvard University, and a PhD in public administration from George Washington University. He served as an infantry officer in the U.S. Army.

Anusuya Chatterjee is a senior economist at the Milken Institute, specializing in issues related to health, longevity, and productivity. She is the lead author of some of the Milken Institute's highest-profile publications, including *Best Cities for Successful Aging* and *Waistlines of the World*. She is a co-author of such impactful work as *An Unhealthy America*; *Jobs for America: Investments and Policies for Economic Growth and Competitiveness*; *The Greater Philadelphia Life Sciences Cluster 2009*; and *Film Flight: Lost Production and Its Economic Impact on California*. Mainstream news outlets, including *Forbes* and the *San Diego Union Tribune*, have published Chatterjee's opinion articles, and have quoted and cited her as an expert. Chatterjee previously held a tenure track academic position at the University of Southern Indiana, worked with the New York State Office of Alcoholism and Substance Abuse Services on funded projects, and helped the Cancer Foundation of India with data collection. Chatterjee received a PhD in economics from the State

University of New York, Albany; a master's degree from the Delhi School of Economics; and a bachelor's degree from Jadavpur University in India.

Pinchas Cohen is the dean of the USC Davis School of Gerontology, executive director of the Andrus Gerontology Center at the University of Southern California, and the William and Sylvia Kugel dean's chair in gerontology. He graduated from the Technion Medical School in Israel and trained in pediatrics and endocrinology at Stanford University. Prior to joining USC, he was a professor and vice chair for research at the Mattel Children's Hospital at the University of California, Los Angeles, as well as the co-director of the UCSD/UCLA Diabetes Research Center. He previously held a faculty position at the University of Pennsylvania. His many research awards include a National Institute on Aging EUREKA Award, the Glenn Award for Research in Biological Mechanisms of Aging, and the Transformative R01 Program grant from the director of the National Institutes of Health. Cohen has published over 250 papers in scientific journals on issues including aging, Alzheimer's, growth hormone, IGF biology, and the emerging science of mitochondrial-derived peptides, which he discovered. The holder of several patents, Cohen is the co-founder of CohBar, a biotechnology company developing treatments for diseases of aging. He serves on the boards of several professional journals and societies, including the American Federation for Aging Research, and sits on multiple National Institutes of Health study sections. Cohen is president of the Growth Hormone Research Society.

Joseph F. Coughlin is founder and director of the Massachusetts Institute of Technology AgeLab. His research provides insights on how demographic change, technology, and consumer behavior will converge to shape innovations in business and government. Based in MIT's Engineering Systems Division, he teaches policy and systems innovation. He is author of BigThink.com's publication *Disruptive Demographics,* and contributes to the *Wall Street Journal*/MarketWatch RetireMentors online. *Fast Company* magazine named him among the "100 Most Creative People in Business," and the *Wall Street Journal* selected him as one of "12 pioneers inventing the future of retirement and how we will all live, work and play tomorrow." Coughlin is a Behavioral Sciences Fellow of the Gerontological Society of America and a Fellow of Switzerland's World Demographic & Ageing Forum. A former member of the White

House Conference on Aging Advisory Committee, he has served on advisory boards for British Telecom, Daimler, Fidelity Investments, the Gallup-Healthways Well-Being Index, Putnam Investments, Sanofi-Aventis, and Toyota. Coughlin has worked with the World Economic Forum, OECD, and the Council on Foreign Relations on demographic change, technology, and strategic advantage. He has been featured on leading news programs and media outlets worldwide. Before coming to MIT, he was with EG&G, a Fortune 1000 science & technology firm. Coughlin received his PhD from Boston University, his MA from Brown University, and his BA from State University of New York at Oswego.

Ken Dychtwald is president and chief executive officer of Age Wave, which guides Fortune 500 companies and government groups in developing products and services for mature adults. Dychtwald is considered a thought leader in the lifestyle, marketing, health care and workforce implications of the aging population. A psychologist, gerontologist, documentary filmmaker, and entrepreneur, he is the best-selling author of sixteen books on aging-related issues, including *A New Purpose: Redefining Money, Family, Work, Retirement and Success*. A recipient of the American Society on Aging award for outstanding national leadership on aging, Dychtwald has been called the most influential marketer to baby boomers by *American Demographics* magazine. His article in *The Harvard Business Review*, "It's Time to Retire Retirement," received the McKinsey Award. Dychtwald was a keynote presenter at the 1995 and 2005 White House Conferences on Aging. His far-reaching forecasts and ideas are regularly featured in leading media worldwide. He is a visiting faculty member at Singularity University NASA's Ames Research Center campus and serves as a senior advisor to the G100. He is a trustee of the American Society on Aging, the Alliance for Aging Research, and USAgainstAlzheimer's. Dychtwald received his PhD in psychology from Union Institute.

Marc Freedman is the founder and chief executive officer of Encore.org, a nonprofit organization promoting encore careers. Freedman spearheaded the creation of Experience Corps (now AARP Experience Corps), which mobilizes Americans over 55 to improve the education of low-income children, and The Purpose Prize, an annual $100,000 award for social innovators in the second half of life. Freedman is the author of four books: *The Big Shift: Navigating the New Stage Beyond Midlife*;

Encore: Finding Work that Matters in the Second Half of Life; Prime Time: How Baby Boomers Will Revolutionize Retirement and Transform America; and *The Kindness of Strangers.* Widely published and quoted in the national media, Freedman is a member of the *Wall Street Journal* group "The Experts." His many honors include an Ashoka senior fellowship. Freedman was named one of the nation's leading social entrepreneurs by *Fast Company* magazine, one of the 50 most influential individuals in the nonprofit sector in 2010 by the *NonProfit Times*, and one of "The Influentials" in 2012 by *AARP The Magazine.* Freedman and Encore.org (then known as Civic Ventures) also received the 2010 Skoll Award for Social Entrepreneurship. A graduate of Swarthmore College, Freedman has an M.B.A. from Yale University and was a visiting research fellow of King's College London.

Sally Greengross is an independent member of the U.K. House of Lords and chief executive of the U.K. International Longevity Center. An expert in the field of social care and an advocate for the interests of older people, Baroness Greengross chairs or co-chairs five all-party parliamentary groups: Dementia, Corporate Responsibility, Intergenerational Futures, Continence Care, and Ageing and Older People. She is the vice chair of the all-party parliamentary group on Choice at the End of Life and treasurer of the all-party parliamentary group on Equalities. Greengross is also co-president of the International Longevity Center Global Alliance, which helps societies address longevity and aging. Previously Greengross served as director general of Age Concern England, joint chair of the Age Concern Institute of Gerontology at King's College London, and secretary general of Eurolink Age. Greengross is chair of the advisory groups for the English Longitudinal Study on Ageing and for the New Dynamics of Ageing. She is president of the Pensions Policy Institute and honorary vice president of the Royal Society for the Promotion of Health. She holds honorary doctorates from eight U.K. universities.

Jody Heymann is the dean of the Fielding School of Public Health at the University of California, Los Angeles. An internationally renowned researcher on health and social policy, she is founding director of the World Policy Analysis Center, the first global initiative to examine health and social policy in all 193 U.N. nations. In addition to her award-winning global social policy research, Heymann led seminal studies on HIV transmission via breast milk in Africa, HIV/AIDS and tuberculosis in

Africa, and how labor conditions impact the health and welfare of families. Previously Heymann was a Canada research chair in global health and social policy at McGill University, where she was the founding director of the Institute for Health and Social Policy. While on the faculty at Harvard Medical School and the Harvard School of Public Health, she founded the Project on Global Working Families. Heymann has authored and edited more than 200 publications, including 16 books, most recently *Changing Children's Chances*; *Making Equal Rights Real, Lessons in Educational Equality*; and *Protecting Childhood in the AIDS Pandemic.* Heymann was elected to the national Institute of Medicine in 2013 and the Canadian Academy of Health Sciences in 2012. Her findings have been featured by leading TV and print news outlets. She received her PhD in public policy from the Harvard University Graduate School of Arts and Sciences, and her MD from Harvard Medical School.

Michael W. Hodin is executive director of the Global Coalition on Aging and a managing partner at High Lantern Group. Previously Hodin was a senior executive for 30 years at Pfizer Inc., leading the company's international public affairs and public policy operations. From 1976 to 1980, Hodin was a legislative assistant to Senator Daniel Patrick Moynihan and a Brookings Institution visiting scholar on U.S. foreign economic policy. A fellow at Oxford University's Harris Manchester College, Hodin is a member of the Council on Foreign Relations. He sits on the boards of the American Society on Aging, the Foreign Policy Association, the Business Council for International Understanding, the New York Blood Center, the American Skin Association, Harris Manchester College, Emigrant Savings Bank, and Partners for a Livable Community's Aging in Place Advisory Council. He also sits on the World Economic Forum's Global Agenda Council on Ageing. Hodin is a featured blogger for the *Huffington Post* and the *Fiscal Times'* Age & Reason blog. He holds a BA from Cornell University, an MSc in international relations from the London School of Economics and political science, and an MPhil and a PhD in political science from Columbia University.

Daniel J. Houston is the president of retirement, insurance and financial services at the Principal Financial Group. He is responsible for the company's U.S. asset accumulation businesses, U.S. insurance solutions businesses, and distribution channels supporting all units. Houston has appeared before the U.S. Senate Special Committee on Aging to discuss the importance of educating the workforce about financial needs in retirement. He also joined the joint forum "Private-Sector Retirement Savings Plans: What Does the Future Hold?" held by the U.S. Senate Committees on Finance and Health, Education, Labor and Pensions. Since joining Principal Financial Group in 1984, Houston has held a number of positions, including executive vice president, senior vice president, vice president, regional vice president, and regional director of group and pension sales. He sits on the boards of the United Way of Central Iowa, Mercy Medical Center, the Employee Benefits Research Institute, America's Health Insurance Plans, Iowa State University Business School Dean's Advisory Council, Morley Financial Services, Principal Financial Advisors, Principal Trust Company (Asia) Ltd., Principal International, Brasilprev, Principal Bank, and Principal Global Services Private Ltd. Houston received a bachelor's degree from Iowa State University.

Steven Knapp is president of The George Washington University. His priorities include enhancing GW's partnerships, expanding its research, strengthening its alumni community, and enlarging students' opportunities for public service. He is co-chair of the Age-Friendly DC Task Force, a Washington, D.C. initiative to address the aging population's needs in areas like affordable housing, transportation, and social inclusion. Knapp serves on the boards of numerous organizations including the Economic Club of Washington, D.C., the Greater Washington Board of Trade, Greater Washington Urban League, and Al Akhawayn University in Ifrane, Morocco. He is chair of the Atlantic 10 Conference Council of Presidents and a member of the senior advisory board of the Northern Virginia Technology Council, the executive committee of the Council on Competitiveness, and the jobs committee of the Federal City Council. A specialist in Romanticism, literary theory, and the relation of literature to philosophy and religion, Knapp taught English literature at the University of California, Berkeley, before serving as dean of arts and sciences and then provost of Johns Hopkins University. He is a fellow of the American Academy of Arts & Sciences and a member of the Council on Foreign Relations. The author of three books and numerous articles, he holds a doctorate and master's degree from Cornell University and a BA from Yale University.

Freda Lewis-Hall is the executive vice president and chief medical officer for Pfizer Inc. A frequent speaker on aging, health care access, and health disparities, she appears regularly on *The Doctors* and *Dr. Phil.* Before joining Pfizer, Lewis-Hall was chief medical officer and an executive vice president at Vertex; a senior vice president at Bristol-Myers Squibb; a vice president at Pharmacia; and product team leader at Eli Lilly, where she founded the Lilly Center for Women's Health. Previously she was vice chair of the Department of Psychiatry at the Howard University College of Medicine and a board member of the American Psychiatric Association Foundation. Lewis-Hall is a fellow of the New York Academy of Medicine, a member of the Institute of Medicine, and chair of the Cures Acceleration Network Review Board and a member of the Advisory Council for the National Center for Advancing Translational Sciences at the National Institutes of Health. She was named the Healthcare Businesswomen's Association's Woman of the Year in 2011 and one of *Savoy* magazine's Top Influential Women in Corporate America in 2012. She is the author of *Make Your Mark: Why Legacy Still Matters* and a contributor to *Balancing Work and Healthcare.* Lewis-Hall holds a BA from Johns Hopkins and an MD from the Howard University College of Medicine.

Michael Milken, chairman of the Milken Institute, has been at the forefront of a wide range of initiatives that have influenced public policy, accelerated medical research, supported public health and expanded access to capital. *Fortune* magazine called him "The Man Who Changed Medicine," and *Esquire* listed him among the most influential people of the twenty-first century. Milken formalized his previous philanthropy in 1982 by co-founding the Milken Family Foundation, a major force for medical research and education reform. In 1998 he led a March on Washington in support of increased funding of biomedical research. When funding increases slowed in 2003, Milken founded *FasterCures*, which works to remove barriers to progress against all life-threatening diseases. He also founded the Prostate Cancer Foundation and joined with leading physicians in launching the Melanoma Research Alliance.

The Milken Institute is a nonpartisan think tank whose annual Global Conference brings 3,500 decision makers from 50 nations to Los Angeles. The event features a track dedicated to successful aging.

As a financier, he revolutionized modern capital markets, making them more democratic and dynamic by expanding access to capital for

3,200 companies that created millions of jobs. Milken graduated from UC Berkeley with highest distinction and earned his MBA from the Wharton School. He and his wife, Lori, were married in 1968. They have three children and eight grandchildren.

Philip A. Pizzo is the former dean and the current David and Susan Heckerman professor of pediatrics and a professor of microbiology and immunology at the Stanford School of Medicine. He is the founding director of The Stanford Distinguished Careers College, which helps midlife individuals transition to new life journeys. Pizzo has championed programs and policies to improve the future of science, education and health care and has devoted much of his career to the prevention and treatment of childhood cancers. He is an author of more than 500 scientific articles and 16 books and monographs, including *Principles and Practice of Pediatric Oncology*. He co-led a committee for the Institute of Medicine that resulted in the 2011 report "Relieving Pain in America." He has been elected to numerous prestigious organizations, including the American Society of Clinical Investigation, the Association of American Physicians, and the Institute of Medicine of the National Academy of Sciences, where he chaired the Board on Health Sciences Policy and was elected to the IOM Council. Before joining Stanford, he was the physician-in-chief of Children's Hospital in Boston and Department of Pediatrics chair at Harvard Medical School. Previously Pizzo was head of the National Cancer Institute's infectious disease section, chief of the NCI's pediatric department, and acting scientific director for the NCI's Division of Clinical Sciences. A graduate of Fordham University, he received his MD from the University of Rochester.

A. Barry Rand is the chief executive officer of AARP, the world's largest nonprofit, nonpartisan-membership organization dedicated to social change and helping people 50 and over to improve the quality of their lives. Since becoming CEO of AARP in 2009, Rand has become a recognized leader and spokesman for people aged 50-plus and a strong advocate for health and financial security. A proven leader of both multibillion-dollar companies and smaller, private equity-driven businesses, Rand has served as chairman and CEO of Avis Group Holdings, CEO of Equitant Ltd., and executive vice president for worldwide operations at Xerox Corporation. Rand has served on numerous boards, both for-profit and nonprofit. He has served as the chairman of the board at Howard University since 2006. He established the Helen Matthews Rand Endowed Scholarship, a $1.5 million program at the Howard University School of Education in honor of his late mother, a Washington, D.C., public school principal, to encourage students to enter teaching careers in urban schools. Rand was inducted into the National Sales Hall of Fame (winning the Thomas J. Watson Award) and is a recipient of the esteemed NAACP Image Award. He also serves as chairman of the board at Howard University. Rand holds a BA from American University and an MBA from Stanford University, where he was also a Sloan executive fellow.

Susan Raymond is the executive vice president for research and analytics at Changing Our World, Inc., a consulting firm for nonprofits and philanthropies. She is responsible for designing and conducting business operating–environment research for nonprofits and foundations as well as developing business plans and program evaluations for new and existing institutions. Raymond previously held positions at the New York Academy of Sciences, where she founded the public policy program; the World Bank; the Center for Public Resources; and the U.S. Agency for International Development. She has worked on philanthropy and economic development projects throughout Africa, the Middle East, Eastern Europe, Russia, and Asia. In 2011, Women United in Philanthropy honored her with the Women in Excellence and Achievement Award. Raymond is a member of the advisory board of the Center for Global Prosperity, a faculty lecturer at Columbia University, and a member of the advisory boards of The Global Index of Philanthropic Freedom and America's Unofficial Ambassadors. In 2012 the director of the National Science Foundation appointed her to the board of the U.S. Civilian Research and Development Foundation. She is a regular speaker at international conferences on the future role of philanthropy in economic growth and civil society. Raymond received her BA from Macalester College and her MA and PhD from the Johns Hopkins University School of Advanced International Studies in a joint program with the School of Hygiene and Public Health.

Fernando M. Torres-Gil is a professor of social welfare and public policy at UCLA, an adjunct professor of gerontology at USC, and director of the UCLA Center for Policy Research on Aging. Previously he was chair of UCLA's Social Welfare Department and associate dean and acting dean at the UCLA School of Public Affairs. The co-author of *Lessons on Aging from Three Nations, Volumes I and II* and *The New Aging: Politics and Change in America*, he has written six books and more than 100 other publications. Torres-Gil is a member of the Academies of Public Administration, Gerontology, and Social Insurance. A leading spokesman on demographics, aging, and public policy, Torres-Gil served as the first U.S. assistant secretary on aging in the Department of Health and Human Services under President Clinton. He also managed the Administration on Aging under HHS Secretary Donna Shalala, organized the 1995 White House Conference on Aging, worked as staff director of the U.S. House Select Committee on Aging under Congressman Ed Roybal, and served as a member of the Federal Council on Aging under President Carter. President Obama appointed him vice chair of the National Council on Disability. Torres-Gil is a board member of the AARP Foundation. A graduate of San Jose State University, he received an MSW and a PhD in social policy, planning, and research from the Heller Graduate School in Social Policy and Management at Brandeis University.

Rita Beamish is the Project Editor for this book. A longtime journalist, Beamish has reported and edited for numerous organizations, including two decades with the Associated Press as a White House, political, environmental, and investigative reporter. Her freelance work has been widely published, including in *The New York Times, The Washington Post, Newsweek, New York* magazine, and AARP publications. Beamish is the author of the nonfiction book *Perils of Paradise,* and was an adjunct professor at Columbia University Graduate School of Journalism. Prior to joining the AP, she reported for the *Ventura Star-Free Press* and the *Los Gatos Times-Observer* in California. She holds a BA from Santa Clara University and an MS from Columbia University Graduate School of Journalism.

Index